Teen Spirits

Media, Education and Culture

Series Editors: David Buckingham is Reader in Education at the Institute of Education, University of London, UK and Julian Sefton-Green is Media Education Development Officer at the Weekend Arts College, part of Interchange Trust, UK.

In response to the increasing diversity of contemporary societies and the significance of the electronic media, cultural studies has developed rigorous and exciting approaches to pedagogy, both in schools and in higher education. At the same time, research in this area has begun to pose fundamental questions about the political claims of much cultural studies theory, and about the relationship between academic knowledge and lived experience. *Media, Education and Culture* will extend the research and debate that is developing in this interface between cultural studies and education.

Also in the series:
Teaching Popular Culture: Beyond Radical Pedagogy edited by David Buckingham
Wired-up: Young People and the Electronic Media edited by Sue Howard
Digital Diversions: Youth Culture in the Age of Multimedia edited by Julian Sefton-Green

Forthcoming:
Schooling the Future: Education 'Youth' and Postmodernity by Bill Green and Lindsay Fitzclarence.

Teen Spirits
Music and Identity in Media Education

Chris Richards

First published in 1998 by UCL Press

UCL Press Limited
1 Gunpowder Square
London EC4A 3DE
UK

and

1900 Frost Road, Suite 101
Bristol
Pennsylvania 19007–1598
USA

The name of University College London (UCL) is a registered trade mark
used by UCL Press with the consent of the owner.

British Library Cataloguing in Publication Data
A catalogue record for this book is available from the British Library.

Library of Congress Cataloging-in-Publication Data are available

ISBNs: 1–85728–858–0
       1–85728–859–9

Typeset in 10/12pt Times
by Graphicraft Typesetters Ltd., Hong Kong

Printed by T.J. International Ltd, Padstow, UK.

In memory of my father
Roy Ernest Richards
9 October 1917–18 September 1984

Contents

Series Editors' Preface

Media and Cultural Studies are currently expanding areas of the curriculum at all levels of the education system, not merely in English-speaking countries but in many other parts of the world. Cultural Studies has made a radical contribution to the study of education, particularly in terms of its emphasis on 'popular' knowledge and on the political dynamics of young people's leisure cultures. Moreover, in the context of anxieties about the apparent decline in traditional cultural values, it also challenges much current thinking about the aims and methods of core areas of the curriculum such as English. Meanwhile, in response to the growing significance of the electronic media and the increasing diversity of contemporary societies, media educators have developed rigorous and exciting new approaches to teaching both in schools and in higher education. In the past decade, media education has come of age – and in the process, fundamental questions about its aims and methods have begun to be asked.

Teen Spirits is one of the first volumes in a new series entitled Media, Education and Culture, which aims to develop original research and debate at the interface between the disciplines of Education and Media/Cultural Studies. The book focuses specifically on teaching about popular music, providing accounts of research and classroom practice using a range of methods and forms of data. The analysis of the data is set within a wider context of theoretical and educational debate about social difference, identity and pedagogy.

Media education has an inconsistent history of engagement with popular music, which has been characterised by long periods of apparent neglect. As Chris Richards argues, this neglect is paradoxical: while claiming to engage the cultural interests of young people, media teachers have effectively marginalized a medium central to the lives of a large majority of them. *Teen Spirits* addresses this absence, suggesting the scope for engagement between media and music education across the conventional curricular divisions, and discussing how teachers might address their students' experiences of popular music more directly.

Consuming music is often seen as a special and personal experience: listening to music can play an important part in how we define our innermost selves, our feelings, identities and histories. Indeed, it is, in part, because music is experienced in these terms, and perhaps particularly by people addressed as 'adolescent', that media education may have veered away from any full engagement with it. Richards acknowledges the genuine difficulty faced by media teachers and, by moving close to the vantage point of teachers themselves, wrestles with it throughout this book.

Some might see these difficulties as arising from an inevitable collision between different 'tastes' in music. Yet, as Richards shows, following Bourdieu, 'taste' is not simply 'innocent' or 'natural', and never just 'personal': on the contrary, it is central to the tactics we adopt in defining and performing our social identities. Most obviously, taste has a distinct generational dimension. Few teachers enjoy the same kind of music as their students; and if they do, they are likely to engage with it (or at least to talk about it) in rather different terms. As Richards illustrates, talking about music is difficult in any case. But teaching about popular music always involves crossing boundaries between school knowledge and everyday knowledge, thus intensifying the tensions and disjunctions typical of institutional encounters between teachers and their students. Students located in different class cultures, with access to sometimes divergent forms of cultural (and subcultural) capital, are likely to respond to such initiatives in very different ways.

Richards' case study of teaching popular music thus raises some challenging questions about the whole enterprise of media education. The sometimes rather propagandist interventions of earlier generations of media educators are clearly inappropriate here: pop is not the most obvious object of concern for the missionary forms of ideological 'demystification' that have characterised some media teaching. While this approach has largely been superseded, media educators are still often uneasy when faced with subjective meanings and popular pleasures, preferring instead to remain with the relative security offered by studying the structures and practices of the industry. In this often fraught and contested domain, it seems much safer to settle for the apparent objectivity of external structures. While the analysis of the industry is certainly an integral feature of study in this field, it can also represent a kind of disavowal of what is most important about the lived experience of popular music.

Through autobiographical reflections, the empirical detail of students' work, and an engagement with teachers' standpoints in everyday practice, Richards also develops a sometimes sceptical challenge to the broad sweep of academic theory in Cultural Studies. While some exponents of Cultural Studies continue to regard schools as merely sites of ideological inculcation, repressive institutions working in the interests of the hegemonic powers of the State, in this book such views will find little support. The everyday cultures of particular groups of young people have often been interpreted – with comparable abstraction – as forms of opposition and resistance to the structural constraints of the educational system. Again, by contrast, Richards' attention to the complexity of teacher-student encounters in schools points to the need to re-investigate schools as places in which young people actively make, and remake, their cultural experience. Schools bring young people together in a variety of ways, not all of which are about the imposition of 'dominant ideologies'; and in doing so, they offer a variety of resources which young people negotiate and make their own.

On one level, schools clearly do attempt to enforce and maintain distinctions between high and low cultures. But they need to be seen as more than mechanistic agencies for reproducing dominant taste cultures. Making popular music into an object of study in the media curriculum creates a space in which complex questions about cultural value and social identity can be explicitly debated and analysed. As Richards argues, this will involve an uneasy interplay between students' knowledge and teachers' knowledge, in which neither can, or should, emerge as privileged or secure. Teaching about music should not become merely a means of submitting popular culture to the discourses and practices of the academic curriculum; but neither should it be simply a matter of celebrating students' existing tastes and identifications.

There are no easy solutions here. As Richards shows, teaching about such areas of student culture is inevitably an uncomfortable one for teachers themselves. It raises awkward questions about their own positions, histories and identities. One of the great original strengths of Teen Spirits is its emphasis on precisely these issues. Unlike many researchers of youth culture, Richards does not seek to render himself invisible, or attempt to claim that he has achieved an empathic identification with the subjects of his research. Such options are not available for teachers in any case. By discussing and problematising his own personal history and his present position, Richards adopts a self-reflexive stance of the kind which is often advocated in Cultural Studies, but very rarely realized. By juxtaposing his own autobiographical recollections with those of the teachers and students with whom he has worked, he points towards a mode of analysis which moves beyond the dichotomies of structure and subjectivity, personal meaning and social significance.

Teen Spirits fulfils several of the central aims of the Media, Education and Culture series. It is firmly grounded by empirical research into the role of the media in young people's lives and, more specifically, into the practice of media education. But it also provokes more far-reaching and unsettling questions, both about classroom practice and about the politics of academic theory and research. As such, we feel that this book will produce new insights and animate debate among teachers, academics and researchers in the field.

David Buckingham
Julian Sefton-Green
London, January 1998

Acknowledgments

This book was written between 1992 and 1995, when I was a Lecturer in the Department of English, Media and Drama at the University of London Institute of Education. I want to thank Gunther Kress and David Buckingham for supervizing the PhD thesis on which this book is based. I also want to thank the following for their widely various criticism, advice and encouragement: Nikki Blackborow, Sara Bragg, Roz Brody, Tony Burgess, Cath Cinnamon, Phil Cohen, Angela Devas, Debbie Epstein, Anton Franks, Pete Fraser, Lucy Green, John Hardcastle, Roger Hewitt, Valerie Hey, Ken Jones, Joyce Little, Janet Maybin, Cameron McCarthy, Peter Medway, Jane Miller, Richard Quarshie, Fazal Rizvi, Muriel Robinson, Julian Sefton-Green, Lyn Thomas and Anne Turvey. The teachers I depended on are named in the preceding list and I can't acknowledge the school students enough; there would be no book without them. I am particularly grateful to Gemma Moss and Joe Tobin for the most detailed and extensive comments on the manuscript for this book.

Some of the material in this book was first presented to participants in the Special Interest Group – Media, Culture and Curriculum at the Annual Meetings of the American Educational Research Association. I want to thank Glenn Hudak and Zena Moore for keeping the connection alive.

Several chapters, originally written as conference papers, have also been published in another form. Extracts from Chapter 1 have been published in *Discourse: Studies in the Cultural Politics of Education*, **16**(3). Chapter 4 was presented to the first Domains of Literacy Conference, at the Institute of Education, September 1992. Chapter 5 was presented to the Media, Culture and Curriculum Special Interest Group at the Annual Meeting of the American Educational Research Association, Atlanta, Georgia, April 1993; it was subsequently published as 'The English Curriculum – What's music got to do with it?' in *Changing English*, **1**(2). Chapter 6 was presented to the second Domains of Literacy Conference, September 1994. An earlier draft of Chapter 7 was presented to the Media, Culture and Curriculum Special Interest Group at the Annual Meeting of the American Educational Research Association in San Francisco, April 1995. A different version of Chapter 8 was presented to the Symposium on Post-Conservative Programmes of Reform, at the European Conference on Educational Research at the University of Bath, September 1995. It has been published as a chapter in David Buckingham (Ed.) *Teaching Popular Culture:*

Beyond Radical Pedagogy (UCL Press, 1997). The post-script, and some of the autobiographical parts of Chapter 1, were presented to the Annual Meeting of the American Educational Research Association, in New Orleans, April 1994 – and subsequently published in *Cultural Studies – A Research Volume*, edited by Norman K. Denzin (JAI Press, 1996).

Finally, I want to thank Elizabeth Rouse (whom I met first in April 1967, and second in the autumn of 1968) and my daughters Fay and Cesca, for putting up with everything and more besides. Thanks also to Saul Richards for a northern angle. By the way, the title *Teen Spirits* (youthful, animated but elusive) was suggested by Nirvana's 'Smells like Teen Spirit' from *Nevermind* (The David Geffen Company, 1991: DGCD 24425). For some of the stories about the Nirvana title, see Gottlieb and Wald in Ross and Rose (1994).

Introduction

This is not another book about youth cultures. To the contrary, it's primarily about students and teachers 'doing' pop music in the context of media education. It argues for the inclusion of popular music in media studies but also explores the complexity of bringing informal knowledge and experience into the formal practices of school – to be rearticulated in discussions, evaluations and assignments. The book is thus located within, and returns to address, a particular social practice – teaching media studies with adolescent groups in school.

Despite some early interest, popular music has been relatively neglected through many years of innovation in media studies teaching and, in the following chapters, I argue that it should be recognized as thoroughly a part of 'media culture' and the concerns of media education. This is the first of three themes pursued throughout this book. I argue, in fact, that this neglect is far from easily overcome and, through Chapters 4–7, I discuss the problems I encountered in my own attempts to try out teaching about popular music with GCSE and A Level students. This is, in part, the story of how easy it is to get wrong-footed in the microcultural politics of adolescence. Nevertheless, against the past neglect of popular music, I pursue its importance in future practice in media studies teaching and bring my argument to a provisional conclusion in Chapter 8 – Endtroducing.

I might have guessed, but, as it turned out, researching young people's knowledge of popular music, and the teaching practices through which such knowledge might be engaged, was a tentative, and somewhat uncertain, process. I could not map out the course of the research in its entirety at the beginning. Only as the encounters discussed in each chapter took place were the next exploratory moves formulated – as, slowly, I began to grasp how, and why, some of my early tactics faltered. In reading through Chapters 4–7, it is important to bear in mind that their sequence represents this process – a narrative of my own progress through the research – and the progression from one limited, and sometimes unsatisfactory, teaching strategy to the next. Such uncertainty is, perhaps, characteristic of much qualitative research – as David Scott notes, for example:

> Qualitative researchers adopt methods which emphasise progressive focusing whereby the shape of the research is not determined before fieldwork begins, but is responsive to the initial data collected, and in turn has an

influence on subsequent methods that are used (Scott, in Scott and Usher, 1996: 81).

But I have tried to fill out this experience of 'progress in uncertainty' by locating my research within an autobiographical framing of three interconnected identities: myself as adolescent, as teacher and as researcher. This autobiographical strand, including my reflections on the tensions between these identities, is the second overarching theme of this book.

The subtheme of *myself as adolescent* also figures in Chapter 2 and, occasionally, in Chapter 3. The subtheme of 'myself as teacher', also introduced in Chapter 1, recurs throughout the entire book but is most evident in the Postscript – where I talk to a teacher doing the job that I once did and from which I do not quite take the usual academic distance. The subtheme of *myself as researcher* is introduced in Chapter 3. As a man aging from 40 to 43 during the period of the research, and seeking to engage students of 15, 16 and 17 in discussions of popular music, I could hardly pretend to be 'hanging out', on terms of familiarity and intimacy, as if I was 'one of them'. For them, I seemed to be a kind of (mature) student teacher or, sometimes, a lecturer 'from the Institute'. Given my visible identity, I explained my interest in popular music – an often peculiarly personalized domain of cultural experience, highly specific to youth and adolescence – as, precisely, a matter of my professional interest in media education. This was not a front adopted in order to gather data about youth cultures – it was the only basis on which I expected to engage in a dialogue with the students I was able to meet and to teach.

Chapter 3 provides an overview of my research, setting out just what I did and why. My data was *not* gathered through a systematic comparative study but arose out of my experiments with teaching about pop music in the two schools to which I had access. I present studies of groups, of individual students, and of teachers involved with attempts to bring pop music into the curriculum. The studies are not strictly parallel. I bring together elements of teacher action research, interviews with adolescents in a classroom setting, and discussion of how teachers represent their efforts to teach pop music. The research is therefore quite eclectic, more of a hybrid than a pure example of just one approach. In effect, I collect various examples of attempts to put popular music into the school curriculum in order to tell a story about how incredibly tricky, and how interesting, making the effort to do this can be.

A third theme involves a contrast between, broadly, working-class and middle-class 'investments' in education and the various ways in which students located in different class cultures represent their knowledge, interests and tastes in popular music in the school context. Though they shared their location in the liminal phase of adolescence, the students in this study displayed divergent orientations: on the one hand articulating an informal knowledge which was immediate and transient, never accumulated and invested in relation to a future self and, on the other, translating informal knowledge into educationally legitimated forms, thus invested in the acquisition of cultural capital, in the energetic pursuit of middle-class career trajectories. The theme of class/adolescence is also significantly complicated by gender and, though I have not discussed this in detail, by the negotiation of ethnicities.

Chapter 2 gives a brief outline of the discursive emphasis of my approach to the data discussed in the central chapters of the book.

The postscript demands a few further words of explanation, not least because it raises some questions which go beyond the main substance of this book. In one respect, it returns to the theme of separations between sectors of education raised in Chapter 1, but it also points towards another, related debate around research and the power of academics to reinscribe the words of others within their own texts – the units of cultural capital on which academic careers are built. In effect, the postscript emerges from my own sense of tension between research and teaching. In fact, the conduct of interviews with teachers somewhat unsettled my own sense of being entitled to reinscribe *both* teachers' and students' words in my writing. Hesitating to write 'on behalf of' teachers tended to highlight, retrospectively, the relative ease with which I had assumed I could appropriate the words of school students. There's no comfortable elimination of this doubt in the following chapters: it appears as a necessary hesitation, an admission, sometimes, that the authority of writing enables me to settle matters that for others remain more open.

*   *   *

In Chapter 1, I begin with several extracts from Simon Frith's book *Sound Effects* (1983). *Sound Effects*, and much of Frith's other writing on popular music, has been widely influential in cultural studies and beyond. Nevertheless, it seems that an example of school based research included in both *Sound Effects* and the earlier *The Sociology of Rock* (1978), has been neglected, remembered only, perhaps, as a footnote to the wider argument about youth and the music industry. I have recovered Frith's school based research because it provides an important precedent for my own study. However, it also provides a marked contrast because, as I have suggested, what I present in the main empirical chapters of the book is not a sociology of the students' lives but an account of the forms in which they represent their experience of popular music in media studies lessons. Rather than attempt to investigate a youth culture 'out there', as constructed in the subcultural literature, I wanted to focus on the intersection, in media studies lessons, of popular cultural knowledge, the social relations of the classroom and the forms of representation required by teachers.

The introductory chapter progresses through four relatively discrete sections. Each provides a particular orientation to the main substance of the book, setting up the themes which are pursued and elaborated in the chapters which follow. The first, *differentiating youth*, argues for more educationally orientated accounts of the cultural experience of young people. The second, *putting cultural studies in its place?*, expands the argument by questioning the distance between academic cultural studies and the work that English and Media teachers do in schools. The third, *media education – a backward glance*, takes a brief look at the history of media education in England and makes a provisional case for a more sustained attempt to develop ways of teaching about popular music. Finally, the fourth section, *approaches through music education*, offers a selective reading of some past attempts to bring 'pop' into school music – a largely performance based subject centred in classical music.

Chapter One

Youth, Music and Media Education

Differentiating Youth

In 1972, in Keighley, a small town in West Yorkshire, Simon Frith carried out a study of young people's involvement with popular music. His research, which was conducted in a comprehensive school,[1] was subsequently incorporated in his book *The Sociology of Rock* (Frith, 1978) and in the later American orientated revision *Sound Effects: Youth, Leisure, and the Politics of Rock 'n' Roll* (Frith, 1983). For a brief, incisive, sketch of pop 'as it was lived' there can be few better places to begin. To show how young people engage with popular music is only a part of Frith's larger study, much of which is devoted to an analysis of the music industry and of the rock aesthetic in the wider field of debates around culture. I want to recover the Keighley research here because it represents a strand in cultural studies, and in the sociology of youth, which should be of considerable value to those who work with young people, especially teachers. Yet, despite their strengths, youth culture studies have only rarely moved on to develop implications for educational practice. As in cultural studies as a whole, questions to do with teaching have been placed as somewhat marginal and perceived as fairly unglamorous. Of course, *Learning to Labour* (Willis, 1977) did, explicitly and at some length, seek to address teachers in its final chapter. But, in the 20 years that have elapsed since, cultural studies has become a more broadly established academic discipline without much sense of obligation to address any particular practice outside higher education itself.

The numerous books and articles which came out of the Centre for Contemporary Cultural Studies in the 1970s and 1980s defined the discipline and, to the extent that they may have been read by teachers, were influential in the larger context of education. *Profane Culture* (Willis, 1978), *Subculture – The Meaning of Style* (Hebdige, 1979), *Resistance through Rituals* (Hall and Jefferson, 1975) and the retrospective collection *Feminism and Youth Culture* (McRobbie, 1991) are all of enduring interest and should still inform teachers in their engagement with young people (for a critical review see Middleton, 1990: 155–71). But these writings do not seek to address teachers explicitly and, like some later monographs, for example *Black Culture, White Youth* (Jones, S., 1988), are unlikely to secure the attention of more than a small minority. Even for teachers directly involved in media education, these titles will seem tangential to their central concern with the media and of little consequence relative to the many books which offer direct advice about how to teach the subject (for example Masterman 1980; 1985). I want to argue in this book that these cultural studies of youth should be central to the thinking of teachers concerned with media education. But I also want to offer, and make a wider case for, studies of youth which more directly address questions of educational practice.

I want to present three quite substantial passages from Frith's account of his Keighley research. In the discussion which follows I do two things. First of all, I want to suggest how Frith's work can be, and to some extent has been, taken further. His analysis of the divisions of class, gender and age within 'youth' is crucial and persists throughout my own account. Second, I want to inject some autobiographical elements into this chapter, partly to provide comparison with and confirmation of Frith's initiative, but also to frame a more extended account of my own motives in seeking to connect cultural studies with media teaching in schools.

The first passage describes a group of mostly middle-class sixth formers:

> Alison and her friends . . . had a busy and self-contained social life, meeting weekly at the folk club . . . at parties in each others' houses, at concerts or the bar at the local universities, at selected pubs. The group tended to come from middle-class backgrounds . . . but they were not particularly well-off in terms of income, spent a large proportion of non-school time studying, and were consequently at home a lot . . .
>
> Music was a background to their lives, radio and records were always on. The records were LPs, chosen carefully and individually and often purchased by saving money after hearing a friend's copy. People listened to music together and often exchanged albums temporarily. Few people in the group had a large record collection . . .
>
> This group was conscious of itself as a group that was clearly differentiated from the culture of their parents, but what really dominated its members' lives was a sense of possibility. They were all preparing to move on – to universities and colleges, to new towns and opportunities, to new sexual and social and chemical experiences; they were all aware that the group itself was transitional and temporary, that individuals had to maintain their individualism within it. They were articulate and self-aware and valued these qualities in music; they turned to music for support as well as for relaxation. They most valued music that was most apparently 'artistic' – technically complex or lyrically poetic – and tastes here went with other interests, in the other arts, in politics, in religion. There were few direct restraints on the activities of this group except members' shortage of money; they were successful at school and at home and rarely clashed with authority. But their life was already a career and the importance of exams and qualifications was fully realized. The resulting tensions made music all the more important – as the context for bopping, relaxing, petting, falling in love, and shouting a temporary 'Fuck the world!' (Frith, 1983: 209–10).

In the second passage, a younger and more decisively working-class group is represented:

> Craig and his friends were in their last year at school, fifth formers itching
> to get out. They would leave school without skill or qualification but had
> been used to failure for years, and school was not so much oppressive
> now as irrelevant. Their lives already revolved around the possibilities of
> (unskilled) work – most members of the group were already working part-
> time – and their leisure reflected this expectation. The group went out
> (why bother studying) to the youth clubs provided by the local authority or
> attached to local churches, to the pubs that would take them, to the fish-
> and-chips shop and the bus station and the streets. None of this group was
> a militant member of any particular gang, but they had skinhead friends
> and relations and could run casually with them and with the emerging groups
> of mods and crombies and knew which side they were on in a fight; Friday
> night, for example, was the traditional time for a trip to Bradford, the boys
> for a brawl, the girls for a dance at the Mecca.
>
> This group had plenty of free time but little money or mobility, and
> their leisure was consequently focused on public places, putting them in
> constant confrontation with the controllers of those spaces – police and
> bus conductors and bouncers. But home wasn't much freer, and so the
> boys went out most nights, doing nothing, having a laugh, aware that this
> was their youth and that their future would be much like the past of their
> working-class parents. Music was a pervasive part of their lives, in their
> rooms and clubs, on the jukebox, at the disco . . . (Frith, 1983: 210–11).

And finally a third group occupying a social position intermediate between the preceding two:

> David's and Peter's friends were younger – age fifteen and in the fourth
> form – but were committed to the academic routine and saw their futures
> stretching out through the sixth form and college . . . They were young and
> lacked the resources and the mobility and the freedom for student life, and
> in chafing about this they were more aggressively hip at school, in the
> youth club, and most of all at home, where they'd gather their friends and
> sit around the record player as if it were Moses, bringing messages from
> on high. It was important for this lot to distinguish themselves from every-
> body – teachers, parents, peers. They were hippies, hairies, in their clothes
> and attitudes and tastes and drugs; and they worked at it, read the music
> press, got passionate about their records and about the evils of commer-
> cialism. They were an elite, a group apart from the masses, even if they
> were in the same school and youth club and street (Frith, 1983: 211).

These contrasts between groups of young people differentially orientated by class, education and gender, must be familiar enough to most readers. For some, as for myself, the familiarity may arise because of a youth coincident with the period of Frith's research, but it may be that the outlines of his portrayal are still evident in current patterns of educational differentiation and popular cultural engagement. The classroom studies I present in later chapters represent groups of young people across much the same age range, and of comparable diversity in terms of class. Though all of my research was conducted in London, I have incorporated his descriptions into this text because, as will become apparent, there is a productive theoretical tension between the form of his account and that which I offer in later chapters of this book. Frith's summary comment on his three groups is this:

> The different youth groups' uses of music were different not because some groups were more resistant to commercial pressures than others, not even because some groups were more organized in subcultural terms than others, but because the groups each had their own leisure needs and interests – Keighley's youth culture patterns were an aspect of the town's social structure, its relations of production (Frith, 1983: 212).

However, Frith's account does date from a quarter of a century ago. By contrast, David Lusted (1991) has argued for a view of popular cultural experience which is much less divided by class and age:

> Prime time television, magazines, 'pop' music and high street videos, the tabloid press and paperbacks are among media *forms* that have penetrated the rhythms and routines of living, the social relations and activities of many teachers and students alike.
>
> This cultural revolution, brought by new technologies and changing social and leisure patterns, takes on a particular force in schooling.
>
> New generations of teachers share experience of these features of a swiftly changing culture most directly with their students. This process narrows the culture gap between largely middle-class teachers and especially working-class students, with many more shared cultural experiences, expectations and pleasures . . . (Lusted, 1991: 3).

Lusted shifts focus to a future which cannot be adequately understood within the categories of class, age and gender. For Lusted, even the differences between teachers and their students are no longer as firm as they were. What is useful here is the challenge to the assumption that the 'relations of production' simply determine cultural experience. Thus, though I think he exaggerates the degree of cultural commonality between teachers and students, the possibility that current youth cultures cannot be explained adequately or only in terms of the social locations of their participants is one which I explore in the following chapters. As I have suggested, I want to present school based studies from the 1990s to set alongside those from 25 years ago. In doing so I will make use of theories of discourse and of subjectivity which will contrast quite sharply with the more sociological emphases of earlier work. I don't want to reject Frith's approach but I do want to offer a more complex view of subjectivity – to be more attentive to the detail of people's self-accounts and to their multi-layered negotiations of social identities.

In recent years, a number of studies have moved substantially in this direction. *Cultural Studies Goes to School* (Buckingham and Sefton-Green, 1994) is a closely related account. Elsewhere, in *Changing Literacies: Media Education and Modern Culture* (Buckingham, 1993c), David Buckingham has argued that:

> . . . we need to look much more concretely and specifically at the diversity of *real* audiences, at subcultures of media users, at the domestic uses of media technology, and the interaction between media use and other social practices and relationships (Buckingham, 1993c: 19).

> . . . 'youth' can no longer be seen (if indeed it ever could) as a unitary category. On the contrary, it is now highly fragmented – and here the contrast with earlier eras, for example, if we look back to the invention or discovery of the teenager as a consumer in the 1950s, is quite striking (Buckingham, 1993c: 17–18).

As I will argue in Chapter 3, the emergence of ethnographically orientated styles of enquiry into media audiences (Buckingham, 1993b; Jenkins, 1992; Lewis, 1992; Morley, 1992) has in effect reaffirmed and renewed the case for teachers to go beyond a narrow mission to inculcate scepticism of the media among young people.[2] In the context of public debates which recurrently display adult panic over the meaning of young people's lives, there is every reason for teachers to be informed by, and where possible participate in, continuing research into the cultures of young people.

The second strand of this 'dialogue' with Frith is autobiographical. In some ways, reading Frith's work from the 1970s makes me ill-at-ease. The scale, the sense of social difference compressed within a constrained milieu, is so familiar it is disconcerting. I remember more than I think I want to and the tensions and conflicts are inseparable from forms of music and the affiliations they implied. My own years in the Sixth Form, for example, between 1968 and 1970, in Beverley, a small town in East Yorkshire, can be recovered and located in much the same social terms as those offered by Frith. By then, late 1968 and heading for 17, I'd mainly turned my back on dancehalls, retreated from the sexual rivalry and the rumours of violence and done what I could to put some distance between myself and local mods. Though I'd liked soul and Motown and, maybe, but I'm not sure, The Small Faces, I would not have wanted to admit it in 1967 – not there, in the social scene that defined my adolescence. I tried to put firm boundaries around my self: the Dylan of *Bringing It All Back Home*, *Highway 61 Revisited*, and *Blonde on Blonde* and the look that went with the last of those (unsmiling, out of focus) was how I handled being 15 and 16. At 17, doing A levels, I often slipped away from school with a friend to sit in his bedroom and listen to the Mothers of Invention, sometimes Edgard Varèse and, with some discomfort, *Nashville Skyline*. Most of the time, at my desk at home writing essays, I listened to Frank Zappa – *Hot Rats* (over and over again), and, on Fridays, for a night out with my girlfriend, went into Hull to watch films by Pasolini, Bergman, Godard and Bunuel. If they didn't have subtitles, forget it.

Even when I was 15, I didn't buy many records because I couldn't afford them and because owning them felt like making definite choices about who I was – even to see myself with a Beatles album was just too embarrassing. Bob Dylan, The Mothers of Invention, some blues – at that age there wasn't much else. The point about this austere and self-isolating stance was that it had far more to do with staking out a social identity and sustaining it, than with any more straightforward expression of likes and dislikes in the field of music. Within the small set of friends I had, we defined ourselves by negatives – not hippies, not mods, not even beats really but we probably wouldn't have minded if that's what other people called us. Retrospectively, I can see that we were defining ourselves in terms of a narrow selection of mostly avant-garde cultural heroes – lower middle-class grammar school boys in a provincial town, waiting to leave. We got on with the homework, watched the films with subtitles, read Alfred Jarry, Albert Camus, William Burroughs and Gary Snyder and listened to records neither British nor especially popular – Captain Beefheart or Jean-Luc Ponty, not the Stones or The Beatles.

In school, we read Jane Austen and Henry James, Shakespeare and Milton. We liked it too; just about all of it. Of course, there wasn't any media studies. Earlier, in English, we had done content analysis of newspapers and, in the spring of 1966, we had a student-teacher who set us up to write lyrics – in the style of Donovan or Dylan, needless to say. Otherwise, literature was the core experience for people like us and, whatever the range and diversity of our reading, much of what we could say and what we believed was precisely and inflexibly Leavisite.[3] Within that context, our social investment in a Leavisite discourse was unshakeable: as elite readers of high literature we could hardly concede that the forms we worked at understanding were anything other than intrinsically superior and, moreover, the only proper guide to the larger social world – if not the more immediate one we were then so effectively shutting out.

Since 1970, and leaving both the school and that small town provincial setting, I've no doubt tried to sustain elements of that same social investment but have also thought far more about how peculiarly exclusive that curriculum was and in what ways the division of legitimate from popular culture, with which I coped well enough, might be transformed.

Putting Cultural Studies in Its Place?

To take this autobiographical framing of the issues further, I want to deal with another, later, period. In this case the years are those between 1974 and 1978. The issue is that of cultural studies and its relationship to the education of young people in secondary schools. The account I offer is selective, informed by one particular construction of my own biography. As such, I am aware of engaging a bundle of anxieties now somewhat tidied up for academic consumption. There are always other ways of telling things. Autobiography is no exception; it has no peculiar transparency and no privileged claim to uncontested truth. But, by these means, in just a few pages, I can suggest the awkwardness and tension between differently located educational practices.

In 1974–5 I taught in schools for the first time. I taught black children either brought over from the Caribbean to join their parents or, increasingly, born in Britain to migrants from Jamaica, Trinidad and the other small islands of the British West Indies. For me, teaching was immediately a matter of close dialogue with people whose cultural experience I knew of, but did not know; the sense of difference in working closely with Afro-Caribbean students made knowledge a more relative and negotiable matter than, in practice, it had ever seemed before. Within that milieu my work as a teacher was to support those who might be seen as marginalized or likely to fail, because of cultural and linguistic difference, or because of the way such differences might be interpreted within English education. My previous educational experience – as a grammar school boy and a student – had been a matter of individual ascent in a context of expanding educational provision. Here, the prevailing educational commitment was towards a more inclusive and socially progressive practice.

In the East London schools where I taught, a broadly egalitarian and welfare consensus, familiar since World War II, seemed the unshakeable background to whatever divisions and conflicts might preoccupy the teachers with whom I worked. In the broader economic and educational context, the underpinnings of this egalitarian and progressive orientation were soon to be challenged and, over subsequent years, eroded. The disintegration of post-war consensus and the end of the long post war boom were shocking in their impact and, from 1976 onwards, elements in and around the Conservative Party have pushed towards the reinstitution of hierarchy, the preservation of elitism and the legitimation of exclusion. Between my first experience of teaching in 1974–5 and my return to it in 1978, there was an economic and political upheaval which, in education, might be represented through a contrast between buoyant optimism in 1974 and the alarm of lurching uncertainly into crisis as 1976 took shape (see CCCS Education Group, 1981; CCCS Education Group II, 1991; Jones, 1983, 1989).

From an educational practice which supported some of those most marginal to schooling, I moved, after a few months out of the country, into Birmingham University's Centre for Contemporary Cultural Studies, then a post-graduate research centre. Politically and theoretically its preoccupations were framed by the history of socialism in Britain, reanimated by current innovations in Marxist thought (see Harris, 1992; Turner, 1990). In relation to education, it favoured, though with some complex reservations, the provision of comprehensive state education; culturally, it endorsed and engaged in serious study of all those forms and practices divided from high culture and refused validity elsewhere in education. There seemed therefore every reason to expect some continuity between my sense of (re)formation as a teacher and my involvement with research in cultural studies.

The dissonance in such a transition was surprising and troublesome. I can recall my uneasy perception of a persistent and intractable disparity between the claims of an academic discourse and the ordinary experience of popular culture to which it referred. The enthusiasm of cultural studies for 'the popular' was, perhaps, more for a new theoretical discourse than, at that time, a wish to be attentive to the meanings people might give to their everyday lives. Of course, important empirical research (see Hobson, 1982; Morley, 1992; Willis, 1977) was being conducted by particular individuals but, in the day-to-day work of some subgroups, theory, in its ecstasies, could flip over into theoreticism, where social practices became no more than objects in thought and knowledge of the real, unless constituted at the heights of theoretical abstraction, was disallowed. Of course, a familiar defence of specialized language in the social sciences is that, like the natural sciences, they refer to phenomena which lie beyond the level of everyday experience and therefore require a distinctive, *necessarily unfamiliar*, language. This has considerable validity. But the domains to which cultural studies relates are already interpreted by their participants – the social actors whose subjective agency in part constitutes the worlds in which they live. Interpretation by social analysts is therefore always a matter of working over a pre-interpreted domain, domains of which participants have an existing, if always circumscribed, knowledge (Geertz, 1973; Thompson, 1990). The question I pursue, especially in Chapter 3 and the classroom studies which follow, is that of how to constitute an effective relationship between those who routinely inhabit a particular preinterpreted domain – like a school – and those who produce a specialist discourse representing that domain to others.

At the Centre, two different problems were united; the difficulty and specialization of theoretical discourse was entangled with a lofty refusal of empirically situated knowledges. Together, the effect could be uncomfortably exclusive. And theoreticism itself – which, in the long run, the Centre contested – could produce a dismal paralysis, with the mundane detail of empirical research appearing as dull as mere dirt beneath the shimmering fields of theory. Thus an internal discussion document, from early in 1978,[4] recorded elliptical hints at the difficulties of 'theoreticism' and the 'weakness of research support and ethos' but struggled towards a way of 'capitalis[ing] a massive collective experience' where 'introduction to the Centre is commonly traumatic or intimidating'. In this recollection of an uneasy relation to the radical claims of an increasingly influential intellectual practice, I can admit to an antagonism which surprised me because, in my four previous years of higher education, I had thought of myself as a very theory orientated kind of person. Indeed, it was such a self-perception that led me to the Centre. But, with a year of school teaching cutting between my earlier enthusiasm for Marx, Levi-Strauss and Sartre and my encounter with cultural studies, theory looked different, worryingly distant from those people, like my secondary school students, for whom popular cultural forms and practices were everyday rather than visited as strategic objects of academic study.

At that point of awkward transition, it seemed that the field of contemporary cultural studies was too much driven by the demands of the academic domain to adequately acknowledge or begin to address the question of how its enabling analytical discourse might also connect with the lives of those it explained. To say *connect with* is perhaps too easy, almost an evasion; I mean to say that it did not seem of much concern to think through how the emergent cultural studies might be a radical element in the lives of those who might never experience education beyond the age of 16. Cultural studies was understood by its proponents to be a politically engaged and critical discipline, not just another academic subject; what it lacked was an educational practice in which teachers outside higher education and their students could begin to participate.

Despite some particular efforts to connect cultural studies with schooling since the 1970s (see Buckingham, 1990; Cohen, 1990), there is a continuing need to generate an educationally refocused cultural studies – informed by those practices of teaching which have not depended upon the presence of students already in possession of a privileged cultural capital. The influence of cultural studies in the area of Sixth Form (A Level) media studies is obviously an important gain but the value of cultural studies needs to be realized in a greater diversity of educational contexts than those associated with the Advanced Level route through the 16 to 19 age phase. Who educational initiatives are for, and what purposes they might serve, are central questions for any newly constituted field of knowledge. Cultural studies has a history which should sustain something more than a theoretical attempt to answer such questions. Cultural studies has to engage with the real sense of difficulty which teachers encounter in their work with all those school students whose orientation to education is resistant, disaffected, or, at least, characterized by prolonged indifference. In the transitions through which those of 15 and 16 pass, the problem of what education might offer, and on what terms, is crucial.

The issue of identities has some importance here, both in thinking through a response to the questions posed above and in reflecting on the aspirations of cultural studies as an academic discipline. In both cases, it is worth asking to what kind of identity cultural studies might contribute. What is the claim made by cultural studies in the formation of new subjectivities? What kinds of new intellectual were to be made through cultural studies? What kinds of working practice might cultural studies engender or remake? A part of the answer may lie in the reading of Gramsci (Hoare and Nowell-Smith, 1971) which informed much cultural theory in the 1970s and 1980s; the intellectuals, in this conception, were organic intellectuals of the subordinate class and, politically, their practice was shaped by the project of a hegemonic socialism and by a continuing relation to, though not containment within, the life of the subordinate class. The working practices of such intellectuals could include teaching but might also range across a variety of practices given an appropriate political inflection. This is one, abstract and general, formulation. Certainly, cultural studies, as I experienced it, implied a political positioning within a Gramscian Marxism and, at the time, an identification with a socialist-feminist cultural politics. This explicit and self-conscious politics has, perhaps, lost much of its momentum and is now quite marginal to being a student of cultural studies.

The question of from where, socially, students of cultural studies might come and what their destinations might be has been addressed by some of the polytechnics in which cultural studies for undergraduates was established. Some favoured policies which offered broad access and even preferred to recruit students not reaching higher education through the conventional Advanced Level route. Thus the Department of Cultural Studies at the University of East London, for example, sought to encourage potential students in these terms:

> In our opinion, a subject like Cultural Studies is enriched by recruiting students from diverse social, cultural and intellectual backgrounds as well as from a wide age range. We are particularly interested in offering places to those whose lives have made entry into higher education neither obvious nor easy, and we seek to encourage both school leavers and older students who live in the geographical area of the University and in the wider national and international community.

Such policies were, and where they survive still are, consistent with the social and political project of cultural studies as it was conceived through the later 1960s and into the 1970s. Some of the excitement of cultural studies lay in its potential for challenging the social relations in which 'academic study' could be conducted. A differently constituted intellectual practice might, it seemed, allow the content of cultural studies to be of social and political consequence for its students. The academicization of cultural studies and the wider emphasis on instrumentalism in education over the past 20 years has limited and undermined this potential. In a period marked by an intensification of social and economic inequalities, the separation of the academic–intellectual domain from the broader concerns of mass education has hardly diminished. With some particular exceptions, the realization of a more widely available and diversified educational practice informed by cultural studies has, as yet, proved immensely difficult to achieve.

There was a further element in cultural studies which, in retrospect, seemed also to compromise its claims to reconstruct established academic practice. Through this period, despite an emerging feminist critique, intellectual argument was sometimes conducted in the language of men at war. To appear theoretically under armed, on the field of cultural studies, risked charges of empiricism, the smear of an effeminate cowardice in the thick of mental battle. The language of combat may have derived less from Gramsci's strategic metaphors than from the British Public School tradition and the traces of that masculine elite culture encountered still in our more immediate past (see Connell, 1995; Gillis, 1981; Weeks, 1981). But this was not peculiar to the Centre. The wider context of this discursive formation, beyond its particular 1970s cultural studies variant, has been discussed by Renato Rosaldo (Rosaldo, 1993: 171–3) in his exploration of the vantage points from which ethnographic research might be conducted. He argues, in effect, for more inclusive modes of intellectual enquiry, distinct from the achievement of a combative intellectual stance.

Perhaps I can suggest just how problematic an educational culture cultural studies appeared to be, by offering the rhetorical conjunction of two disparate experiences. First, the memory of my most disaffected moments in Beverley Grammar School: an exclusively masculine and hierarchical institution, intensely competitive with honours boards displayed in the hall, published examination results in the school magazine and entrance to Oxford and Cambridge elevated above all else. Second, in cultural studies at the Birmingham Centre, an implicit hierarchy of subgroups and the intellectual divisions they represented, a ranking of incoming graduates in terms of their attainments and likely performance and, just as at school, anxiety that you could be made to feel stupid for not already knowing what you were there to find out. These crossed memories, of a 1960s grammar school with 1970s cultural studies in the academy, if somewhat elliptically collapsed together, nevertheless underscore that question of what education is for and for whom it confirms a future (Bourdieu, 1986; Bourdieu and Passeron, 1977; Sennett and Cobb, 1972).

I left the Centre in 1978 to teach English in comprehensive schools, and be located thus in a culture of work somewhat sceptical of the academic domain. From that vantage point, the work that I did for the next 10 years was substantially a matter of reappropriating cultural studies, attempting to make its perspectives make sense both for me as a teacher and for the young people that I taught (Richards, 1981/82; 1990). The relationship between different kinds of intellectual practice is difficult – institutionally separated and governed by widely divergent priorities – but it is essential to connect theory and research with teaching, and other practices, in educational settings not available only to a tiny elite.

I want to conclude this section by looking back, briefly, to the work of Iain Chambers, a former student at the Centre for Contemporary Cultural Studies[5] and, along with Dick Hebdige, Paul Willis and Angela McRobbie, one of the few to devote substantial attention to popular music. Chambers contributed to the journal *Screen Education* and has since written more extensively about popular music (Chambers 1985, 1986). In 'Pop music: A teaching perspective' Chambers suggests:

> One of the advantages (and difficulties) of teaching pop music is that it immediately involves the common experience of the students . . . listening to Boney M while sitting at desks is different from dancing to the music at the local discotheque, but . . . these experiences are organised through a continual employment of such common-sensical categories as 'entertainment', 'leisure' and 'pleasure', and this has pertinent consequences for a teaching situation (not the least being friction that can arise if it is felt that the student's leisure space, the realm of the 'private', is being violated and transformed into a public exercise in academia). At the same time, the initial 'shock' that this provokes can be strategically exploited to prise open the contradictory, but often extremely rich, knowledge that the students have of the material. In transforming pop music into a problematic area of study within the context of the students' own everyday knowledge there emerges the potential for that important tension between how the cultural experience of pop music is lived and of how, through a critical exploration, it can be made to speak with new accents (Chambers, 1981: 35).

This, though referring to teaching in higher education, identifies some of the most awkward aspects of that process of making an emotionally 'personalized' dimension of everyday life the object of some public scrutiny. But Chambers compounds what he describes by writing as if teachers are a cultural branch of the military police, trained to 'violate', 'strategically exploit', and to 'prise open'. Thus, though he is reporting a difficulty which many other teachers might recognize, he writes as if the privileged knowledge of the teacher is not itself open to question. Here, the power of academically constituted knowledge appears as the means to compel the 'cultural experience of pop music' to speak in terms the teacher wishes to hear. Chambers never provides an account of a particular teaching situation and, though the force of his metaphors becomes more muted, their combative tenor has much in common with a more pervasive masculine imagery of battle and conquest in cultural studies writing. Whatever the wider issue, the implication I want to emphasize is that, in Chambers' teaching perspective, the study of popular music is still too firmly anchored within the orthodoxy of the professional competence of teachers and academics. The 'correct' form of knowledge of this dimension of students' experience is, ultimately, to be determined by the teacher.

Chambers goes on to make a case for more attentive analysis of music:

> . . . the pertinence of particular cultural relations in the formation of pop music must not be permitted to obscure the specific instance of the music. That aural reality, the specificity of the sounds of British pop is, after all, where our discourse begins. How can we avoid a seemingly inevitable bifurcation between musicological approaches, on the one hand, and cultural analyses, on the other? (Chambers, 1981: 36).

To overcome this 'bifurcation', he maps out some priorities for teaching the history of British pop music placing, for example, particular stress on Afro-American sources. These priorities are important (see Green, 1988), but what disappears from his account is the particularity of encounters with students, the dialogues which might take place in such encounters (between students as well as with a teacher) and the possibility that the knowledge he advocates might be reconstructed – or at least somewhat challenged – through the various cultural experiences that, in another way of teaching, might be permitted their place in the classroom.

In the following chapters, rather than elaborate the body of knowledge – popular music – as teachers and academics in the field may wish it to be, I have made the students' existing understanding of music in their own experience a more distinct presence than in other accounts. Teaching can be conceived in terms which always make the higher value of the teacher's knowledge prevail; such teaching might therefore notice all that students lack in their knowledge of popular music, giving priority to the task of transmitting more academic accounts of the field. Of course, I would not want to neglect such academic accounts (see especially Middleton, 1990) but, whatever their scope or sophistication, they are always constrained and reformed in their reception by particular groups of students. Such constraints and reformations may be experienced by teachers as just frustrating impediments to the knowledge they wish students to understand. It's not surprising if teachers see students as failing to progress beyond their existing positions within excessively particular, and relatively closed, forms of knowledge. But such a perception does assume that the forms of popular knowledge, as yet unarticulated within education-ally constituted discourses, are therefore always inchoate, waiting to be rendered meaningful, and to be given depth, by a retrospective commentary from another, more authoritative, vantage point.

Of course, I can hardly exempt my own account from its implication in this process. However, I do want to argue that teaching should create the conditions in which the cultural logic of students' experience can emerge – conditions which favour *dialogue* rather than *interrogation*. This can entail a provisional suspension of the knowledge a teacher believes to be important and an effort to adopt a degree of mobility between cultural positions. This is not a simple cultural relativism but an attempt to grasp that what teachers may regard as 'limits' may be, for students, meaningful boundaries. There are excellent studies of this kind of disjunction, and how it might be overcome, in Shirley Brice Heath's ethnographic study *Ways with Words* (Heath, 1983); for example, between young children from different commu-nities and their teachers there are widely divergent understandings of what it means 'to tell a story'.[6] Following the implications of Heath's research, the purposes of teaching about popular music may need to be redefined through an effort to engage, however provisionally, with the positions voiced by students. As she has shown, sustained attention to the meanings of students' cultures and to their negotiations of the classroom context are central to the development of an effective, reciprocal, practice of teaching.

Media Education – A Backward Glance

Media education has gathered its momentum in a period marked by expanded and intensified patterns of material consumption and by the diversification of techno-logies of communication. The cultural centrality of print has been undermined by a wide array of media in which combinations of visual and aural forms of representa-tion predominate. Media education has addressed these shifts in the configuration of cultural forms and has, over the past decade, achieved a provisional coherence and credibility. At its centre has been the study of television and film and of other media in which visual images are a significant component. But relative to the visual media, the study of popular music is unevenly developed and still regarded as a less than essential concern (despite Murdock and Phelps, 1973). Sound technologies gen-erally have received less attention – despite their wide social use. Young people, perhaps particularly those 'in adolescence', are often intensively involved with such technologies and yet media education has not realized, in its practice, an adequate means of exploring this dimension of cultural experience.

There is no single reason for this neglect. Certainly, there is a real difficulty for teachers, already formed in their professional identities, in rethinking their prac-tice and in securing the time to develop the knowledge and skill which the study of popular music requires. It is relatively rare for teachers of media studies, themselves educated most often within the limits of English or related literary studies, to be proficient in reading or performing music. Music education has itself been quite marginal to most state secondary schools. My own education included no musical training. With exceptions, the formation of teachers of media studies has meant that few have the cultural resources, or the confidence, to teach about a medium of which, in common with most people without formal musical education, we find it difficult to speak.

There are additional explanations for the slow emergence of work on popular music in media studies. For much of its history, media education has been dominated by a concern with the protection of pupils from manipulation and mystification by the media industries. The practices of news and advertising have therefore drawn the most consistent and productive attention. Of course, popular music has, from time to time, been targeted with a similar intent but it has not been regarded as a domain of comparable importance, perhaps because it has been seen as addressing only young people, an audience often assumed to be a powerless, pre-political minority with necessarily ephemeral interests. If growing up, and out of, a youthful saturation with 'pop' could be regarded as inevitable then, despite such immediate obsessions, the school student of the media should be directed towards more enduring problems of the kind which teachers, and other adults, recognized and found disturbing. From within this demystificatory perspective, other, overlapping, reasons for avoiding pop could be suggested. First of all, it is notoriously difficult for teachers to know more than students about popular music or, often, to persuade students that what teachers know is *more* and important. Second, because an enjoyment of popular music in youth is intense and vigorously defended by school students, to approach with a critical, demystificatory intent is likely to meet determined resistance. Third, though pop is an industry it is also, and this has been widely acknowledged, also a collection of genres in which much that is innovative and, sometimes, politically challenging can be articulated. For these reasons, pop is too ambiguous an object of study and has been left to one side in pursuing what teachers could either attack or advocate with more confidence.

In a relatively recent and influential collection, *Media Education: An Introduction* (Alvarado and Boyd-Barrett, 1992), it is remarkable that the most emphatic assertions of the importance of popular music are to be found among extracts dating from the early 1960s and 1970s. The first comes out of the early formative years of cultural studies. Stuart Hall and Paddy Whannel published *The Popular Arts* (1964) in the same year that the Centre for Contemporary Cultural Studies was established (Hall *et al.*, 1980). Despite their use of *jazz* to represent popular music, their comments include observations of continuing relevance:

> The opportunist teacher who embraces the leisure interests of his (sic) pupils in the hope of leading them to higher things is as frequently unsympathetic to the really valuable qualities of popular culture as his colleague who remains resolutely hostile ... Even when this doctrine is presented in its more progressive dress as 'beginning with the child's interests' it remains unsatisfactory. The assumption is that we can begin with jazz but

with the intention of moving towards concert music . . . Now jazz music and the movies have their own special virtues but it is doubtful if these can be revealed when they are regarded as only stepping-stones in a hierarchy of taste. If these virtues are not revealed, if in handling jazz and films we do not confront their essential qualities, then their study will not result in a real growth of awareness (From Alvarado and Boyd-Barrett, 1992: 25).

Subsequent references to Cole Porter and Ella Fitzgerald, at a time when The Beatles were becoming massively popular and when early Motown was achieving some success in Britain, compromise the intentions of their argument. But the place they give to music, alongside film, and their refusal of a 'hierarchy of taste', constitute orientations for the study of popular culture which have yet to be adequately realized and which have been significantly marginalized in legislation for a National Curriculum.

An extract from *Mass Media and the Secondary School*, a sociological survey rather than a media education text, (Murdock and Phelps, 1973) also represents some important advocacy, in this case from someone the authors describe as 'a young music mistress in a large mixed comprehensive school in London':

I think it is essential that any music teacher today should take account of the vast amount of music the pupils hear through the mass media. I do not mean that entire lessons should be given over to 'pop' but that it should be treated as a branch of music, with an equal right to be enjoyed as much as any other. The teacher must then go on to help the children decide for themselves what they like or dislike *within* each type (From Alvarado and Boyd-Barrett, 1992: 16; see also Murdock and Phelps, 1973: 140–50).

Of course, as with Hall and Whannel, there are elements of the Leavisite discourse of 'discrimination' in these remarks but their importance here is to register the gulf between the recognition of these cultural priorities in the 1960s and 1970s and the continuing difficulty of developing their implications 20 and 30 years later.

It is only in the late 1980s that a stronger interest in the pleasures of media consumption and a more empirically informed grasp of audience engagements with popular texts began to emerge among media teachers. Such elements may have coexisted with the more demystificatory strand in the practice of many teachers, but they were not easily articulated amid discourses privileging moral and political critique. Though Hall and Whannel (1964) were able to record some acknowledgement of popular pleasures, it should be recalled that they wrote as Labour entered power after a long period of Conservative government. By contrast, the political circumstances of the later 1970s should be seen as having elicited a more combative rhetoric from media studies. The sense of crisis in politics and education after 1976, and the emergence of the authoritarian populism of the Thatcher era, generated a need from within media studies to make teaching a credible political response and, from without, it was necessary to make media studies appear a serious and rigorous discipline, not compromised by attention to what might appear frivolous.

It is not surprising, therefore, that many of the teaching handbooks which defined the discipline in the late 1970s and 1980s made little mention of popular music at all. For example, *Teaching about Television* (Masterman, 1980) was both widely read and influential in the shaping of media teaching in schools. Meanwhile, *Mass Media and the Secondary School* (Murdock and Phelps, 1973), which advocated significant attention to pop but didn't offer practical advice, had little significant influence. Masterman made television the central medium for study: more pervasive than film, more powerful (visual) than radio and thus a priority for classroom analysis. As in many other media studies books of the period, pop music was represented by the BBC 1 weekly programme *Top of the Pops*. Somewhat ironically, therefore, Masterman allowed popular music only that degree of visibility permitted by a medium criticized for its exclusions and neglect of cultures beyond the horizon of the dominant ideology.

It is worth recovering some of the detail here. Masterman's text, completed in 1978, draws upon his own practice, and that of colleagues, through the 1970s. A kind of classroom democracy is identified as responsible for *Top of the Pops'* entry into his lesson; he makes it clear that he did not choose the programme:

> For the purposes of this exercise any programme will do – a point worth stressing, for what is being taught is a method of analysis which will yield insights across the whole output of the medium. Deciding by majority vote the class choose, unsurprisingly, *Top of the Pops* (BBC1) (Masterman, 1980: 62).

The exercise, consistent with much subsequent media teaching, is conceived conceptually. The concepts to be taught were iconography, narrative structure, spectacle, genre and mediation. The difficulty is that, despite Masterman's enthusiasm for progressive teaching, the meaning of the students' choice, and the meanings of the programme, are subordinated to *his* definition of what the lesson is to mean for them. His own account of the meaning of the programme seems to arise out of an accidental juxtaposition with *Gardeners' World* rather than through any comparison with other programming addressed to young people or, indeed, any account of the broader field of popular music at the time (the early days of punk, the emergence of reggae into widespread popularity, particularly Bob Marley). His comment on the programme is this:

> It isn't a chronological age which has drawn together the blooming young and fast-fading disc-jockeys and stars, but an attitude. To be young in this sense is to exist butterfly-like in an a-causal world to which one has a totally passive relationship. Here-and-now, celebrated because it *is*, becomes emptied of meaning (cf. the aimless meandering talk of all disc-jockeys everywhere) . . . the attitude locks wonderfully well into the interests of capitalism. Likewise the expression of a tentatively emerging identity, a 'natural' desire to be different, to be an individual is achieved through an ownership, particularly of records and clothes, which presupposes the

possession of money, and an absence of adult constraints in spending it
. . . it holds out the promise of eternal youth through constant consumption
(Masterman, 1980: 64).

The sharp edge of Frankfurt School critical theory is here, merging with elements of a Leavisite distaste for commerce. The effect is to position young people
as the recipients of a corrupting consumerism and the media teacher as intervening
to challenge the transmission of such an ideology. Though still a powerful tendency in media education, the contrary emphasis, on modes of consumption in which
cultural agency has some part (see Buckingham, 1986; 1987; 1990; Lusted, 1991),
has at least begun to exert a greater influence, though in Masterman's later book,
Teaching the Media (Masterman, 1985)[7] there is no further discussion of popular
music at all. Indeed, it is only in the 1990s that media education texts have begun
to include any substantial discussion of popular music.[8] Such recent acknowledgement and advocacy of teaching about popular music may yet have had little impact
on the wider practice of media teaching but it is notable that new course outlines
for examinations in 1997 do include music.[9] Meanwhile, in music education, there
is evidence of a more consistent history of interest and innovation through from the
1970s and it is to this that I turn in the next section.

Approaches through Music Education

Between 1976 and 1982, Graham Vulliamy and Ed Lee edited three collections of
essays in which teachers, mostly of music, described and proposed studies of pop
and other 'non-classical' genres. Vulliamy, in Whitty and Young (1976) outlined
his concern:

> . . . to apply some of the insights of contemporary sociologists of education
> . . . A major focus of recent work in the sociology of education has been
> a critical consideration of the school curriculum and what counts as valid
> knowledge in educational institutions (Whitty and Young, 1976: 19).

In common with the intentions of what was called the 'new' sociology of education, exemplified in Young (1971), Vulliamy questioned the orthodox separation and
privileging of subject-based (school) knowledge relative to the everyday knowledge
acquired by children in informal contexts. The case of music, polarized between what
is *serious* and what is *pop*, was presented as a particularly explicit instance and one
where his critique could contribute to significant curricular change. He argued for a
curtailment of serious music's claim to absolute aesthetic superiority:

> It can . . . be argued that different types of music necessitate different cri-
> teria for aesthetic judgement and the 'objectivity' of such judgements is
> relative to public truth criteria within that particular type of music . . . music

would seem to be an area where change could take place as a result of a shift in the 'subject perspective' of music teachers (Whitty and Young, 1976: 29).

Though he did acknowledge a variety of material constraints upon the change he advocated, he seemed otherwise committed to a rationalist pedagogy, believing that 'rational analysis' could simply displace affective identifications, thus advocating a dispassionate evaluation of 'sets of criteria':

> ... many young people are extremely critical in their appreciation of various types of 'pop' music and approach the latter *with clear sets of criteria* concerning the relative worth both of various styles and of various records within one style (Whitty and Young, 1976: 31) [My italics].

Such optimistic rationalism underestimates the complex formation of identities and the commitments involved in statements of taste:

> The process of musical education should be concerned with expanding pupils' horizons ... encouraging all forms of musical expression without as far as possible holding preconceived ideas about which forms of music are intrinsically better or worse than others (Whitty and Young, 1976: 31).

As the experience of many teachers has confirmed, even if they are striving to bracket their 'preconceived ideas', students are unlikely to make any comparable effort to suspend their ideas, feelings and identities.

Nevertheless, the intention to recognize and work with the cultural experience of students was an important theme in this account of music education. It can be seen as intimately associated with concepts of *child-centred* teaching – an approach which, in media studies, was regarded as pathetically liberal and was thus the object of some intense theoretical anxiety. If, in media studies, popular cultural experience was always compromised by the invasive contamination of dominant ideology, in music education few such doubts, and none of the neo-Marxist theory of ideology, appear to have secured a place.

Vulliamy and Lee's (1976) editorial comments are illustrative of this difference in perspective:

> A general problem with pupil-centred learning is that teachers tend to fear a loss of control ... the teacher might also argue that in this case the situation could be made even more difficult by his [sic] own ignorance, often exaggerated by rapid changes of fashion in pop ... we feel that pop should not be taught in the traditional manner, in which the teacher is the master of a body of facts ... the whole operation being directed by him. Instead the teacher should start by seeing his pupils as already possessing a considerable knowledge of pop music, which they are strongly motivated to

expand. What he brings to the situation, which they do not have, is a body of ideas and concepts about music . . . the possibility of a real dialogue emerges, particularly if the teacher is willing to recognise the limitations of his own knowledge in this area . . . the pupils, in having to communicate with the teacher, could take a more active part in the educational process (Vulliamy and Lee, 1976: 2).

Though some elements of this kind of statement could be found in media education texts in the late 1970s, it lacks the anxiety about what young people might learn from pop which, with a variety of political inflections, entered virtually any account of media teaching. This is both an advantage and a weakness. The valuable aspects of Vulliamy and Lee's statement lie in the potentially productive sense of a relationship involving some fluidity in subject-positions: being learners or teachers become unfixed, negotiable positions. However, their wish to validate popular music also excludes issues which media teaching would identify and question: for example, the form of gender relations within the field of popular music, almost entirely ignored in their studies, might well be given a central place. In this respect, their neglect of wider ideological questions follows from their exclusive focus on the elitism of a dominant aesthetic ideology.

Vulliamy's own essay, 'Pupil-centred music teaching', offers further evidence of the assumption that, if only the division of music between high and low culture could be overcome, then the conditions for a radical 'open' practice would follow. He suggested, following a discussion of Murdock and Phelps (1973):

. . . one might hope that a more open approach . . . would break down . . . barriers between classical and pop . . . but also *within* pop . . . The process of musical education should be concerned with expanding pupils' horizons and the best way to achieve this is by encouraging all forms of musical expression . . . (Vulliamy in Vulliamy and Lee, 1976: 57).

The implicit proposal that education could provide a kind of liberal public forum in which divisions might be eliminated by the rational pursuit of mutual knowledge bore some similarity to tendencies within multiculturalism in the 1970s; and, just as the multicultural discourse became both more necessary, and less credible, so too did Vulliamy both repeat the need for hierarchical divisions to be eliminated and actually present evidence of how they might be reproduced. Indeed, Vulliamy appears to favour 'rock' notions of authenticity (Frith, 1983) but at the same time, drawing upon evidence from Murdock and Phelps, connects the use of such critical criteria only with middle-class students. He comments:

In rock music . . . the originators of the material tend to account for the total product: not only do groups now write, orchestrate and play their own material, but in many cases they also produce their own records thus eliminating the possibility of outside control over the finished product (Vulliamy and Lee, 1976: 58).

In this respect, Vulliamy risked validating one particular set of criteria, thus colluding with a process he intended to challenge.

Some of the contributions to Vulliamy and Lee (1976) were marked by a suspicion of popular music and, with a more explicit intention than Vulliamy, sought critical standpoints within an educational distancing from pop. To some extent, the polarity of mass culture versus authenticity was reasserted:

> ... the anti-social behaviour of teenage fans at soccer matches, and the conduct of some famous footballers ... has no connection with the nature of the game itself, and certainly does not prevent it from being played in schools. There is a clear separation in the minds of physical education teachers between soccer as a social phenomenon and soccer as a game. We must, as music educators, also be aware of a similar separation between 'pop culture' and music making in 'pop' and related Afro-American styles such as the blues, as a valid musical recreation for young people (Spencer in Vulliamy and Lee, 1976: 100).

This implied a strategy of appropriation. By seeking to abstract from the popular domain those forms which can be seemingly stripped of their cultural meaning and reconstructed on the terms which teachers dictate, the teacher was called upon to exert an extraordinary cultural authority. In this scenario, the meanings young people gave to pop, or to football, were to have no place. It was the teacher's attribution of meaning which should determine the way in which popular music ought to be engaged. Elsewhere in the same essay the writer reintroduces the discourse of a defensive cultural minority, struggling to preserve authentic value, claiming that 'despite their outward conformity to pop culture, the creativity of teenage children remains intact' (Vulliamy and Lee, 1976: 107). Indeed he concludes his contribution with a somewhat hopeful plea for the restoration of a folk creativity, conceiving schools as engaged in rivalry with, and in opposition to, the media:

> I am convinced that an increase of creative pop music making in schools where, given resources and encouragement, children will find that they are capable of producing more interesting pop music than is sold to them by the mass media, will lead to schools creating an alternative teenage musical culture based on *doing* rather than just listening. This could prove a formidable rival to the 'establishment pop' of the mass media (Vulliamy and Lee, 1976: 121).

If students produced their own music successfully it seems unlikely that they did so *in opposition* to the domain of commercial popular music. More recent studies show the fragility of any attempt to sustain a version of creativity in isolation from current popular culture (see Fornas, Lindberg and Sernhede, 1995).

A further contribution, of a similar kind, is worth noting here. In this, despite the positions to which Vulliamy and Lee, as editors, attempted to commit themselves, the construction of school music in opposition to media music emerges as a discursive limit beyond which the argument cannot progress:

Since musical education for the over-fourteens was concerned mainly with a preparation for post-school leisure it was unrealistic to ignore the music they were listening to out of school and would continue listening to, or at least be bombarded with, after leaving. With the powerful influence of broadcasting media, popular music of all kinds has become a major part of our lives. It is difficult for teachers to touch pop music, not only because they are no longer musically young but also because of certain non-musical characteristics in pop, which are related to the adolescent's need for an independent identity. Also commercial exploitation has made pop – as it has other popular music – disreputable. Yet thanks to the dominance of younger musicians and to the continuing influence of Afro-American musical values, pop and rock music have tremendous vitality. The music teacher's job is to educate and to combat the limiting and desensitising aspects of the mass-media presentation of pop . . . it may be necessary to begin their musical education by starting from what their interest actually is (Nicholls in Vulliamy and Lee, 1976: 131–2).

This delineation of a boundary between the 'popular-authentic' and the 'popular-media' seemed to constrain otherwise constructive efforts to rethink the relationship of school practice to students' cultural experience. Though not displaying quite the fear of a loss of control suggested by the analogy with football, here too the narrowing of music to a concern with active performance makes the social meanings of music extraneous, awkward impediments to a more proper attention to form and its enactment. In this way the social practice of listening, and all the complexity of practices of music consumption and use, became subordinate matters, if they were recognized at all.

In a later publication (Vulliamy and Lee, 1982a), the editors made a wide array of suggestions for the development of popular music in school. They suggested that:

. . . the popular audience is more concerned with dancing, social participation, and in some cases making music, than with attentive listening and analysis. The teacher who understands and attempts to implement these insights will find a need for some reassessment of his values and some readjustment of his professional role (Vulliamy and Lee, 1982a: 22).

They therefore proposed that music become linked with dance through both dance based social events and through explorations of the variety of dance styles known to students. They also advocated the production of rock musicals, viewing pop related films, and developing project work around pop graphics. In these respects, their emphasis upon forms of reception and upon the inter-related character of pop music and the media offered promising developments. Other examples of media-orientated work on pop music, and perhaps more securely grounded in actual practice, did exist. For example, Paul Farmer described his own CSE Mode 3 course (1977) at Holland Park School. He included work on the music industry:

This covers the recording and manufacture of records, music broadcasting, pop journalism, the media and other related areas. Visits to radio stations and record company offices are organised, and visiting speakers from the industry are invited to talk to the pupils. Specific topics include: the development of recording equipment and techniques; the organisation and management of a performer; the marketing organisation of record companies; the disc jockey; 'bootlegging' and 'piracy' (Farmer in Vulliamy and Lee, 1982b: 59).

The practical component of the examination also specified the submission of 'a short radio-type music programme, recorded, mixed and edited entirely by the pupils, who use their own choice of records.' In these respects, music education did offer important precedents for media studies, itself largely sustained by the mostly teacher initiated CSE Mode 3 in that period.

So, having looked back through the past two decades and more, it is worth pausing briefly to summarize the main approaches to teaching about popular music which have emerged from media studies and from music education. In media studies, until very recently, popular music has drawn very little attention and has tended to be either displaced by, or absorbed into, the approaches associated with the wish to demystify the media for young people. Earlier and more constructive proposals, from Hall and Whannel (1964) and from Murdock and Phelps (1973), have been neglected, almost forgotten, it seems, in the more definite formation of media studies as a curricular subject through the later 1970s and early 1980s. By contrast with the primarily combative, 'anti-ideological', paradigm of media studies, music education has carried a more diverse range of initiatives around popular music though, in the studies gathered together by Vulliamy and Lee (1976; 1982a; 1982b), there is a strong tendency for them to converge around a wish to identify and develop 'authentic creativity'. The constraints perpetuated in both media studies and music education, despite their marked differences, are thus both underpinned by the logic of discrimination from an implicitly superior cultural position.

In media studies and in English, there have been significant moves beyond demystification (see Buckingham, 1986; 1990; Moss, 1989) but the implications for work around popular music remain relatively undeveloped (see, however, Buckingham and Sefton-Green, 1994). In music education, the most fully argued case for teaching which engages with popular music can be found in the work of Lucy Green (1988). In the next part of this section, I want to introduce some of her key ideas and consider their implications for media education. The complexity and detail of her argument have been compressed in the following account but, at the very least, I want to *initiate* a dialogue between these otherwise dissociated curricular domains.

Music on Deaf Ears (Green, 1988) was published in the early years of the new GCSE examination. Indeed, a part of her argument is concerned with the claims made for the GCSE, particularly as a means to 'overcome' the separation of classical and popular music and the social interests they represent. However, she is also concerned with elaborating an historical and dialectical theory of musical meaning which has more general implications for the study of music. My purpose, in reading

Green, is to consider the implications of her argument for the approach to popular music adopted by media teachers and their students.

A key distinction for Green is that between 'inherent' and 'delineated' musical meaning. It is a distinction which Green insists is strictly analytic and thus listening to music can never be a matter of attending to one kind of meaning to the exclusion of the other. However, the terms are useful to the extent that they orientate any attempt to analyse the meanings of music towards temporal structures and sonic qualities, on the one hand, and more contextual, cultural, meanings on the other. It is evident, though, that in Green's exposition there is a considerable struggle to keep the theoretical objections at bay. The terms *inherent* and *delineated* are awkward, letting in too many troublesome connotations which then have to be methodically expelled. Inherent seems to imply that meanings are located in the musical text itself, independent of audiences and their contexts of reception. It suggests a level of formal meaning quite distinct from the social domain in which actual meanings are produced, interpreted and constantly reworked.[10]

Like the uneasy history of the concepts of denotation and connotation in visual semiotics, inherent and delineated meaning emerge as a pair to be always accompanied by their disclaimers, reiterated warnings that *inherent* meaning only refers to 'a formal, or logical, moment' which does not include 'the meaning of music as a historical object' (Green, 1988: 26). Musical experience, she argues, cannot be divided, and the conceptual distinction is, she repeats, 'a purely formal move on my part' (Green, 1988: 12). So what is the value of her argument for work on popular music in media education?

It is in her discussion of delineated meanings that her argument, and her examples, intersect both with media education and with cultural studies. She suggests that:

> Images, associations, memories, queries, problems and beliefs inspired in us by music are musical meanings that . . . point outwards from music and towards its role as a social product . . . Music delineates a profile of its position in the musical world amongst these social relations, and thereby also delineates ideas of social relations and social meanings to us: I will call these *delineated musical meanings* (Green, 1988: 28).

In a reworking of Willis' ethnography of hippies and bike-boys (Willis, 1978) she stresses the close inter-relation of inherent and delineated meanings:

> Aspects of [rock 'n' roll's] inherent meanings – its beat and forward impulse, its ability to be remembered, to get in the head, to accompany dance – are undistinguished from its delineated meanings – dancing as a sociable activity, motor-bikes, speed, machismo and aggression . . .
> . . . The bike-boys liked the music not only for its inherent meanings, but also because what inheres in it carries further delineated meanings: dancing as a sociable activity, fast motor-bikes, machismo, leather jackets, camaraderie. These were shared social markers; they were associated with

the music, itself a social marker, its inherent meanings having given rise to a set of learnt responses which, once learnt, were integrated with a set of activities in the social world. Hence with all the arbitrariness of the linguistic sign, the music comes to delineate these activities . . . However, in the bike-boys' minds, the inherent and the delineated musical meanings were integral and inseparable, and in their activities, undistinguished (Green, 1988: 40–1).

This is one significant, and interesting, example of how she puts her conceptual pair to work. But there are some significant uncertainties to be drawn out more fully here. To reiterate, inherent meanings are, in one moment, seemingly pre-social, acquiring social meaning only when incorporated into the field of delineations. Furthermore, the relation between these 'moments' is understood to be 'arbitrary', as if sets of empty musical signifiers have an existence somehow prior to the 'attachment' of, contingent, social signifieds. I have doubts about the value of describing this as 'arbitrariness' and, once again, the problems seem to arise because the terms she brings into play carry implications which, in the larger context of her argument, she appears not to intend. Thus, against the notion of arbitrariness, I want to emphasize that the inherent meaning of the music, rock 'n' roll, is already social – it is, like any other music, a socially produced form in which particular agents make, and have made, choices between possible formal alternatives. Its characteristic features are never therefore a neutral material onto which social meanings are imposed but are themselves meaningful elements in a particular socially located communication – rock 'n' roll produced for a specific social audience. Other kinds of music could not be substituted for rock 'n' roll, and not just because they have the wrong delineated meanings – the qualities of the music are motivated (Kress, 1993a; 1994). Indeed, the social subjects involved in the production and reception of such music are not usefully understood through an abstraction of consciousness from its social constitution; the mythical generality of the listening subject, stripped of social interests, does not pre-exist the acquisition of learnt responses.

The importance of Green's case really only emerges in her discussion of what she calls 'musical fetishism', where it becomes clear that her priority is in fact to challenge the view that the only *social meanings* of music are those which can be translated into verbal language. To the contrary, she wants to argue that music is itself a social medium but not one which can be entirely assimilated to a verbal semiotic. Thus, her discussion of 'musical fetishism' emerges as the crucial turn in her argument, pointing much more affirmatively to a social account of inherent meaning:

The concept of musical fetishism relates directly to the ideological assumption that music is autonomous: because fetishism posits delineated meanings as the only ones that are communicable, it simultaneously posits inherent meanings as autonomous essences. We have access to the former but the latter, it appears, elude us. Whereas this is true in so far as we communicate *about* music in natural language, it is untrue in so far as we also communicate *through* music via musical inherent meanings. We are just as much the creators and reproducers of inherent meanings as we are of delineated meanings. Because it ignores this, ideology posits humanity as the slave of a music that has its own natural and unalterable laws, not as raw sonic material, but as pre-extant musical meanings (Green, 1988: 87).

The implication of her argument is that an educational practice which does not make music heard, and through which musical meanings can be exchanged, will thus collude with, and reproduce, the ideological construction of music as a non-social medium (see McClary, 1991). This is an important challenge for media education and one which raises questions for educational practice which inevitably extend beyond the scope of my own research for this book.

The rationale for the somewhat provocative title of her book is made clear when she comments:

As soon as one attributes particular qualities to musically-aroused emotional states without further enquiry, the inherent meanings are posited as inexplicable essences. Once unquestioningly incorporated into an educational setting, the mode of study which is engendered by such an approach is one that therefore distances the inherent meanings of music from the act of learning: it is a sort of paramusicology, the study of music without the music (Green, 1988: 88).

Media teachers, often also English teachers, might assume that verbal language is the pre-eminently social medium and that whatever cannot be translated into, and therefore 're-expressed', through its forms is beyond the semiotic domain. To accept that there are other modes of communication which are distinct from, though sometimes combining with, the verbal is not easy in a *logocentric* culture. Through the history of media education, a massive effort has been committed to the task of explaining visual material in verbal terms and, no doubt, the same challenge confronts a social semiotics of music. This verbal imperative is important but, as Green suggests, might compound the common attribution of a mysterious, non-human quality to music. Thus without by any means wishing to abandon the need for talk about music, it is essential to bring musical sound into a practice often constrained, by a combination of institutional regulation, limited resources, and mere diffidence, to hesitate whenever listening to, or the production of, music becomes necessary.

Though media education can hardly centre itself in the teaching of musical performance skills, there is a case for a much more extensive use of musical quotation and representation in media work. In any case, the proliferation of the new technologies of musical production has opened up possibilities beyond the traditional concern with the achievement of instrumental skill. All the popular uses of such technologies, in hip-hop culture (Gilroy, 1993) for example, suggest the futility of maintaining hard educational boundaries between what counts as music and what belongs to *media studies*. Forms of production in media education have become more central in recent years and there is every reason to support a sense of cultural agency, and of the sociality of musical meaning, through an exploration of precisely those practices which do not depend upon an elite social milieu. At the same time, it is essential to acknowledge that successful production, in practice, actually requires more intervention by teachers and more developed skills than the wish simply to undercut elite conceptions of knowledge might allow (see Buckingham, Grahame and Sefton-Green, 1995).

Conclusion

In this chapter I have provided four distinct, but interrelated, vantage points from which to view the rest of this book. These four sections – Differentiating Youth, Putting Cultural Studies in Its Place?, Media Education – A Backward Glance, and Approaches through Music Education – may not map onto all the positions from which readers take up the following argument for popular music in the media curriculum. But, as a guide, they each point towards features of the account which I offer.

Simon Frith's sociological sketch of young people's lives in Keighley, with which I began this chapter, provides one vivid example of what a particular discipline enables us to know. But it is, like my own research, inevitably constrained, partial and provisional. Certainly, questions of identity, of subjectivity and of musical form have gained greater prominence since such issues were addressed by Frith (1978) and by Willis (1978) from within sociology and cultural studies. My own concern, traced through the four sections of this chapter and pursued in the empirical research for this book, is to consider how to refocus the social themes identified by Frith, in particular, in relation to the possibilities for practice in media education. At its simplest, I just wonder in what ways a teacher of English, conceivably of media or social studies, could have used Frith's account back in the early 1970s? Further, in what ways can my own more particular concern with the interface between informal and formal knowledge in classrooms inform the practice of English and media teachers?

In what follows, I move closer to classrooms, considering first of all the discursive constitution of adolescence and its persistence in current forms of exchange between teachers and students. As I go on to show, in Chapter 3, I focus my account within the classroom practices of media studies, addressing questions of knowledge and learning rather than seeking to provide an ethnography of youth cultures. How young people engage with music outside of school was not beyond the bounds of my curiosity,[11] but I never attempted to 'hang out' with young people in clubs or in record shops, nor did I ever seek to visit them at home. Sometimes (see Chapters 4 and 5) there are *accounts* of activities in other places but, in this study, these accounts are taken as shaped by the school context and by the identity of their addressee – myself as a kind of teacher. The larger question is thus, throughout, that of how young people represent their informal cultural experience in the formal institutional context of school and specifically in the context of the subject media studies. Within that context, my concern has been, both as a teacher and in this research, to consider problems of *agency* and of *identity* from the vantage point of English and media studies teaching.

Notes

1 Frith comments:

> My sample was 105 pupils from one of Keighley's two comprehensive schools and was representative of the school's social and academic mix. In the town as a whole only upper-middle-class children were creamed off to direct-grant or public schools. I also talked to pupils' friends who were at the other comprehensive school or had already started at college and university (1978: 216).

2 See Buckingham and Sefton-Green (1994) and Buckingham, Grahame and Sefton-Green (1995).
3 Leavisite refers to the highly influential literary criticism of F.R. Leavis.
4 *Priorities* **2** 77–8, dated February 4th 1978.
5 He contributed to the Summer 1975 issue of *Resistence through Rituals*, see Hall and Jefferson, 1975: 157–66.
6 See Heath (1983) Chapter 5 and the Epilogue.
7 In Masterman, (1985) there is some discussion of what Masterman calls the 'ideology of sound', pp. 153–6, but no discussion of music.
8 See Buckingham and Sefton-Green (1994); Buckingham, Grahame and Sefton-Green (1995); Fleming (1993); Hart (1991). For teaching materials see Blanchard, Greenleaf and Sefton-Green (1989) and Ferrari and James (1989).
9 See, for example, the Southern Examining Group syllabus for the 1997 GCSE examinations in Media Studies (Southern Examining Group, 1994).
10 For recent, and substantial, developments in Lucy Green's own work see *Music, Gender and Education* (1997). The introductory chapter includes a very clear restatement of the inherent/delineated distinction.
11 See the work of John Shepherd and Jennifer Giles-Davis, 'Music, text and subjectivity', (Shepherd, 1991) for an interesting, and challenging, precedent.

Chapter Two

Questions of Agency and Adolescence

Introduction

Studies of *adolescence* and of *youth* are so numerous (see Griffin, 1993) that, rather than attempt to review even a substantial subcategory, I intend this chapter to fulfil a different purpose. I want to identify, as briefly as possible, some of the approaches to questions of agency and of youth which have helped me to make sense of young people's responses to 'being taught about' pop music in school.

An important argument both for the constitution of *youth* as a category, and for its subdivision into *childhood* and *adolescence*, is that physical development determines a whole array of social and psychological characteristics of young people. It would be difficult to disagree that physical size and sexual development are both relevant to the differentiation of young people from adults and of children from teenagers. However, the meanings attributed to changes in size, in body shape and in sexual development, are socially produced and, for young people themselves, their own understanding of such changes is not an expression of the biological but is, rather, an appropriation of a complex array of socially available discourses – those of popular biology and psychology, of law and of education, but also those of the various cultural media (see Connell, 1995). My particular area of concern is, therefore, that of the cultural-discursive material through which, within a particular historical location, childhood and youth are constituted and demarcated.

Though the organization of families, economic and legal structures, and the institutional sequestration of young people, are powerful determinants of their lives, I want to dwell mainly upon the meaning of adolescence as a subjective phenomenon. The relationship between social practices and subjectivity is a complex matter but I want to emphasize that one crucial dimension of that relationship is shaped by the continuing discursive construction of social actors. For example, the categories of *adolescent* and *adult* have radically different implications for the actions of people assigned to each category and, perhaps most importantly, different degrees, even different kinds, of agency are attributed to each. It may be that the agency of adolescents is construed as less rational, certainly more emotional and more erratic, than that of adults; such preadult agency is not therefore safe, unless contained by social identities which project a continuity with 'respectable' adulthood. Identities more strictly circumscribed by the complex requirements of a middle-class education are likely to be linked, by adults, with concepts of maturity and responsibility.

Adolescence *is* a highly problematic concept. In current use, it is widely distributed across popular discourse, though still deriving some of its aura of technical authority from psychology. It is commonly used to label and explain, in an elliptical and routine way, the combination of sexual maturation (often represented in terms of 'raging hormones') with the confusion of being in-between childhood and adulthood. It is thus, crucially, understood to be an inevitable and unavoidable stage or phase through which all must pass, if with varying degrees of torment and distress. However, the delineation of such a phase, and its construction as a natural and inescapable feature of individual development, tends to reflect and confirm the institutional authority of a psychological problematic. There is, it seems, a familiar circularity: psychology recognizes adolescence, adolescence is a problem which psychology can explain.

A Historical Perspective

In the aftermath of 1968, John Gillis produced a history of youth which, though limited by its masculine focus, suggests a view of adolescence as an historically circumscribed feature of economic and familial organization. In *Youth and History* (Gillis, 1981), he opposes the view that adolescence is a natural developmental phase, a perspective which he attributes to the universalizing discourses of medicine and psychology. Indeed, Gillis argues against any simple relation of cause and effect between puberty and adolescence. To the contrary, the emphasis of his account falls upon the sets of social and economic relationships within which sexual maturity might be understood in different ways and given varying degrees of importance.

The achievement of the social preconditions of adolescence is represented as, first of all, peculiar to the middle-classes of the developed West. During the later decades of the nineteenth century, 'low mortality and low fertility made adolescence possible' but, he continues, 'the real crucible of the age-group's social and psychological qualities was the elite secondary school' (Gillis, 1981: 105). The extension of schooling and the deferral of young people's entry into more adult domains are seen as fundamental to the formation of the new adolescent age phase, between 14 and 18. The emphasis, in this middle-class construction, was upon the 'conformity, self-denial, and dependence' required of children in whom time, money and the expectation of continuing respectability and class privilege were invested.

This sketch of the origins of a discourse, for that is how I am appropriating a study which is neither primarily concerned with discursive analysis nor with the experience of school students in the present, provides one way of critically disengaging my own analysis from a complicity with the still prevalent discourse of adolescence. In the account offered by Gillis, adolescence emerges as a social mechanism through which children, maintained as subjects to whom teachers, parents and youth workers have access, might pass into the settled and regulated life of adult respectability; lacking such access, adolescents would be at risk, subject to their own unguided agency. There is clearly still a case for emphasizing the continuing effectivity of the discourse of adolescence and, in my account, I argue that young people themselves take up positions as adolescent and, in part, constitute themselves as subjects within its terms.

Academic Discourse: Representing Youth

There is a case for arguing that *we* as adult subjects, and as academics, however old, are not simply beyond youth but carry the traces and consequences of our own location as youth/adolescent at another time and, in doing research on youth, might constructively recall such moments in our own formation (see Griffin, 1993; Hollway, 1994). Here, for example, it is appropriate to add a little more to the autobiographical notes presented in the previous chapter. There is a relation between the production of the present text and the coincidence of my own youth/adolescence with schooling in an institution concerned to inculcate traditional middle-class culture and to emulate the regimes of masculinity associated with the elite public schools. At 15 and 16, in 1967 and 1968, I was intensely preoccupied with being elsewhere, locating myself in a cultural space defined by the fading of American 'beat' writing, much of it dating from the early 1950s, into the more immediate allure of West Coast 'counter-culture'. I took off, whenever I could, to try out another kind of identity – if in effect to thus return with subcultural, and sexual, capital to set against that of my ex-best friend, then into being a mod, sex and scooters, fighting and The Small Faces. Hitching down to London alone in the spring of 1968, I began a series of ventures into other people's lives, smoking joints with people 10 years older, stumbling into (mis)calculated sex in streetlit rooms. The day I finished my GCE O Levels, I took a Chemistry practical exam in Beverley in the morning, and took LSD just off Kensington High Street, in London, in the afternoon. My illicit absences led me to a threat of expulsion. To define myself through this cultural other scene fulfilled, if with considerable damage, several purposes. At the very least it set me up, like those in the third of Frith's case-studies, as 'aggressively hip' in the context of school and as more of an enigma, and maybe a challenge, to my mod (formerly childhood) friend. But somehow, and unlike my friend who did get expelled, I retrieved myself into the expected educational narrative and, high on high literature, did the Sixth Form.

The tension between the cultural order of the school and the construction of a self-identity located in another, if equally masculine, cultural scene has persisted in the negotiated compromises that have shaped my adult, and academic, preoccupations. Karl Mannheim remarks that young people are 'dramatically aware of a process of destabilization and take sides in it' and that, meanwhile, 'the older generation cling to the re-orientation that had been the drama of *their* youth' (Mannheim, in

Jenks, 1982: 268). This can be construed as critical of the self-bounded concerns of 'the older generation' but it also points to that persistence of past identities which, I want to argue, rather than impeding youth research, actually facilitates recognition of what, as adults, we may not otherwise allow much conscious time. It is through work upon the (dis)location of the supposedly mature, unitary, adult subject that the position of young people as participants in research can be (re)placed beyond the confines of adolescence. Thus, in any dialogue between ourselves as adults and young people, there should be some effort to reflectively deconstruct our own vantage point.

Agency . . .

I'll say more about how adults might relate to, and represent, young people in the next chapter. Here I want to ask in what sense young people, resident with parental figures, positioned as children, and yet also located culturally as growing up and rapidly entering into adult sexuality, can be the agents of their own self-identity. This 'double-positioning' (see James, 1993: 106) precedes adolescence but becomes more intensely contradictory in its demands during the later years of compulsory schooling. Responsibility for the self becomes a more insistent theme in those educational discourses which address secondary school students and, to some extent, *agency* is itself a construction which offers, and compels, the assumption of adult status. It would not be difficult to adopt a mostly celebratory view here, arguing that if such agency is expected of those still legally resident with their families (or guardians), then the forms of that agency far exceed the narrow terms of normative responsibility which schools may prescribe. To some extent, this is an argument I want to endorse but it would be simplistic and naive to cling to the phrase I used above – 'agents of their own self-identity'. This may be a motif in particular popular discourses around youth but it is overwhelmed by all the particular social and material conditions in which young people are charged with being more responsible for themselves. Though the recognition of the cultural agency of children and young people is a desirable counter-point to their portrayal as passive victims (see Griffin, 1993: 140–1), it is not credible to attribute to *them* a capacity for autonomous self-construction which *we*, as adults, might feel we have lost and wish, by means of displaced fantasies about 'the young', we could recover.

. . . and Discourse

Now, I want to offer just a brief outline of an approach to agency through *discourse*. Discourse, and the discursive emphasis of my argument, allows attention to language within its historically circumscribed uses. While making language a crucial dimension of subjectivity, the term discourse marks out a more fluid and variable encounter with language than that associated with accounts of language which stress its structural order, its stability and its duration across long phases of history. Such accounts cannot grasp the transformative agency of speakers. Discourse, however, is a socially located use of language, never reducible, at the level of meaning, to the generality of the 'official' language (see Bakhtin, 1994; Volosinov, 1973). Discourses may be very strongly bounded and institutionally regulated but, equally, they may be much less sharply defined, varying in their degrees of differentiation from other discourses, sometimes, perhaps, seeming to coalesce. For example, a discourse such as that of official medicine is of the first kind and those of folk, proverbial and alternative medicine might be of the latter. Within discourses, particular subject-positions are in play: thus, most distinctively, doctor and patient. Particular kinds of social relation are also inscribed within discourses and the subject-positions they sustain. To refuse to speak 'as a patient', to a doctor, is, if nothing else, a discursive aberration. However, there is evidently considerable scope for any person positioned as a patient to both maintain something of the mutually understood discursive relation while simultaneously elaborating, reworking and perhaps contesting that given subject-position.[1]

Tentatively, it is useful to think of being an adolescent in some of the ways that it is possible to think of being a patient. I want to argue, in effect, that just as people are only sometimes, and in widely varying circumstances, patients, so it is useful to say that people are, sometimes, adolescents. To be more precise: I want to argue, not that the young people, introduced through Chapters 4 to 7, are simply *adolescents*, but that being an 'adolescent' is one of the available self-identifications which they can adopt, contest and elaborate. This is not to deny the power of subordination associated with the discourses in which adolescence has been produced. The point is, rather, that there is considerable scope in the use of adolescence for its appropriation in the construction of self-understanding across a much longer time-span than the very few years, technically and prescriptively, associated with physical/sexual maturation. Children, in various circumstances, use being a child as a strategy in their negotiation of those social relations within which adopting such a subject-position may confer some advantage; equally, they may seek to refute the ascription of such a subject-position when, and where, it is a hindrance or involves conceding the power of others. Similarly, being an adolescent or a teenager, can be both a strategy in negotiating relations with others and a provisional mode of self-identification and, perhaps, self-understanding. To some extent, then, it is helpful to say that people produce themselves as young, as children, as teenagers and do have some degree of agency in their construction of self-identity at the level of their own inscription into different available discourses, and in their remaking of those discourses. But, also, as for patients, there is sometimes very little choice at all. In some circumstances, the constraints of the position to which people are assigned may be too intractable, and involve too many compromises, to be tolerated; in schools, for example, being positioned as a pupil and a non-adult is, for many, weirdly and impossibly inconsistent with the broader array of positions available elsewhere.

The relation of discourse to subjectivity requires some further discussion; the formulation of subject-positions in discourses cannot, after all, exhaust what is constitutive of subjectivity. It may be that some discursive acts are highly self-conscious and others routine, barely available as objects of conscious reflection until, and unless, the need arises. Giddens has proposed a distinction which seems close to that implied here (Giddens, 1979; 1991) – he argues, for example, that:

> . . . the accounts that actors are able to offer of their conduct draw upon the same stocks of knowledge as are drawn upon in the very production and reproduction of their action. As Harré expresses this, 'the very same social knowledge and skill is involved in the genesis of action and accounts . . . an individual's ability to do each depends upon his stock of social knowledge'. But we must make an important emendation to the point of view Harré appears to take. The 'giving of accounts' refers to the *discursive* capabilities and inclinations of actors, and does not exhaust the connections between 'stocks of knowledge' and action. The factor missing from Harré's characterisation is practical consciousness: tacit knowledge that is skilfully applied in the enactment of courses of conduct, but which the actor is not able to formulate discursively (Giddens, 1979: 57).

One aspect of conduct is, of course, the production of discursive acts – to speak is an *action* entailing the production of discourse. Thus, though this is not Giddens' central point, to some extent discursive acts are themselves dependent upon 'tacit knowledge' which the actor may not be able to reflect upon discursively. If, for example, young people speak as adolescents this might combine, in some moments, both a self-reflexive consciousness of such positioning and a tacit understanding of how to produce discourse from such a position. As Giddens argues, this should not be collapsed into the category of the unconscious. Indeed, even when the possibility of self-reflexive consciousness is not realized by an actor, there is no need to explain their actions as 'unconscious'. Giddens' argument here is this:

> The reflexive monitoring of action draws upon 'tacit knowledge' which, however, can only partially and imperfectly be expressed in discourse. Such knowledge, which is above all practical and contextual in character, is not unconscious in any of the senses in which that term is usually employed in the structuralist literature (Giddens, 1979: 40).

The 'contextual' use of tacit knowledge, in Giddens' terms, includes 'the monitoring of *the setting of interaction*, and not just the behaviour of the particular actors taken separately' (Giddens, 1979: 57). In relation to my concerns, this may help to clarify the sense in which young people in secondary schools, located there as adolescents, consistently take account of such an institutional setting and produce actions which constantly reproduce, but also re-inflect, the form and meaning of the positions they are called upon to occupy. Their agency is not therefore a matter of entirely self-conscious (knowing) tactics, nor is it to be sought in moments which appear to transcend the institutional setting. However, agency can be identified in the capacity to draw upon a multiple, and often diverse, repertoire of cultural knowledge in ways which enable actors to interpret and to project action beyond the positions to which they are assigned. Thus the codified formality and regulated conduct which schools attempt to sustain is, if powerful, also precarious.

The unconscious dimension of agency should not be neglected here. But it is exceptionally difficult to explore within the contexts which educational research allows. More generally, the practices of social research have not developed adequate means to document unconscious meanings and motives (see Hollway, 1994; Hunt, 1989). Nevertheless, there is a case for attending to the possible effects of emotional dynamics in contexts where, routinely, such an understanding of subjectivity is excluded. Giddens, again, argues for some recognition of the complex combination, or 'layering together', of discursive and practical consciousness with the unconscious:

> ... a theory of motivation also has to relate to the unacknowledged conditions of action: in respect of unconscious motives, operating or [sic] 'outside' the range of the self-understanding of the agent (Giddens, 1979: 59).

Indeed, he follows this assertion with a more detailed consideration of the terms in which the formation of the subject, and of agency, might be reappraised through a selective reading of Lacan. The attraction of the Lacanian account lies in its 'radical' reading of Freud – emphasizing that 'the "I" is already "internally divided" through the very process of achieving that status.'[2] This is, of course, a significant move beyond the approach to subjectivity allowed by most kinds of discourse analysis; their limitation, if also their provisional advantage, is that questions of an 'intra-psychic' nature are bracketed out. Such questions were not fully engaged in my own research and I draw attention to them here in order to suggest the constraints of my own approach and the possibilities for further research which does more to bring psycho-analytic concepts into play.[3]

In later chapters, I place considerable emphasis on the importance of sexuality in school students' negotiations of their institutional position. This might well be read as confirmation of the inevitability of adolescence and of its crisis ridden sexuality. Certainly, in the social and institutional conditions which have prevailed in the recent past, there is no doubt that sexuality figures centrally in the cultures of youth and is critical to many of the conflicts which arise between young people and adults.[4] Simon Frith and Angela McRobbie, for example, place sexuality as central both to rock music and to the concerns of its audience:

> Of all the mass media rock is the most explicitly concerned with sexual expression. This reflects its function as a youth cultural form: rock treats the problem of puberty, it draws on and articulates the psychological and physical tensions of adolescence . . . (Frith and McRobbie, 1978/79: 3).

There is a risk in this, as in my own account, of reducing the question of adolescence to one seemingly inevitable dimension – sexuality – and of thus, whatever the intention, of reinstating the view that this is necessarily the crucial formative moment in the making of sexually positioned adult subjects (see Taylor and Laing, 1979). However, as I have argued, it may be more appropriate to see 'adolescent sexuality' as, in part, a discursive figure taken up (by some of those positioned as adolescents) and used in the construction of a sense of autonomy or agency, and therefore actively drawn into forms of contestation of adult and institutional power. Certainly the sexual elements in the resistances to schooling documented by Paul Willis and by Angela McRobbie[5] can be understood, not as natural expressions of an emergent adult sexuality, but as enactments of those forms of behaviour for which schools themselves, and other institutions in which the discourse of adolescence circulates, produce the pre-conditions. Thus the ambivalence (see James, 1993) of the positioning to which school students are subject is, for all concerned, lived as a contradiction beyond which it can seem impossible to progress.

Agency: Consumption and Schooling

The question of agency, which clearly cannot be resolved satisfactorily by invoking the natural achievements of growth and development, can also be considered from a perspective in which consumption is somewhat redefined in terms of active self-construction. The publication of *Common Culture* (Willis *et al.*, 1990) represented a significant conjunction of this more celebratory theory with empirical studies of youth.

Willis *et al.* make two specific claims which are central for the development of my argument here. One is that adolescence is crucially formative of long-term identities; the second is that music is a pervasive cultural form in young people's lives. First, then:

> The teenage and early adult years are important from a cultural perspective
> . . . it is here . . . where people are formed most self-consciously . . . It is
> where they form symbolic moulds through which they understand them-
> selves and their possibilities for the rest of their lives (Willis *et al.*, 1990: 7).

The production of subjectivities within the phase of adolescence is represented as marked by particular cultural engagements which endure as framing orientations for adult identities. Such adult identities are understood to be grounded in the cultural routes which characterize the transition from child to adult status. Of course, identities formed in the 'informal cultural domain' are, even there, subject to the constraints and conditions marked out by work, family, wealth and education.

The second claim, about music, is this:

> By listening to music together and using it as a background to their lives,
> by expressing affiliation to particular taste groups, popular music becomes
> one of the principal means by which young people define themselves (Willis
> *et al.*, 1990: 69).

Music, in short, is not just something young people like and do. It is in many ways the model for their involvement in a common culture which provides the resources to see beyond the immediate requirements and contradictions of work, family and the dole (Willis *et al.*, 1990: 82).

Certainly, relative to the assumptions which have informed the growth of media studies in schools, where film and television have been the privileged media, these observations stand out as warnings that the most intensely pursued interests of young people lie more in music than in the media which preoccupy their teachers. However, the intensity of their involvement is diffuse, merging into their preoccupation with other media forms – such as video and computer games – and inseparable from tastes in clothes or attitudes to drugs and the many other culturally significant commodities of consequence for them. Music is embedded in a whole array of media forms and cannot be simply isolated out as preeminent in youthful patterns of consumption.

In this recognition and celebration of consumption, there is a danger of indulging a romantic politics – a wish that working-class youth be revealed as possessing agency in their self-definition through music, as proving a capacity for resistance to official institutional regulation of their lives or to ideological incorporation as amenable subjects of the national political culture. What Willis does not adequately address is the need for a specifically educational practice which projects identities beyond those already available within particular subordinate cultures. But it is possible to have it both ways: there are dimensions of working-class youth culture which are resistant in ways which can effect change in educational practice, and 'to make resistance into more than challenge',[6] and therefore for teachers to pursue a developing engagement with students' informal cultural practice, is a necessary step beyond simply acknowledging or affirming the agency of those they teach.

Whatever the risks, the agency of young people can be usefully considered in terms which derive from theories of 'active consumption' (see de Certeau, 1984; Fiske, 1989b). For example, an educationally orientated version of this case is made in the conclusion to an article by Stephen Wagg:

> Developments during the 1980s in the social world of children produced a contradiction which, to a greater or lesser extent, all British children face. The media . . . increasingly address and define children as *consumers*. Today, in a growing volume of writing across the political spectrum, consumption means choice, fulfilment and the finding of the self. So an area of behaviour – consumption – previously thought *passive* is increasingly seen as *active*. But in other, parallel and equally vital areas – notably *education*, wherein the greater part of a child's waking life is spent – the opportunity for self-determination is more firmly closed off than ever (Wagg, in Strinati and Wagg, 1992: 174).

If children and young people are addressed now as having agency within the domain of consumption, then the question of what constitutes student identity needs also to be reviewed in terms which support some degree of consistency across the separated domains of school, family and popular consumption. In reality, of course, such domains overlap and it is their representation in varieties of official discourse which persuade otherwise. To make the most optimistic case, in teaching about popular music there is the potential for a wider engagement with the cultural agency of young people. Though seemingly remote from what is understood to be a politics, there is, in the combination of sexuality, of age-phase identification and the various forms of 'borrowing, mixing and fusion',[7] a refusal of the authority and prescriptive power of those educational policies which presume to address and confine young people within more traditionally circumscribed versions of childhood. A curriculum which can make popular music a presence can, at least, establish a space for the exploration of identities which are not contained within the terms which the educational policies of the 1990s prefer.

Conclusions

In this chapter, I have argued for a discursive understanding of subjectivity and of positioning in the age-phase of adolescence. As I will go on to show, it is important that through the detail of empirical research, some close attention is given to the terms in which young people themselves define their own subject positions. These vary with context and addressee, but may also represent a diversity which the concepts of youth and adolescence simply cannot acknowledge. The homogeneity of youth, in some of those official discourses which circulate in schools, cannot be sustained where the degree of social diversity, and of more tactically complex differentiations, is considerable. Moreover, it is in the students' interpretative remaking of their own social and institutional positions, and in their self-differentiation through dress and through tastes in music, that some sense of their agency can be convincingly identified. Given the difficulty of the transition in which they are placed, it is not surprising that their choices are among small things (see Hebdige, 1979; Mac an Ghaill, 1994) and that, just as they distance themselves from children, their activities might also seem no more than mere play to adults. However, the meaning of objects and activities for those who value them cannot be read solely from the apparent authority of an adult perspective. Small things, and the differentiations they facilitate, are largely a matter of indifference to non-participants in their contexts of use. Their meanings and the affective weight given them need to be examined through the words and actions of those for whom they are a familiar language.

Notes

1   This example was suggested by conversations with Dr Dina Dhorajiwala.
2   Giddens (1979): 121.
3   See, for example, Cohen, 1986 and Cohen's essay 'Against the new vocationalism' in Bates *et al.*, 1984.

4   See Hebdige's (1979) reading of punk style.
5   See Willis (1977); McRobbie in Women's Studies Group (CCCS) (1978); also, Nava and McRobbie (1984).
6   See CCCS Education Group II (1991).
7   See Johnson in CCCS Education group II (1991): 71.

Chapter Three

Classroom Research: Contexts and Identities

Introduction

In this chapter I want to describe my approach to the classroom research. To begin, it's important to say that, in general, investigating questions of subjectivity and identity is highly problematic. In what follows, I discuss my doubts about representing the 'identities' of school students. So, in the chapter as a whole there are three distinguishable, but interconnected, concerns: first, the question of what is meant by the term *identity* and its contrast with *subjectivity*; second, the problems of research which claims to represent the identities of others; third, the more particular methods used in my classroom research.

During the three years through which I did my research, I tended to locate what I was doing as 'on the side of' the ethnographic claim.[1] In fact, the research was not, and could not be, ethnographic in the sense that its professional advocates would give to the term. Hammersley and Atkinson (1983) give this definition:

> ... for us ethnography (or participant observation, a cognate term) is simply one social research method, albeit a somewhat unusual one, drawing as it does on a wide range of sources of information. The ethnographer participates, overtly or covertly, in people's daily lives for an extended period of time, watching what happens, listening to what is said, asking questions; in fact collecting whatever data are available to throw light on the issues with which he or she is concerned (Hammersley and Atkinson, 1983: 2).

By contrast with this, the methods adopted in my research correspond more closely to models of 'reflective practice' and to forms of action research (see Winter, 1989). Bryant (1996), for example, characterizes *action research*, though preferring the term *reflective practice*, in terms which usefully define my own sense of participation, *not in an ethnographic mode*, but as a practitioner:

> ... action research is carried out by practitioners or at least ... researchers
> are actually participating in the practices being researched, and working
> collaboratively with practitioners. The point here is that action research is
> concerned both to understand and to change particular situations, and that
> researchers who are not in and of the situation are not in a position to do
> either. They cannot share the informal theory of practitioners and cannot
> possess the situated knowledge essential for change (Bryant, in Scott and
> Usher, 1996: 114).

My own earlier educational research (Richards, 1990) was carried out while teaching GCSE media studies, and other subjects, full-time in a tertiary college. Though I was not a school teacher during the course of this research, my entry into media studies classrooms, and my actions within them, depended upon that earlier formation (1978–89) as an English and media teacher. Thus, whatever the disjunctions between myself as a researcher and the teachers with whom I collaborated, I also had the resources of a practitioner appropriate to the very particular contexts of my research. In Hackney, for example, there was between myself and Richard, the Head of English, a reciprocal sense of a common 'habitus': a way of being, and knowing how to act as, a teacher within that context. In fact, for almost five years I had taught in a comparable school in the adjacent borough of Islington. I did conceive of my enquiry as one involving participant observation – but participation in the classroom as a teacher, not, despite my early attempts to just observe, participation with the students as some kind of friend or acquaintance.

This kind of participation doesn't make the research ethnographic, even if, more broadly, it was informed by studies produced in an 'ethnographic style',[2] and especially by those examples of ethnographic research which do directly seek to inform educational practice (see, for example, Heath, 1983; Willis, 1977). Despite the importance of these precedents, my own research could not attempt to equal their scope or detail. My concerns have been much more narrowly defined through and informed by participation in the practice of media teaching – exploring the implications of including popular music from within its concerns. Out of such a limited focus, I aim to complicate, and add local detail to, the generality of theoretical accounts of ideology, social reproduction and class which have provided the background to the development of media education in Britain.[3]

Even such apparently constrained classroom research can present significant problems for that form of media education which has aspired to intervene, on behalf of students, to reveal the ideological purposes of the media (see Buckingham, 1990; Buckingham and Sefton-Green, 1994; Moss, 1989). From within the limits of participation in classroom practice, it is possible to view the 'dominant ideology thesis', for example, as a less than adequate support for the further elaboration of media education. The assumptions sometimes encouraged by that thesis, that, for example, children might be especially subject to 'mystification' (see Buckingham, 1986; Richards, 1992), have often been recognized as simplistic by teachers themselves seeking to engage children in the deconstruction of the dominant ideology. Theoretical critiques of that thesis, notably Abercrombie, Hill and Turner (1980) and the post-structuralist theories of Foucault (among numerous others), have contributed to the continuing need to rethink the account of media education offered in some of its formative moments (see, for example, Masterman 1980 and 1985). But much of the impetus for reconsideration has come from within the practice of media teaching itself, from teachers seeking to understand the purpose and outcome of their efforts in institutional conditions radically removed from those in which academic debate is conducted.

In keeping with this history, my own research is located, not in the professional concerns of any one academic discipline, but in the practice I seek to address. For example, the methods of elicitation of data I adopted deliberately replicated those that media teachers use in the conduct of their teaching – setting up discussions and writing/practical projects which draw upon the informal cultures of students. Because I regard it is a central responsibility of my research to inform the practice of teachers (in this respect sharing the commitments of action research), I conceived of the research activity as both exploring some existing and familiar teaching strategies (see Chapters 5 and 6) and introducing, in the context of media studies, more innovative practices (see Chapter 7). Furthermore, I have drawn both on my own past experience of teaching and, as additional data, the accounts offered by teachers themselves. But, during the research, my position was also somewhat removed from that of teachers and my preoccupations were shaped by the particular academic context in which I worked – the Department of English, Media and Drama at the Institute of Education. Thus, as I argue later in this chapter, my production of this text has involved the *appropriation* and *reinflection* of the words of both school students and teachers. In this text, they are not, in any simplistic sense, 'given a voice' but are quoted within the structure of my account, an account in which I also address others beyond the dialogue from which their words are taken.[4]

Identities

As I argued in the preceding chapter, I want to make a case for agency and, though I dislike the degree of fixity and reification implicit in the concept of *identity*, I want to use it to refer to the uncertain experience of acting to remake *oneself* in continuity with the 'self-as-it-was' and yet in the particular circumstances of multiple, and changing, social worlds. Identity can thus be used to imply more than being identified, or identifiable, the object of others' attributions: it suggests a degree of agency in subjective self-construction, though nevertheless always limited by particular discursive, cultural and material resources and thus socially contingent (see Giddens, 1991; Harré and Gillett, 1994). I use identity to name a set of practices which subjects may adopt in sustaining both individual and, to varying degrees, collective continuity. Among the social practices through which people 'do identity', forms of narrative ordering are commonplace (Giddens, 1991; Shotter and Gergen,

1989) and may be anchored in collecting (records, books, souvenirs) and in other modes of self-recording (photography, diaries). Other practices are more elusive, more transient: the conversational performance and negotiation of identity, for example (see Buckingham, 1993a; Widdicombe and Wooffitt, 1995; and Chapter 5, in this volume). Widdicombe and Wooffitt, in their analysis of interview data, argue that they:

> . . . view identities as *achieved*; not fixed but negotiated products of the ongoing flow of interaction. By this we mean that identities are features which people can occasion as relevant in their day-to-day dealings with each other (Widdicombe and Wooffitt, 1995: 131, italics in original).

> . . . identity is not seen as a thing that *we are*, a property of individuals, but as something *we do*. It is a practical accomplishment, achieved and maintained through the detail of language use (Widdicombe and Wooffitt, 1995: 133, italics in original).

This perspective usefully corresponds to my own effort to describe agency in the school-based discussions considered in this book and, in common with Widdicombe and Wooffitt, I use the term *identity* because an emphasis upon agency is less consistently implied in the current understanding of *subjectivity* and *subjects* (see Kress, 1995: 87).

However, in this context, it's also essential to recognize the power of schools to *identify* children, to position them in ways which don't necessarily enhance their experience of subjective agency. In schools, children are routinely identified and classified in a highly regulated social domain; identities are seemingly overdetermined through multiple discourses of attribution. To be identified as a student is to be placed within a particular educational category: to be in a position which entails learning, being taught and, most often, being younger and subject to authority and judgement. But even thus positioned in this category of ascribed identity children draw on both popular and educational discourses and practices in negotiating a continuing sense of self-identity, of identity-for-themselves in that more assertive sense.

It is worth noting that, though I am using the term *student* here, this is, in British schools, a formal 'backstage' category, only infrequently spoken with any consistency and, when it is, self-consciously, as an attempt to invite children to take up more scholarly and self-motivated modes of action than those of which they are customarily thought to be capable. In British school discourse students are pupils, kids, children and sometimes youngsters, young people, young adults and learners. These finely differentiated subject-positions, and their deployment in pedagogic discourse, are worthy of further close investigation. Here, I am less concerned with the nuanced differences between these terms than with their common tendency to position young people as subordinate; for the purposes of my argument, this variety of terms can therefore be provisionally subsumed within the category *student*. It should be remembered, nevertheless, that each variant implies a differently inflected relation between teacher and taught. Moreover, it is important to consider what young people in schools call themselves and to note that the various adult discourses of teachers are unlikely to be taken up, simply, by those thus positioned. Together in the school setting, young people produce other social identities (see Hewitt, 1986).

Indeed, the overdetermination of student identities in educational institutions cannot be regarded as a closure, as if such institutions form their subjects entirely in their own terms. Biographical reflection, even among academics, can suggest something of how incomplete the inculcation of the school's preferred cultural identity might be (see, for example, Kuhn, 1995: 84–103). For many people, in recalling their educational histories, it is not so difficult to revive a sense of tension between, on the one hand, the class and career destinations legitimated by school and, on the other, self-projections into an alternative future. Such imagined identities, if mostly contingent on the conditions of adolescence, can also be a cultural argument with the pragmatic attainments on offer in the educational exchange.

My own example, outlined in Chapter 1, is just one kind of account, but its importance here is methodological. Some degree of reflexive consideration by researchers of their own formation can – though with no guarantees – provide a means to construct accounts of other identities, differently constituted of course, but at least thus less 'objectified' in their otherness (see Hollway, 1994). The relational dimension in *doing research* is a significant concern: the habit of reflecting on one's own presence as a social actor entails both a record of one's public presence and of elements of mood and memory produced in the research context. Thus, in doing the research for this book, what I said, what I did, and even what I wore on particular occasions had some salience to the task of interpreting what was said to me, providing hints at the students' understanding of my identity and purposes. For example, it seems likely that my initial observer status and my often informal clothing (jeans, T-shirts, running shoes) led some of them to identify me as a student-teacher. But I also noted personal recollections (not voiced features of my self-presentation) which may have contributed to my display of interest on particular occasions, animating the conversation and motivating unplanned questions. In talking to Stephen about pirate radio for example (see Chapter 4), I recalled (for myself) that, at 14 and 15, I lay awake late at night, every night, listening to the music of off-shore pirate radio stations (mainly Radio 270, anchored in the North Sea off Scarborough), without, after all, needing or wanting to let teachers know about any of it.

So, some recollection of my own relation to schooling and to adolescence has been a significant element in constructing an account of students' school identities. In fact, the more open forms of interview and discussion I adopted tended to exceed a more narrowly conceived intention to elicit responses to research questions. Talking to groups of school students involved particular social events – complex social interactions in which relational dynamics, and their continuing outcomes, complicated any tendency to assume that data could be simply gathered or extracted. In Chapter 5, for example, I discuss data which comes out of sessions which took the form of group evaluations, semi-formal discussions familiar to students as part of the assessment process in media studies. In such a context, my actions were very much those of a teacher concerned to keep discussion going, to open up issues, rather than be constrained by only those questions which I had planned in advance.

Doing research in schools is also an intervention and can produce social relationships which are more uncertain than those formed routinely between teachers and students. In my approach, it was apparent that I occupied and approximately reenacted the position of a student-teacher, getting to know the class by observing lessons, talking informally and eventually moving into teaching. By introducing uncertainty of that kind – my own identity hovering between (mature) student and teacher – subject positions otherwise excluded or marginalized perhaps became more available than in more settled exchanges between teachers and students. Such settled exchanges are vulnerable to some disturbance when more informal discourses are allowed, invited or insisted upon (by the students). Thus the situation described by Fairclough (1989) is, as his account of discourse argues, far from stable:

> . . . there is a sense in which we can say that the teacher and the pupil *are what they do*. The discourse types of the classroom set up subject positions for teachers and pupils, and it is only by 'occupying' these positions that one becomes a teacher or a pupil. Occupying a subject position is essentially a matter of doing (or not doing) certain things, in line with the discoursal rights and obligations of teachers and pupils – what each is allowed and required to say, and not allowed or required to say, within that particular discourse type (Fairclough, 1989: 38, italics in original).

To some extent, the presence of a student-teacher or a researcher acting like one, can open up the routine exchanges of the classroom and make apparent the limits, the customary circumscription implicit in being positioned as a school student. Moreover, my research also involved engaging teachers somewhat beyond the boundaries of their professional identities. Thus, for both students and teachers, there was the potential in such a 'researched situation' to speak, if only temporarily, in terms a little less constrained by their institutional positioning.

To conclude this section, I want to clarify the sense in which this kind of research, especially because it invites discussion of popular culture, can be productive for classroom practice itself. There was no easy commonality between the students (or all of the teachers) and me, but a move into the field of popular culture did open up conversations beyond those allowed by the more fixed, and singular, subject positions assumed in the formal discourses of schooling. To some extent, such reciprocal acknowledgment of informal elements of people's lives, can undercut the polarity of student-teacher subject positions and can thus contribute to a prefiguring of new forms of educational practice. If only provisionally, an educational practice which goes beyond validation of present cultural dispositions[5] can be introduced into the redefined context which research can encourage. Doing research can help to produce a shift in social relationships between those involved in the classroom setting. To effect change in dispositions of both teachers and students is a concern given further consideration in Chapter 8.

The Context of the Research

I want to turn now to say more about the contexts in which I did the research. The students to whom I talked, in those discussions reported in Chapters 4 and 5, were in their last years in a comprehensive school. A great deal has been written about young people positioned in this way, especially since the raising of the school leaving age in the early 1970s. Inevitably, I am reiterating aspects of familiar arguments in what follows but, equally, I want to set out the terms of my own perspective here.

The first of the schools I want to describe, in Hackney, is a comprehensive. The school, though set within the inner city, is not quite so entirely working-class in its intake as that might suggest. The area is socially diverse and, through the 1970s and 1980s, attracted elements of the new professional middle-class. The students, without uniform, dressed casually and displayed, in an unspectacular way, an array of styles amongst which some were read by students themselves as signifying a particular youth cultural affiliation. For example, 'raggas' were picked out by one black student, who commented that they have 'roll up trousers, baggy, too baggy . . . expensive trainers . . . a lot have caps . . . and sometimes they do some stupid stuff like they cut up their trousers'.[6] But, mostly, dress styles were not strongly differentiated among young people at the school. Of course, within such an apparent homogeneity, markers of difference, slight in my eyes, may have signalled much more than I, as an outsider, could understand. A properly ethnographic immersion in the culture of the school might well have illuminated this but, as I have emphasized, my attention was devoted to classroom practices within media studies rather than the wider cultures of the students themselves.

However, I can offer a little more descriptive detail. On one day in September 1992, several of those to whom I talked were dressed, much as usual, in the following way. Margaret, white, wore a black Black Hawks T-shirt, dark trousers, laced black boots, numerous bracelets and rings, red lipstick, eyes made up, dark hair loose, chin length; Stephen, a black student, a black zip-up top, green trousers, trainers, short hair, gold earring; Alan, white, a green, white and purple sweatshirt, blue jeans, trainers, short hair; Asiye, a Turkish speaking girl, black jean jacket, striped open neck shirt, jeans, patterned socks, black shoes, hair tied back, probably no make up. Though I cannot classify and explain these details of their clothing in any very precise way, I can suggest that between Margaret and Asiye there was a difference in the degree both of sexual self-positioning and affiliation with music oriented culture. Margaret dressed with a self-regarding care and, in her use of black, perhaps hinted at traces of 'Goth' style. As her comments in Chapter 5 confirm, she was self-consciously concerned with displaying music/youth cultural connections in a way that Asiye was not. Between Alan and Stephen there was, again, very little difference except that Stephen, like Margaret, also dressed with the suggestion of more self-conscious care than Alan. The difference was no more than that between the appearance of a more consciously considered ensemble and what, to the contrary, was a more personally arbitrary collection of elements. But, however I might have read their dress, it is important to note here that, with no school uniform, something of the students' 'out-of-school' identities was routinely made visible between them (see Asiye's comment on dress style in Chapter 5).

The second school, in Edmonton, selects its students at 11, by competitive examination. The area itself is broadly working- and lower middle-class – an outer London suburb which does not attract professional middle-class residents. The school draws its students from a very wide area, including most of North and North-east London and rural areas beyond the city itself. Though the intake of students is ethnically mixed, my focus, the Sixth Form A Level media studies group, was predominantly white. Boys and girls attend in all years and wear uniform through to the end of Year 11. The Sixth Form students to whom I talked did not wear any elements of the school uniform and, on the whole, dressed in much the same casual and economical style as the group in Hackney. However, most of the girls wore their hair very long, as did a few of the boys (Spencer, for example), and in many respects they had already acquired the look of university students. Certainly there were very few markers of any strong sub-cultural affiliation.

Though I knew the school very well, and had visited it on many occasions, I confined my research there to the first year (Year 12) A Level class alone. They were at a stage in their course which allowed me to involve them in some music related work and to do so without consuming time that, as I emphasize in Chapter 7, they had committed to achieving their futures through education. Whereas I spent most of a year visiting and teaching the class in Hackney, in Edmonton I was defined much more explicitly as an academic visitor and confined myself to a specific project supported by their A Level media studies teachers.

By contrast with the Edmonton students, the Hackney school with no 'Sixth Form' did not offer any clear route to a future identity. September 1992 was the first month of their last year of compulsory schooling. Being a student is a necessarily transitional identity and requires some sense of movement from one condition to another – to those more adult identities in which a past educational history is a necessary element. To be a student without some credible sense of the future to which it connects is merely to live out the duration of that identity; lacking such a future, most imagine other kinds of adult life. It has been argued by Paul Willis *et al.* (1990) that such futures are conceived through an engagement in informal culture of a kind marginal to life as a school student. Among some of those I interviewed, mainly though not exclusively boys, there was a marked distance from the prospective orientation of student identity and a restless impatience with time passed in classrooms. Both of the next two chapters illustrate this to some extent. In particular, it is evident that in the more working-class milieu of the Hackney school, the students do not make cultural capital out of their informal experience with the same sense of investment in the self which became so apparent in the research with the Edmonton students.

However, the Hackney students, if mainly the girls, did make something out of the work they were asked to do and, in Chapter 6, I examine the texts they produced in some detail. So, to qualify Willis' view, I want to stress that working-class students negotiate routes through schooling, combining elements of what student identity entails with positions available in other cultural domains. Meanwhile, of course, for middle-class students, identities are still most often made substantially through their experience in education (though see Aggleton, 1987). For the Edmonton students, adolescence is certainly not just 'boring' but time invested. So, in this book, in devoting attention to classroom practice – to what students actually do in media studies – I am reaffirming the importance of schools as still significant sites for the formation of young people's identities.

The scale of this research needs some clarification. It is a qualitative study of an aspect of classroom practice which is rare in British schools, if increasing with the relatively recent inclusion of popular music in GCSE media studies and in some A Level courses. The scope for comparison and replication was very limited indeed. I worked with only a small number of students – a class of about 17 in Hackney, of whom several participated in interviews and discussions. In Edmonton I worked with a class of about 30 but selected only a limited set of examples of their writing for detailed consideration. The Hackney study produced less data than I would have liked – though that, as I have noted, was itself a fact of some significance, and the Edmonton study produced rather more than I could include in this book without squeezing out the Hackney study and losing the sense of contrast between middle- and working-class students.

I was in contact with the first group across a period of 11 months, beginning in the year when they were 15 and ending when they were 16. I was involved in 23 sessions with the Hackney group, 13 of those as a teacher. I saw the second group, in Year 12 (16–17), across a period of three months but returned to talk to the group into Year 13. My direct involvement in taught sessions with them was possible on only four occasions but I was able to visit the school and talk to their teachers rather more frequently.

Methods

The period of my classroom research in Hackney began in June 1992 with observation in media studies lessons with a Year 10 class. As an observer, I wanted to see what kind of teaching they were experiencing and how that might define the version of media studies with which they were becoming familiar. At first, I had little opportunity to speak to them either as a group or individually. I tended to find myself unlocated in terms of the social relationships which constituted the class as a group and the teacher as their teacher. I was a stranger without a publicly understood identity or purpose. I had not wanted to be identified as, or with, teaching and, as an adult in a classroom, therefore found myself without a position from which to engage their attention. I noted what I could as an observer, but was increasingly aware that this was superficial, enabling me to record a series of impressions through which I could discern the teacher's priorities and typical modes of address and something of their self-organization as a class, their habits of talk and styles of engagement with the teacher, but not much more.

After observing several lessons, frustrated by the lack of opportunity to develop any sustained dialogue, I arranged to take out a small group to discuss my interest in music with them. When I did so, I was still uncertain of my identity for them and offered only a brief explanation of my interest in being there – recorded in my classroom notes thus: 'I want to ask some questions about music because it often gets left out of media studies courses and I'm trying to work out some ways of including it . . .' I recorded the discussion with them – a discussion which I kept alive by asking a number of preconceived questions about their knowledge of, and interests in, popular music. I have given an account of the discussion in Chapter 4. I also draw upon three individual interviews, also taped, with members of the group involved in the prior discussion. This had the considerable advantage of alerting me to the variability in the kinds of statements made in differently constituted social situations. Indeed, it was important to have statements made by the same individuals but in different situations and thus to be able to identify contrasts in their self-accounts and in their referencing of various kinds of music. I knew something of them in the classroom context to begin with; I was then able to record the way in which four of them together, away from the lesson, represented themselves and, further, to compare the responses of three of those four in a one-to-one interview situation. Subsequently, all of these individuals were also involved in the group evaluation sessions (see Chapter 5). Furthermore, I was able to accumulate more classroom based observational material in both the Autumn and Spring Terms of 1992–93 and to develop a detailed reading of their written assignments produced during the first weeks of the Spring Term 1993. Across this variety of material, differences in the constitution of discussion situations, in the audiences for their talk and writing, and in their precise location within the context of the school allowed a sense of how 'tactical', of how socially embedded, their 'knowledge about music' might be. It was essential to keep in focus the institutional setting and the particular practice within which they spoke or wrote, and thus not to conceive my task as that of extracting just the verbal data (a point of contrast with Widdicombe and Wooffitt, 1995). Indeed, my evidence is not only the verbal data – transcripts and students' writing – but also includes both knowledge as a teaching participant in the classroom and discussions with the teachers more continuously involved with the students.

When I returned to observe the class and to talk to them in the first term of Year 11, the year in which they would all have their sixteenth birthdays, I had no secure sense of a continuing, active relationship with the students.[7] In the classroom context, I could not, as an adult, 'participate' with them; indeed, the same would have been even more apparent in virtually any other context. It became clear that I had to take up a version of a teaching role and therefore abandon my initial, awkward, attempts to distance myself from the authority of teachers and from the particular form of relationship that would entail. In the Spring Term, the mid-point of their final year, I established myself as a co-teacher responsible for planning and taking them into a unit of work specifically focused around music. This produced a much stronger sense of reciprocal engagement: I had to be there every time they had a media studies lesson; I had to address the class, help them with their work, know where to find things, give them permission to leave the room, read and respond to their writing. However, not all the consequences of becoming a teacher followed. Sometimes, when the Head of English was out of the room, they would take off into rows with each other, swearing profusely in a way which I never witnessed when their own teacher was present. Towards the end of this phase of teaching, having become known to them as a teacher, I conducted the two group evaluation sessions, one with girls, one with boys, and recorded them.

I kept copies of all that the Hackney group produced as work for assessment. Such work, it should be emphasized, was also a production of research material and was an invaluable means to explore issues of self-representation not accessible through talk alone (see Sefton-Green, in Buckingham, 1993b: 138). Their projects, discussed in Chapter 6, provided the most substantial data from the class. Having explored both the pedagogic and the research limitations of talk, I carried out the research in Edmonton with the production of written data as the central objective. But, as I have suggested, rather than work within the limits of existing practice in media studies, I invited the A Level students to write autobiographically about six music tracks of their choice. This task was inserted into a block of teaching focused on popular music and the production of pop videos. However, the writing they were asked to do was not for formal assessment and was thus much more of an experiment than anything I could ask the Hackney students to do. The detail of this project is discussed in Chapter 7. So, the evolving shape of the research involved a taught unit in Hackney, conceived within the limits of existing practice in media studies, followed by a further project in Edmonton, located within work on pop music, but seeking to make some innovation in the normal practice of A Level media studies teaching.

Methods of Analysis

In this section, I want to clarify the relationship between *interpretation* and *analysis*. These are terms which will prove to be less than satisfactory, but they are the familiar currency of debates around methods and methodology and can be used to stand for what seem to be provisionally distinguishable phases of much the same process. Beyond this, I particularly want to comment on the status of my analysis of the students' words and the relation between that analysis and the students' own self-understanding. Of course, their *self-understanding* is elusive but should not therefore be eliminated from what is a necessarily speculative discussion.

I always transcribed the whole of each interview and each discussion that I recorded. I didn't make a predetermined selection of moments on the basis of the themes that were my interest. It was important to transcribe everything because I wanted to read the text thus produced as a representation of a whole event. My approach has therefore emphasized the relation between speakers in a particular school context and through the time of a distinctive occasion. The transcripts have often enabled me to recover speech I did not hear or could not remember and, inevitably, these texts have tended to stand in for the real event of which they are just one limited document. Nevertheless, my own memory of these events has invariably informed my reading even if such memory was largely of the way the occasion 'felt', rather than of the details of what was said. The transcripts represent dialogues in which the speakers have interpreted the situations, the questions and the issues, and have spoken accordingly. Evidence of the work of interpretation, involving all those present, is partially inscribed in the words recorded and transcribed. To some extent, I have tried to identify, through such evidence, how the students understood the situation and their positions within it. I was inevitably making such interpretations within the time of each event but, of course, I have also devoted much more time to the task of retrospective interpretation. I have read and listened repeatedly to an event which, for those others involved, had only its one unique time. I have read these events *for my particular purposes*. The conditions of my retrospective interpretation are thus radically different from those available to the other participants; the enlargement of time, repetition and transcription have combined to allow me a special kind of interpretative relation to these events. In effect, they became texts for me to read and, importantly, to discuss with others – the teachers and, sometimes, the students themselves.[8] Much of this applies also to the written texts produced by both the Hackney and the Edmonton students. Whereas school writing is typically read for assessment, once or twice and quite rapidly, I returned to their writing repeatedly and read it for purposes clearly far broader than the need to assess.

Analysis, though prefigured in the questions I chose to pursue, and thus not strictly separable from interpretation, has been the outcome of further processes of classification, a matter of determining what kinds of discourse were produced and what interests they served. However, such a process of classification was dependent upon the text being already read, and, to some extent, interpreted. Of course, the adoption of different modes of discursive analysis does not leave interpretation as it was; over a period of months, even years, my interpretation has changed in relation to the analytical perspectives I have encountered. Certainly I have tried to be attentive to the words the students used but, both in my own analysis and to some extent as a teacher, I have wanted to connect them to more general categories in a larger system, following, to some extent, Vygotsky's (1962) distinction between spontaneous and scientific concepts. I have also attempted to analyze words as somewhat unstable in meaning and, more particularly, as multiaccentual and thus often the point of intersection of participants' differing social interests (Bakhtin, 1994; Volosinov, 1973). Sometimes, such interests have seemed immediate and tactical, at others to be indicative of more enduring social differences; often, of course, both have combined in the same moment. My analysis of discourse in such educational settings has also been informed by perspectives which, rather than attending primarily to learning, have made the issue of power central. Kress, for example, has suggested that education is about 'the processes of classification, repositioning individuals with respect to potent social/cultural classificatory systems' (Kress, 1985: 63). From this point of view, I have attempted to attend particularly to those moments in which the relationship between informal classificatory systems and those formally validated by schools became apparent in the students' negotiations of either a written task or of a dialogue with myself. It has been essential, therefore, to have *both* data derived from talk and from the more formal, specifically educational, practice of writing (Kress, 1994).

A further dimension of analysis, but one which suggests the insufficiency of the term, has been pursued through the process of reinscribing the students' words in this text. Of course, much analytical work has preceded the production of this text but *reinscription* suggests the larger process of *remaking* the discourse of others to serve different purposes. Their words are thus relocated, and their meanings incorporated in what is itself an extended discursive act. However, this is the case in any work of re-presentation and I don't regard this incorporation as also a disauthentification. Their words, spoken or written, were always also particular discursive acts, not 'testimonies of the self'. I am not suggesting, therefore, that this text is the culmination of a process in which self-expressive utterances are alienated from their speakers. To the contrary, I want to argue that language, spoken or written, to whomever it may be addressed, is always both less and more than an expression of the self; it always fails to express and to fix who we are, even if we think we want it to achieve that purpose. Thus, I want to refuse any tendency to take words just as testimony, as simply the voiced truth of either past or present identities.

Though I do not offer a psychoanalytically conceived discussion of the data – words – it is at least of some consequence to acknowledge a psychoanalytic perspective upon their instability. Thus, for example, Jacqueline Rose, in her analysis of 'the impossibility of children's fiction', argues that:

> ... the concept of the unconscious has been refused at exactly that point where it throws into question the idea of our subjectivity as something which we can fully know, or that ultimately can be cohered ... Deception is, however, for Freud, in the very order of language. When we speak, we take up a position of identity and certainty in language, a position whose largely fictional nature only the occasional slip, and at times the joke, is allowed to reveal ... (Rose, 1984: 15–18).

With more particular reference to the educational context, Elizabeth Ellsworth, in a critique of 'critical pedagogy', observes, similarly, that:

> Conventional notions of dialogue and democracy assume rationalized, individualized subjects ... Yet social agents are not capable of being fully rational and disinterested; and they are subjects split between the conscious and unconscious and among multiple social positionings (Ellsworth, 1989: 316).

I have not attempted to translate such psychoanalytically informed perspectives into methods for the analysis of the data in the following chapters. However, the refusal of an 'expressive' transparency of words in relation to subjects suggests an approach which attends to the particular contexts of their utterance or inscription and places some emphasis on the multiple interests they might fulfil. As I suggested in Chapter 2, analysis within the limits of discourse enables me to describe situational positionings but it cannot adequately explain the force and persistence of particular identifications. Equally, by invoking psychoanalysis here I am not claiming great depth, as if I have been able to uncover concealed meanings. To the contrary, I am acknowledging a degree of uncertainty in appearing to fix the identities of others by means of words pinned down in particular circumstances.

I have emphasized that my reading of both transcripts and written assignments has depended on knowledge of the setting and the social relations peculiar to it. The question I want to address now is that of the status of my analysis in relation to the participants' own interpretations. To do so, I want to refer to a discussion of methodology provided by John B. Thompson in *Ideology and Modern Culture* (Thompson, 1990). He makes a substantial case for 'depth hermeneutics', arguing that 'the object domain of social-historical inquiry is a *pre-interpreted domain* in which processes of understanding and interpretation take place as a routine part of the everyday lives of the individuals who, in part, make up this domain' (Thompson, 1990: 21, italics in original). As one moment in a more elaborate structure of ideological analysis, Thompson advocates attention to the interpretations produced by participants in their own social worlds. Thus, studies which seek to represent the past might resort to the methods of oral history (see Bertaux, 1981; Humphries, 1981) and, in contemporary settings, attention to participants' preinterpretations demands some form of ethnographic enquiry:

> By means of interviews, participant observation and other kinds of ethnographic research, we can reconstruct the ways in which symbolic forms are interpreted and understood in the varied contexts of social life (Thompson, 1990: 279).

Thompson insists that in reinterpreting a preinterpreted domain we are 'engaging in a process which can, by its very nature, give rise to a conflict of interpretations' (Thompson, 1990: 22–3). Indeed, Thompson argues that the 'interpretation of ideology is depth hermeneutics with a critical intent', the aim to disclose 'meaning in the service of power' (Thompson, 1990: 23). In producing interpretations of ideology:

> ... we are putting forward an interpretation which may diverge from the everyday understanding of the individuals who make up the social world. The interpretation of ideology may enable individuals to see symbolic forms differently, in a new light, and thereby to see themselves differently (Thompson, 1990: 25).

In the process of enquiring into identity, or into the uses made of media forms, the practice of research itself, in so far as it produces different interpretations from those produced by research subjects themselves, might therefore contribute to changes in self-understanding. However, this more political outcome is exceptionally difficult to specify in any particular practice. Thompson's general case is presented hypothetically:

> *The depth interpretation becomes a potential intervention in the very cir-*
> *cumstances about which it is formulated.* A depth interpretation is itself
> a symbolic construction, capable in principle of being understood by the
> subjects enmeshed in the circumstances which form in part the object of
> interpretation (Thompson, 1990: 323, italics in original).

In fact, there is no path, solely through theory, beyond this reiteration of 'potential',
of plausibility 'in principle'. Moreover, Thompson recognizes that the practical
obstacles to 'potential intervention' are 'numerous, formidable'. However, there are
important reasons, arising from within these larger political ambitions, to consider
the 'ethnographic moment', or, in my research, the 'classroom moment', not as one
from which to move on but rather as one from within which to explore the relationship between those interpretations produced by a researcher and those shared, or
otherwise, by the other participants. Doing empirical research and, in particular,
specifying the relation of researcher to participants can help to situate Thompson's
more abstracted formulations. It was clear to me that as an adult observer and subsequently as a teacher, I necessarily entered into a set of overdetermined relationships from which I could hardly extract myself or the young people to whom I spoke.
To offer interpretations independent of such a particular set of relationships was,
of course, impossible. Thompson says '. . . an interpretation which is plausible may
stimulate a process of critical self-reflection among subjects who, as actors capable
of deliberation, may regard the interpretation as plausible and worthy of recognition'
(Thompson, 1990: 324). But it is the specificity of the social relations in which this
might occur which shape that possibility. Both Rose and Ellsworth should be recalled
at this point (see also Harding, 1991; Stanley, 1990); their perspectives, by their contrast, reveal the grand rationalism of Thompson's theoretical exposition.

Unfortunately, I was not able to return to the Hackney class at the stage when
I had produced, through an analysis of their writing, more considered interpretations; unlike several of the students in Edmonton, they had no opportunity to read
what I had written. Nevertheless, in the course of my research, interpretations, my
own and those of everyone else involved, were thick on the ground – and by that
I mean that *interpretations* did not stand as abstracted sets of propositions but were
made by, and from, all the various positions sustained by located social actors – in
this case in the school classroom and other, adjacent, areas. Difference, or conflict,
between interpretations cannot be understood in isolation from the social interests
pursued by the various members of the class and by myself in the particular institutional settings that we occupied. Interpretation is a part of social practices, tactical,
multivalent and somewhat provisional.

It may be helpful at this point to outline in brief just one example which is
drawn into my argument in Chapter 5. The question is that of how the participants
in this context interpret ragga, a relatively recent development in Jamaican music.
My own interpretation of ragga was, though not voiced explicitly, neither singular
nor coherent: I could have said I liked the sound and found its 'Jamaican' characteristics enjoyably familiar but that it also seemed, lyrically and iconographically, and
in the larger context of pop, mostly a matter of male sexual boasts and misogyny.

In the classroom, there was little overtly interpretative discussion of ragga. However, one of the group evaluation sessions, in this case with the girls, provided a context in which quite specific criticisms of some ideological elements in ragga culture were voiced. Ragga was, though valued for some aspects of its musical form, sharply criticized for its antipathy towards gays and its arrogance in relation to women. The kind of dialogue that was produced in that context, where girls without boys could present themselves to other girls and to myself, as an interested teacher, could be read as evidence of their pre-existing subject positions and their already critical engagement with ragga as one genre in their currently familiar repertoire. They selectively dismantled and re-presented this particular 'symbolic resource' from an implicitly feminist position. Equally, the statement of such criticisms in the context of a recorded discussion could be seen as a way of securing some educational credibility where, they might have known, anti-sexism is an institutionally legitimated discourse. Also, because they are girls in school, they would probably have found it more difficult to acknowledge and criticize their position, as young, as female, as school students, in relation to myself as a middle-aged, male, teacher than they did to challenge the popular forms around which teacherly anxieties and interventions are so often seen to converge. Ragga might thus have become an object around which, through an act of public interpretation, a particular competence in a critical discursive practice could be safely displayed. Thus, it is possible that in voicing one oppositional interpretation of a 'masculinist' ideology, they were simultaneously enacting their acquiescence in other ideological relations. Of course, in terms of Thompson's interpretative schema, much more elaborated discussion and investigation should follow, but my point here is that the social contexts of interpretative work are fundamental to social actors' negotiation of such tasks.

Concepts in Action

I want to consider the relation of analysis to the students' self-understanding again, in this concluding section, by discussing the distance between *grounded* and *analytic* concepts. As I have noted, the modes of enquiry which I pursued were framed by the classroom context and, effectively, '(student-)teacher–student' relations. To some extent, therefore, discussions tended towards explanation in terms which were reasonably clear to me – as if my power required *some* movement from *spontaneous* to *scientific* concepts, however uncertain. A word such as 'taste', for example, was a part of most students' vocabulary and was also a term which I sometimes introduced and made a more deliberate focus of attention. As a grounded or spontaneous concept, however, taste seemed to have a mainly common sense set of meanings; typically taste was used to suggest preferences which were radically idiosyncratic and arbitrary. However, through the form of my questions and other comments, I represented a more sociological set of meanings and, to some extent, dialogues developed in which the relationship between these variable meanings was explored. Similarly, an analytic contrast such as that between the 'authentic' and the 'inauthentic' had its less abstractly defined counterpart in the students' more *spontaneous* references to *imitation, sampling, mixing* and *tiefing* [thieving]. Furthermore, discussions of generic terms such as *acid, hardcore, ragga* and *rap* demanded the effort of constructing some shared understanding of how these words were being used, with what range of reference and with some awareness of their mutability and their often divergent meanings.

In Edmonton, I was not able to be present as a teacher and was not therefore personally instrumental in attempting to pursue the kind of relation between analysis and understanding in which I felt involved in Hackney. In both cases, however, my analysis was not solely a retrospective matter of work upon data but was a continuing part of the act of enquiry itself. This approach, broadly framed through Vygotsky's discussion of the relationship between spontaneous and scientific concepts, also suggests some further thoughts on *interpretation*.

In fact, the concept of interpretation does not fully explain how I have represented the social encounters reported here. There is some advantage in redefining this process, as I argued in the preceding chapter, as one in which discourses are reinflected and remade by all those involved and in terms of their own situated interests. My remaking of their discourse, though doubtless an interpretation of a preinterpreted domain, is also a discursive act in which I privilege a particular repertoire of concepts and seek to select and reorder the students' discourse in terms of the relationships between those concepts. However, the material on which this further analytical work has been conducted is already more than my interpretation of their preinterpreted domain; the material represents a process of negotiated exchange between discourses and between institutionally positioned social actors. Much of the subsequent development, brought to a conclusion here in a more overtly analytical form, had already begun *in situ*. Of course, a theoretical discussion of subjectivity, agency and identity was not an explicit part of any of my school-based discussions but there were, as I have suggested, necessary mediations between concepts from our differing discursive repertoires. Here, the elaboration of my analysis, in terms of discourse and subject-position, social practice and institutional regulation, produces a reordering of classroom speech and writing for an audience, not of school students, but of teachers and academics. The priority in this discursive act is to address such an audience. Potentially, the school students, whose speech and writing is reported in the next four chapters, could, at some point, read and further reappropriate my discourse in conversations about what it is that I have done. But, in this book, to also address school students is obviously not a part of my intention (see Feld, 1982).

Conclusion

The value of moving from a predominantly working-class school in Hackney to the much more middle-class milieu of a selective school in Edmonton was that it enabled me to grasp how differently the students were placed in relation to my enquiries. In Edmonton, the students took up my invitation to write about their music in terms which suggested how accustomed and how committed they were to that transformation of informal experience into cultural capital. They 'invested'[9] their informal knowledge in the educational context, knowing tacitly that there it would acquire a value, a value to be reinvested in themselves and their futures. In Hackney, there were few students, with some exceptions, who had an interest in using my research as a means to any comparable accumulation and investment of their informal and transient knowledge in the school context. Methodologically, the early Hackney data may seem unsatisfactory but its retention illustrates, if tentatively, a class inflected relation to the acquisition of educational and cultural capital.

However, I also want to reiterate, finally, that the logic of the following chapters is primarily pedagogic – they explore questions about the teaching of popular music in media education and do so through research located in modes of teacher–student exchange. What I did later, in Edmonton, was a little more inventive, perhaps more sophisticated, than what I did earlier, with the students in Hackney. In what follows I try to tease out patterns of difference in the students' responses to my attempts to introduce work around pop music. But, and it's important to remember this, I also tell a story about my own progress, about what I learnt as a teacher and classroom researcher.[10]

Notes

1   My curiosity about ethnography goes back to the very early 1970s and reading such books as *Soulside* (Hannerz, 1969). It was also seriously tested by a period of about seven months in a Japanese village in 1976, alongside my wife who was doing research in the mode of traditional anthropological fieldwork.

2   I have borrowed this phrase from Brian Street who spoke on the topic of academic literacies at the University of North London, June 6th 1996. For some critical comments on the 'ethnographic claim' in the work of the Birmingham Centre for Contemporary Cultural Studies, see Connell (1983). See also Radway (1988), especially p. 367.

3   See Buckingham (1990); Buckingham (1993b) Buckingham and Sefton-Green (1994); Walkerdine in Burgin, Donald and Kaplan (1986) and Morley (1992).

4   See Clifford and Marcus (1986) for the debate around the textual representation of others in anthropology; see also Harding (1991) for a feminist critique of traditional epistemology and the case for *standpoint theory*.

5   For example, see Green in CCCS Education Group II (1990: 296). On dispositions and 'habitus' see Bourdieu (1986), especially pp. 170–5.

6   A comment made by Stephen, a black student, 15 July 1992.

7   In fact, I went in wanting several of them to complete 'time–use' diaries of their domestic consumption of music but this resulted in very meagre data indeed. Margaret lost the notebook I gave her and the boys produced only very brief notes.

8   This was possible with several of the students in Edmonton.

9   Bourdieu comments, of teachers:

> ... the *specific* profits, and the consequent propensities to invest, are only defined in the relationship between a field and a particular agent with particular characteristics. For example, those who owe most of their cultural capital to the educational system, such as primary and secondary teachers originating from the working and middle classes, are particularly subject to the academic definition of legitimacy, and tend to proportion their investments very strictly to the value the educational system sets on the different areas (1986: 87).

For more elaborations of this perspective, see 'Price Formation and the Anticipation of Profits' in Bourdieu (1992).

10   For a lengthy and much more detailed account of my research methods see Richards (1998).

Chapter Four

Knowledge about Music?

Introduction

This chapter borrows a question from the controversies surrounding the introduction
of the National Curriculum for English: 'knowledge about language'. I want to turn
this into a question about music, to ask what 'knowledge about music' would be if
attention was turned to it in the context provided by English and media education. It
is a question, or rather a puzzle, to which there is no straightforward answer; I had
no answer to it when I began the research for this book in 1992. My own preoccupation was with the knowledge *about* music that students might already have, with how
such knowledge might be a resource in media teaching, and with how students might
be involved in reflection upon the social dimensions of their knowledge. The teachers
to whom I talked, and with whom I collaborated to varying degrees, were much more
concerned with the knowledge about music they thought the students should have
but to which they did not have access. But, as the research progressed, some convergence between our positions did develop.

In fact, it is worth elaborating on this convergence because, as I have suggested,
my research was carried out in dialogue with one particular teacher, Richard. I interviewed him early in March 1994 and thus introduce here retrospective observations
made almost a year after the main study was concluded. They stand, often, as well
judged *criticisms* of what I was doing but I was able to use them to define issues
which became much more central in later phases of interpretation and analysis. For
example, in the following comment it is as if he addresses both a notional 'other'
(a younger teacher perhaps) and myself as an academic researcher too preoccupied
with what I thought they might know, rather than with what I might teach them:

> . . . in a way you're just picking up what they know and that's an import-
> ant aspect of it but sometimes – What are the sources of their own know-
> ledge and so on? And you're sort of taking that as a kind of something
> given and almost y'know with a sort of reverential attitude but just as
> with everything else that they know, it's a mixture of real insight, their
> own development, their own purposes, as well as received wisdom and

prejudice and all sorts of things and I think you do actually have to have
a better, a clearer theoretical stance and be, be more upfront about times
when you need to be a bit more didactic and make an input, I think . . .

There are elements in this of a Gramscian perspective: the students' knowledge is
represented as uneven, mixing together 'good sense' with more limited, and limiting,
beliefs and (mis)conceptions. Teaching, in relation to such knowledge, is necessarily also a mix: of validation and recognition but with a more distinctly authoritative
voice, both telling and challenging. Through much of the initial research, and especially in the very earliest stages represented in this chapter, I did adopt a minimally
interventionist classroom presence, in order to sustain my sense of enquiry into their
knowledge about music.

On the other hand, Richard also made the question of what might constitute
knowledge about music very much a matter of elusive and complex social positioning and, further, of particular modes of knowing:

I think what fascinated me was the sources of their knowledge . . . I mean
we think that there's something they should know more about, the history
for example and so on. But it's actually where they got their knowledge
of it from and I find all that very strange . . . there were some things you
would hear at raves so called or that, just from the radio or buying things
and it didn't, it seemed to reflect different types of music as well, that you
would listen to certain types of music on the radio whereas you would buy
or borrow, you know, other kinds of music from your friends . . .

. . . I think I said jokingly too that I kept wanting to go to Vortex but
hadn't been, this jazz club . . . I wasn't quite sure what to wear and that was
a facetious remark . . . but that seemed actually to be (laughter) connected
for them . . . that these were particular roles you took on and so on . . .

. . . my brothers seem, I've always been very poor personally at learning
and being able to kind of talk in a fluent and coherent manner about things
which I have learnt impressionistically and from my own experience, I
think I have got an academic mind, not in terms of cleverness, but in terms
of my approach . . . I find it much easier to absorb something if I read a
book and read about it from preface to index than actually kind of absorb
it from living it and I'm fascinated that these children are able to do it so
well and one of my brothers is very good at that . . . he can kind of give
you a history of, you know, rock 'n' roll or something, which I'm completely unable to do, simply because he's listened to records not because
he's read books about it, whereas I would be able to if I read about it, I
think that . . . a dry and dusty way of experiencing the world . . . (laughter).

These themes, of the embeddedness of music in the thick of social life and of the
means to (re)constitute such experience as *knowledge*, unclear in my early research,
were actually defined through a retrospective reading of this discussion. In the following comment, through reflections on the 'mobility' of Margaret's self-positioning,

Richard also provides an oblique, but incisive, criticism of my initial enquiry, casting some doubt on my early attempts to recompose the forms of lived cultural experience as organized knowledge. In this respect, from a vantage point within the day-to-day life of the school, he provided early clues to the argument I have pursued through Chapters 4–7: that the quest to (re)categorize, and perhaps delimit, a disparate and embedded experience as knowledge about music would be fraught with problems and might well be frustrated:

> I think much more interesting than the actual content is the process of learning and of making sense of it and indeed of, I mean from a kind of, even from your more academic point of view, of actually what constitutes a field of knowledge because in a way we were artificially saying it was music because they were, it had to do with dress styles, it had to do with language, the words they use to speak about it and it, I mean Margaret, for example, is basically a speaker of standard English but she would then sort of switch into a slightly self-conscious, well not self-conscious, a kind of deliberate use of non-standard forms in talking about music, you know, so there was the dress, there was the sense of cultural identity, the alternativeness of the culture, the references to booze and drugs and so on and I think that would be interesting if you could actually look at how you might recategorize things and what it, this vague process of how you make sense of something constituting it as a kind of distinct domain to be thought about . . .

So here, in this account of my earliest discussions with students in the Hackney comprehensive, and in the next three chapters, I suggest that to constitute music as a phenomenon about which one has 'knowledge' is problematic in contexts where popular musical references are invoked somewhat tactically, in the negotiation of immediate social relations. Moreover, to constitute popular music as 'knowledge', and thus within more precisely bounded and enduring educational modalities, was an activity unwelcome, or irrelevant, to students with little interest in sustaining an investment in their educational futures.

The data discussed in this chapter are derived from a brief pilot study involving only four students in the Hackney comprehensive. The students involved were 'given' to me by their teacher, Richard. They seemed willing, and were perhaps flattered, to be chosen to talk to me away from their media studies lesson. I did not choose the students myself according to some predetermined plan. On the contrary, I depended upon Richard's pre-existing relationship with the class and upon his knowledge of the students. Though I had my own rationale for this initial enquiry, the research took shape, as I have noted, through a negotiated collaboration with their teacher, an already knowledgeable participant in that classroom setting. The students were chosen, then, in the context of that continuing dialogue between us. Thus, these were students selected as perhaps more interested than others (among those present on that particular day) in the questions I wanted to ask – more likely, then, to offer knowledge about music.

Most simply, I wanted to elicit some suggestions about how media studies might engage with popular music. But the discussions, one with the group and three individual interviews, didn't flow easily. They didn't offer knowledge about music in the terms that, perhaps, I expected: they were neither detailed nor explicit and tended not to elaborate in response to probing questions. At first, I found this puzzling – I thought that as young people they would know about music and be interested in telling me about what they listened to. But it became apparent, though much more fully in retrospect, that they were not in the habit of extracting from, and making knowledge out of, their everyday experience of popular music. In fact, they had no strong interest in translating such experience into the forms in which, in school, knowledge is accumulated and invested in the formation of future, educated, selves. Later, through the contrast with students in Edmonton (see Chapter 7), their relative lack of interest in making cultural capital out of their experience became more sharply defined. However, within the Hackney group there was also no simple class homogeneity and, as will become apparent, gender, and to some extent ethnicity, significantly complicated their relation to my enquiries.

At the beginning of my first group interview with the students, I defined my interest and explained my presence as motivated by a wish to explore and develop the role of popular music in media studies. I was thus offering an educationally bounded legitimation of my enquiry and one which, as students of GCSE media studies, they might accept as inviting them to be plausible and experienced respondents. I certainly wanted to defer any intrusion beyond their school identities. I didn't, for example, suggest that I might be interested in them because they were students from a working-class area or because they were an ethnically mixed group. My intentions thus involved a more narrowly defined address to their contextually specific, institutional identities. However, within my explanation, there was also the implication that there was something more with which media studies should engage, that the subject as they knew it might be less of a space to examine their own familiar popular culture than they might have been entitled to expect. Perhaps, I thought, as an outsider, I was someone to whom any dissatisfaction with media studies might be expressed. In fact, at this stage, they had no particular criticisms of their course and had, as yet, no evident interest in constituting their experience of popular music as knowledge to which credit might be attached in the school context.

The Group Interview

The group discussion took place in July 1992. The four students were Alan, a white boy; Stephen, an Afro-Caribbean boy; Asiye, a bilingual (Turkish/English) girl, and Margaret, a white girl from an Irish family background. Margaret spoke a great deal, the boys in response to my questions, and Asiye very little.

The discussion was an attempt to draw out accounts of how music is used in their everyday lives and was especially directed towards the domestic contexts of their use of music. Following the recent upsurge in research concerned with the domestic contexts of television viewing (see Morley, 1992) and as I was inclined to see this as a promising area for media teaching, I wanted to open up this context for discussion in the classroom. But even with the individual interviews – with the possible exception of Margaret – I realized that this was a domain of experience which would require far more extended interviewing in depth than my research focus on classroom practice allowed.

There was an advantage in talking to them together as a group, apart from making them feel more at ease, because together they provided some evidence of the socially tactical meanings music might have in relations between them. It is this dimension of the discussion that I want to consider first of all and which is explored further – through additional group discussions – in the next chapter.

Asiye never volunteered a response and was only drawn in by very direct and specific questions, mainly at the end of the session. By contrast, Stephen was quick to answer from the beginning, if not interested in developing responses at length. In this context he seemed able to establish some degree of credibility to which others might defer. Certainly Margaret, despite her own confidence in speaking, seemed at times to turn to Stephen for affirmation or clarification of a point she wished to make. But the first part of the interview was dominated by a dialogue between Stephen and me, a dialogue into which Margaret and Alan entered though not in any sustained way. It is not so much that Stephen kept them out but that, having successfully drawn my attention to his knowledge of black pirate radio, I colluded with him in giving time to a topic to which the others found it difficult to contribute. The discussion thus appeared as one anchored somewhat by this first relatively prolonged exchange and the opportunity it gave Stephen to present himself as a credible and serious respondent.

At various points my dialogue with Stephen faltered. Certainly I found it very difficult to know what kinds of questions to ask and repeatedly found my own bookish knowledge of popular music a hopelessly inadequate resource on which to draw. In those first weeks of the research, I didn't have the familiarity with current popular music to improvise in conversation with the students. I felt ill-at-ease, floundering in a cultural world to which the published works of Dick Hebdige (1987), Simon Jones (1988) or David Toop (1984) provided no reliable guide (see Richard's earlier comments).[1] For the students, it may not have been surprising that I knew so little, but my confidence declined as the discussion unfolded and the extent of my own ignorance became apparent. But perhaps even Stephen knew less than his self-assured manner suggested, and we were thus both, perhaps all, warily avoiding the admission that we did not know quite what we were talking about.

CR: What's Station FM?
Stephen: It plays soul, reggae . . . it's a pirate station . . .
CR: And it's just in this area . . . so if you're living in west London you probably couldn't pick it up . . . Could I pick it up, where would I find it on the dial?
Stephen: . . . just know where . . .

CR: You just know where . . . and do you know exactly where it's broadcast from, roughly well 'round here, any ideas?

Stephen: Stoke Newington . . . 'round Dalston I think

CR: . . . 'round Dalston . . . and is it on what, 24 hours a day or less?

Stephen: If they don't get caught yeah . . .

CR: How often do they get caught?

Stephen: I don't know . . . they had a station before but they got done . . .

CR: So what're they doing, transmitting from a building somewhere . . . from the top . . . And what do they play?

Stephen: Reggae, soul, rap, ragga

CR: And is it stuff that's new to you or is it all very familiar?

Stephen: It's familiar

CR: But do they sort of import stuff and play stuff you've never heard before?

Stephen: A bit

CR: . . . probably can't get it where I live, I live in Haringey . . . do you have your own radio, do you listen to that alone at home . . .

Stephen: (inaudible response)

CR: And if you want to get the records they play . . . where do you to get them?

Stephen: . . . yeah . . . down Ridley . . .

CR: What, in the market?

Stephen: . . . sometimes Our Price but not a lot

CR: Do they actually advertise the shops? By name . . . they don't do any advertising at all . . . so they're not making any money like in that way . . . so they never mention shops, they don't tell you where to get things . . .

Stephen: . . . some yeah but on occasions they do, but not much 'cause they wanna keep it to themselves . . . where they get it from to themselves

CR: So I mean what's new in reggae . . . does new reggae come from this country or from Jamaica?

Stephen: Jamaica

CR: Really? So what's new from there then?

Stephen: (inaudible response)

CR: I don't know any recent reggae from Jamaica at all . . . I really don't . . . I know stuff that's very old, from years ago . . . I saw a poster the other day for Burning Spear . . . doing something on the 10th I think, I don't know where, I saw this poster in Finsbury Park but I wouldn't know of any new names at all . . . (turning to Margaret) . . . What was the station you mentioned?

Stephen's inaudible mumble at the end of this exchange and my own final, unsuccessful, struggle to connect the past with the present ('I saw a poster the other day for Burning Spear') illustrate just how my desire to be given 'knowledge about music' was, in this context, frustrated.

A comparable exchange occurred much later in the interview. Again, it is essential to have quite an extended extract from the transcript:

CR: What's the difference between ragga and reggae?

Stephen: The other one's got . . . just a faster beat

CR: What, ragga's faster?

Stephen: . . . yeah . . . in reggae . . . more singing

Margaret: Reggae's more slow

Stephen: . . . slow

Margaret: Ragga's more fast, faster . . . you can dance to it

CR: I mean I suppose the kind of reggae I know is pretty old stuff like there's obviously all of Bob Marley's stuff but I mean . . . what else?

CR: I like Bob Marley

CR: Reggae seems to me to cover a lot of different things that's all, it's a name that people use for sort of ska and lover's rock and all sorts of stuff

Stephen: Yeah, lover's rock

CR: So when you say reggae, you're including those yeah?

Stephen: I don't think ska is reggae though . . .

CR: You don't think ska is reggae, no?

Stephen: I think it's just an old kind of acid . . . it doesn't sound like reggae . . .

Margaret: What's that?

Stephen: Ska

CR: What about rocksteady? Do you know about that? I mean they're really difficult to separate out one from another, it's just that in the 60s and early 70s people used to talk about different things and I mean here people used to talk about Blue Beat just 'cause it was the name of a record label . . . so reggae means generally what . . . give me some names

Stephen: Peter Tosh

CR: I mean Peter Tosh used to be with the Wailers ages ago, yeah

Stephen: John Holt . . . C (inaudible) . . . I can't think of any more . . .

CR: Is there any connection between that kind of music and rap? Or are they completely separate?

Stephen: Between what?

CR: Between reggae and rap?

Stephen: (inaudible response)

CR: There isn't at all?

Stephen: Not much no . . . maybe a little but not a lot . . . in rap sometimes they use a little reggae as a beat

In this, by locating Peter Tosh as both already familiar to me and as belonging to the distant past I indicated that Peter Tosh didn't count as the 'knowledge' I wanted to elicit. To give me any names at all may have been just a necessary concession, stuck with an adult visitor with several minutes of lesson time still to go. On the other hand, as I asked about reggae, I got precisely the 'old' information elicited by such a backward looking generic category! And perhaps he offered no more because, speaking as an adolescent to a teacher, to become a more expansive informant would have entailed giving up the distance from within which he could control, and frustrate, my efforts to know adolescent cultures. Indeed, on another occasion he brought in a ragga tape for me to listen to and was undoubtedly pleased when I admitted that I couldn't understand it.

However, without in any way contradicting these possibilities, it is also plausible to argue that coexisting with quite a sparse knowledge of the detailed contents of genres was a strong cultural claim upon black music as a public marker of his identity. For Stephen, a sense of participation in Afro-Caribbean and African-American music perhaps enabled him to speak from a position which, in the field of popular music, has a substantial and distinctive power (see Hewitt, 1986: 26; 94). Thus, though he indicated knowledge of other music, it is to black traditions that he returned and to which he seemed committed. Such self-positioning in a black Atlantic culture was achieved without needing to have, or at least constituting his experience as, knowledge.

He combined reference to a pirate station in the immediate area, the Stoke Newington and Dalston districts of Hackney, with reference to a range of black music establishing a connection with Jamaica and North America. The local area of Hackney and the pirate Station FM emerged as nodes within a network of relations between black musical cultures, crossing national boundaries. Such cultures, however sharply differentiated one from another, are nevertheless allied to each other by their implicit separation from the white musical cultures of the nations in which they are located. There is a larger argument to pursue here, an argument in which the significance of Station FM for Stephen can be connected with a perspective outlined by the economic geographer Doreen Massey:

> Instead . . . of thinking of places as areas with boundaries around, they can be imagined as articulated moments in networks of social relations and understandings, but where a large proportion of those relations, experiences and understandings are constructed on a far larger scale than what we happen to define for that moment as the place itself, whether that be a street, or a region or even a continent (Massey, 1991).

Some of the students with whom I talked were well positioned to grasp the perception of global relations suggested by Massey, if, initially, from the more personal space of their own subjectivities and their formation in particular familial histories. Following Massey, I want to stress that the meaning of Stoke Newington and Dalston as places, though delimited perhaps by the transmission range of Station FM, cannot nevertheless be contained within what are accepted as the usual, commonsense, definitions of the *local* or, even, the *East End* (see Gilroy, 1993; Hall, in Hall, Held and McGrew, 1992; Hannerz, 1992). Stephen's relation with the place is both medi-ated through the pirate station and informed by the particularity of his involvement in a history of black migration and settlement. But a white student, such as Margaret, could also participate in this understanding of place, partly through an interest in black music, but also through her own location in another history of migrations. For example, she referred to family connections with Ireland and Nova Scotia and these figured in her domestic experience of music. Indeed, in later discussions with other Hackney students and in the writing produced by students in Edmonton, it became apparent that pop music is a medium through which individual subjects often, though certainly not always, reposition themselves in geographically wide-ranging cultural networks (see Frith, in Grossberg, Nelson and Treichler, 1992; and Jones, S., 1988).

Station FM was, additionally, characterized by Stephen as relating to its audi-ence through a somewhat contradictory strategy: though it makes available reggae, soul, rap, ragga, it does so without informing the audience of their sources – 'they wanna keep it to themselves . . . where they get it from to themselves'. It may be that the 'otherness' of Station FM is also implicit in this lack of involvement in advertising, in its apparent distance from the practice of addressing the radio audi-ence as paying consumers of music. To some extent it seemed important for Stephen to produce an account of the station as a pirate operator, taking risks, carrying no advertising, somewhat obscure, clandestine and unpredictable and thus the 'other' to the mainstream commercial music station Capital, for example (see Thornton, 1995: 147). Stephen thus placed himself as having particular access to an arcane domain; in the recent history of local radio in Britain pirate stations have been primarily a black concern. Thus, his barely audible mumbles and meagre references, whatever the lack of knowledge they may have concealed, could have actually enhanced the power of his claim to a *culturally distinctive* presence in the group. He could be seen as doing just like the black pirate DJs: 'keep[ing] it to themselves'.

A further dimension of Stephen's tactical claim to cultural prestige requires some consideration here. Though none of the students ever makes any explicit claim in terms of a distinction between authenticity and inauthenticity, there are implicit tactics of differentiation in their utterances which can be read as drawing upon a variety of discourses in which the logic of that distinction is evident (see Goodwin, 1993; Middleton, 1990; Redhead, 1990). For example, black music is set against the music of *Top of the Pops*, the BBC-TV chart show originating in the mid-1960s. Stephen seemed to watch with the expectation that something other than pop might appear – rap was his example (see Cubitt, in Masterman, 1984):

CR: Do you all watch *Top of the Pops*?

Stephen: I do sometimes . . . if there's something good on but, but *Top of the Pops*, I don't like most of the music on there . . . if it's got rap or something like that, you know, I watch it . . .

Margaret: yeah . . . *The Chart Show* . . .

CR: Do they ever have rap on *Top of the Pops*?

Stephen:	Only sometimes . . . only once every . . . they only . . . the only thing that comes up is like Omar, stuff like that . . .
CR:	I'm trying to think what other music programmes there are . . . Do . . . did you ever watch Rapido? (mild derision) . . . they did stuff on rap occasionally
Stephen:	Yeah I saw
Margaret:	I like *The Chart Show*, I like watching it

There were no overt challenges to the status of black music in this discussion and Margaret, in particular, repeatedly and with some reciprocation, affirmed Stephen's view, if also introducing another programme against which to disauthenticate *Top of the Pops*. Analytically, *authenticity* provides a provisional means to compare otherwise apparently unrelated tactics in the comments made by Margaret and by Alan, both in the group and, more fully, in the individual interviews which followed. In Stephen's account black music had a prestige implicit in its constituent genres themselves, rather than, on the whole, in any strong subdivision among its exponents. I'll return to this issue later, in discussion of the individual interviews.

Though I have referred to this discussion as *the group interview*, they only constituted themselves as a group[2] at particular moments and, most evidently, by taking a common distance from whatever they regarded as laughable or boring in popular music. In particular, *Top of the Pops* seemed a kind of stock item in a repertoire of objects against which they could position themselves. It, perhaps, had a particularly enduring place among the more ephemeral resources on which they could draw in positioning themselves as adolescent:

Margaret:	On TV they end up playing what they wanna hear like on *Top of the Pops*, they don't play . . . people, they play things like what they want us, what they want people to like . . .
Alan:	That's what they want, it's not what we want
Margaret:	yeah
Stephen:	Yeah it's true
Margaret:	. . . try like to make us like it but no one likes it . . .
CR:	. . . yeah but isn't it already on *Top of the Pops* because it's sold I don't know x number of copies?
Margaret:	Yeah but *Top of the Pops* is trying to be for people our age and people older but people our age and older just don't like that sort of music really . . .
CR:	So how old . . .
Margaret:	The majority of people . . . it's normally younger kids who listen to that sort of music . . .
CR:	So what age of people do you think watch *Top of the Pops* . . . 7, 8? What do you think?
Stephen:	I watch it
Stephen/Margaret:	Everyone watches it . . .

This repeats the motifs of a familiar discourse in which the BBC, in particular, is charged with misaddressing young people, usually with some combination of moralistic and aesthetically prescriptive intent. Here, it is tactically necessary to be misaddressed by a more inclusive, adult, 'they' against which an adolescent 'we' can enjoy being misunderstood, mistargeted as 'they', year after year, go on getting it wrong. And thus they say they continue to watch, if only to keep alive the context of their difference.

Interestingly, they mocked the programme which, for Masterman more than a decade earlier (Masterman, 1980), was the object of some critical anxiety. It has been a programme dominated by what many regard as the safe middle ground of pop, and particularly by music probably more popular with younger, pre-teenage, audiences (see Cubitt, in Masterman, 1984). Furthermore, Thornton (1995) comments, in the context of her account of *club culture*, that *Top of the Pops* 'is seen as the unrivalled nemesis of the underground and the main gateway to mass culture' (Thornton, 1995: 123). However, for these 15-year-olds *as a group*, it was more salient as a means to put some distance between themselves and both childhood and the adult world. But, within the same discussion, they could also constitute themselves as individuals through a further differentiation of their negative relation to the programme. Margaret, for example, in her endorsement of *The Chart Show*, shown on commercial television, was drawing more upon the subcultural discourse identified by Thornton. In the more subcultural logic of discrimination teased out in Thornton's (1995) research, there is an inversion of authenticity which results in video being privileged above live performance. Thus to appear live on *Top of the Pops* is to sell out to an extent to which having the video shown does not, or did not, correspond. Self-positioned as an adolescent group, they watched *Top of the Pops* but claimed to dislike it. They marked their individuality along different axes of escape: pulling out to rap and ragga (Stephen), to video (Margaret) or, in the case of Alan, whom I discuss below, to musicianship.

Before I turn to examine their individual accounts in more detail, it is important to consider how else they may have collaborated to constitute themselves as adolescent, against childhood, and against myself as an adult, grey haired and 40. My questioning was too insistent, too journalistic in its urgency. Moreover, I was asking questions which intruded into a domain constructed as more personal, and more peculiar to youth, than, for example, television. Indeed, they did speak of television more easily, as if the programmes they watched could not be read as so revealing of their interior selves. Impatient to provoke some more expansive discussion, I asked:

CR:	But are there any kinds of music you really dislike, any of you, anything you really wouldn't want to listen to?
Margaret:	Sonia . . . (laughter) I can listen to Kylie, I can listen to it, I can, but I can't . . .
Stephen:	I can't stand Erasure
CR:	You can't stand what?
Stephen:	Erasure

CR:	Why not?
Margaret:	Pet Shop Boys . . . I can't stand them . . . they get on my nerves
CR:	Why, what's wrong with Pet Shop Boys?
Alan:	They're just boring
CR:	Why are they boring?
Margaret/Stephen/Alan:	(Overlapping, mutually confirming, condemnations – noted but untranscribable)
Stephen:	It's just like the same . . . it doesn't change
CR:	And what about Erasure?
Stephen:	That's what I mean, it doesn't change
CR:	The same stuff
Margaret:	They put me off
Alan:	You see them on *Top of the Pops*

Rather than reject whole categories of music as boring, they spoke only of named singers and groups, each the object of some derision: Sonia, Kylie, Erasure, Pet Shop Boys. What seemed to matter in this context was to mark out their distance from prominent names still current in the field. Their refusals thus suggested a more precise and immediate self-positioning than that achieved by distancing themselves from Mozart or BBC Radio 2 – examples I had suggested but which had very little pertinence for them. To locate themselves against what might more plausibly be seen by others (adults) as for *them* was evidently more important. But, more than that, it is clear that Sonia and Kylie belong to a (girlish) childhood, Erasure and Pet Shop Boys to a somewhat ironical, adult and sexually ambiguous, play with and parody of pop music. They're not the least bit explicit about any of this: 'boring', 'the same', 'they put me off'. But in these refusals, they confirm for me, and for each other, their location within adolescence and (hetero)sexuality. On the other hand, by mocking these figures they also succeed in defying the intrusive aspect of my questions. Not liking, or not taking seriously, Sonia, Kylie, Erasure and the Pet Shop Boys, does not involve any significant personal statement: these are (or were) the almost stock figures to be drawn, safely, into their public account of tastes in music.

Three Individual Interviews

Now, I want to reconsider the speakers already discussed but to examine, more closely, their individual concerns in relation to music. I mean 'individual' here to stand for a rhetorical self-construction which cannot be equated in any simple way with a 'personal' subjectivity. As will become increasingly apparent in subsequent chapters, the wider discourses of music journalism (see Redhead, 1990; Thornton, 1995), and of other everyday talk about music, are appropriated into their accounts and thus, though they position themselves individually, they do so by means of a particular repertoire of socially available distinctions (see Bakhtin, 1988; 1994).

Alan, for example, explained his liking for Simply Red in the words of a rock discourse dating from the 1960s, distinguishing between rock and pop (Frith, 1983):

CR:	. . . are you saying then that the kind of music you listen to is hard in the sense that you need to be quite skilled or something like that?
Alan:	I listen to Simply Red . . . like they use all their own instruments . . . if you did like rap or acid you just take bits from other records, there's no skill in it at all . . .
CR:	Does, I mean can you say a bit more about Simply Red then and what you like about Simply Red?
Alan:	It's just sort of what appeals to me . . . really good . . . Mick Hucknall writes all the songs, all the music . . .
CR:	Do the words matter?
Alan:	I think it, with them it does yeah . . . like they tell us what they're saying . . .
CR:	And what are they singing about?
Alan:	Mostly it's love and relationships, things like that . . .
CR:	And . . . how would you describe the music, what's it most like? I don't just mean the name of another band or something like that but if you had to put it in a category, say what kind of music it is, what would you say? What would you say it'd be?
Alan:	. . . don't know

Asking for some kind of generic classification virtually brought this interview to a premature end. Though later in the research I might well have learnt enough to ask the question differently, his emphasis on authorship, musicianship and emotional honesty can be read as antagonistic towards an emphasis on similarity within genres. Certainly, he only named genres to criticize them: '. . . everyone these days just wants acid and rapping but it don't really appeal to me'. More specifically, he rejected rap, and acid, on the grounds that it is:

> . . . just boring . . . just imitation all the time, the same thing . . . like they just get bits from other tracks and play it all over again, just mix it all in . . . it's not hard is it really? . . . if you did, like rap or acid, you just take bits from other records, there's no skill in it at all.

There was a kind of rock nostalgia here, as if at 15 he was weary of the inauthenticity of imitation, the severing of music from musicianship and the alienation of words from their speakers. Apparently, he had no affection for post-punk, post-modern cultural bricolage. His words, spoken here without the presence of Stephen, Margaret and Asiye, sounded like those of an absent parent, reanimated in this instance, perhaps, as a challenge to the prestige of black music.[3] With Alan, but also with the others, utterances sometimes appear to 'call up' the voices of parents and older siblings, suggesting the continuing tension between various discourses around music. Here *individual consciousness* is complex and divided:

The tendency to assimilate other's discourse takes on an even deeper and more basic significance in an individual's ideological becoming, in the most fundamental sense. Another's discourse performs here no longer as information, directions, rules, models and so forth – but strives rather to determine the very bases of our ideological interrelations with the world, the very basis of our behavior; it performs here as *authoritative discourse*, and an *internally persuasive discourse* (Bakhtin, 1988: 342, italics in original).

There are other ways of situating this, perhaps puzzling, cultural conservatism. The fact that Alan had recently bought a CD player had emerged in the group interview. I followed this up with him:

CR: ... if you've got money – what do you spend it on, do records come first, is that important, or do you tend to find other things to spend money on much more easily?

Alan: No, I've got a Saturday job, that's why

CR: Yeah well I realize that you must have

Alan: And I bought a system a couple of months ago from a catalogue so I have to pay that off first ...

CR: Right

Alan: About £20 goes on that a week ...

CR: How much do you get from your Saturday job?

Alan: I get 35 'cause I go in there after school as well ... (inaudible comment on the proportion committed to necessities)

CR: Thirty-five per week right

Alan: And the rest of it's just for me, whatever I want

CR: And what happens during the holidays, does that job become a full-time job?

Alan: If I wanted, I can go in there

CR: What're you doing, what kind of work is it?

Alan: It's just working in a bakery shop

CR: What, where they actually bake stuff or doing deliveries?

Alan: No, it's just doing deliveries
        [section omitted]

CR: But I, I'm just trying to work this out ... if you're spending 20 quid a week paying back for a system that includes what, cassette, CD ... and other things or is it just the CD?

Alan: Just the record player as well

CR: I mean it must matter to you quite a lot to have that though, yes?

Alan: Yes

CR: You know what I mean, 'cause there's plenty of other things you can spend your money on ...

Alan: I just wanted a new one 'cause I had one before but it was all tinny and didn't sound right ...

CR: Yeah

Alan: So I thought to myself that I might as well buy another one . . .
CR: What make is it?
Alan: Murphy

It is of some importance that Alan is willing to talk about his job and the money that he earns. In the traditional terms of working-class masculinity, he can thus address me from a position which points outside and beyond his current place as a school student and a 15-year-old boy. Moreover, generically, this is an easy conversation to have; we can talk together about earning money, what to spend it on, the quality and brand name of the technology it can buy. This is just the common small talk of conversations between men; the topic and its constituent subthemes are secure and confirm the everyday content and limits of a public masculinity. But why should he commit so much, proportionately, to the possession of this Murphy system?

There is a wider argument around the culture of post-modernity within which, tentatively, his comments can be located. The economic geographer David Harvey (1989) offers a perspective which may define the relevant context for Alan's attachment to his new Murphy stereo system and his Simply Red CD:

> Photographs, particular objects (like a piano, a clock, a chair), and events (the playing of a record of a piece of music, the singing of a song) become the focus of a contemplative memory, and hence a generator of a sense of self that lies outside the sensory overloading of consumerist culture and fashion. The home becomes a private museum to guard against the ravages of time–space compression (Harvey, 1989: 292).

This may sound like a description of the habits of much older people or, conceivably, the supposedly more defensive 'bedroom culture' of girls. But it is important to set aside old 'youth culture' preconceptions of male adolescence as played out on the street and recognize that boys do also live within families (McRobbie, 1980) and appropriate domestic space within them. Alan's self-positioning actually seemed to involve a slightly defensive centring in a domestic technology and the private experience it allows. Though Alan's 'private museum' has been inaugurated with the recent products of consumer culture, his music is chosen because, in his aesthetic, he can claim that it is least contaminated by the impediments of manufacture, copying and technological contrivance and the Murphy system is at least less 'tinny'. Thus out of consumption, Alan constructs a version of authenticity and the anchoring of the self which an aesthetic of expression supports. In other respects, also, Alan implicitly drew upon craft notions of authenticity in work, thus making a nostalgic claim to a work-identity rooted in traditional skills. As I have suggested, he disdained as facile the practices of sampling and mixing, favouring effort and traditional musical skill.

Stephen has already figured extensively in the earlier discussion. Most of what I want to add here underlines the reading of his comments in the context of the group interview. He responded to a general question about the importance of black music to him in these terms:

It's what, like what I've grown up with, that's why I'm used to it more than the other kids who like pop . . . My brother listens to reggae and ragga, the old, the old type reggae 'cause he's a musician as well . . . he plays music and he's taking it at college . . . My sister listens to reggae and soul. My two younger sisters listen to reggae and soul as well . . . like that kind of music as well.

This very firm anchoring of himself and his relation to black music through its place in his *family* experience constructs a kind of historical depth at odds with the perception of musical taste as somewhat uprooted and contingent, as if it is no more than what an individual might happen to choose from what the market makes available. At the same time, his location in black music is double-edged: he invoked the past (elsewhere referring to 1960s soul and Motown for example) but also tended to place himself with what is new and innovative, perhaps here marking himself off from some other, (mainly black?) youth: '. . . most people're still into hip hop and stuff . . . but we listen to ragga.' As I have suggested, Stephen was at ease in setting himself apart from pop, but also implied some mobility within the field of black music. Without claiming to be 'a ragga' he could align himself with it as Afro-Caribbean and thus, from one discussion to the next, move in and out of, and beyond, the limits of African-American (black) music. This could be compared to the 'classless autonomy of "hip" youth' (Thornton, 1995: 101); this was also a feature of Margaret's self-account.

Margaret presented her involvement with music in quite a variety of ways. In fact, she sometimes seemed to contradict herself but, in marked contrast with Alan and to a greater extent than Stephen, was perhaps significantly more interested in representing herself as able to engage with a music on several levels. In the group interview, in addition to those contributions already discussed, she presented a possibly exaggerated, perhaps self-mockingly 'typical', account of her everyday use of music:

I listen to anything . . . I listen to rock, classical, anything . . . if I'm driving a car, well I don't drive, but if I'm going in a car . . . without music . . . and like my personal stereo . . . I don't like walking places without listening to music, any music . . . if I'm going on a long walk . . . Put it on [speaking of music radio] leave it on all day . . . leave it on . . . can't be bothered to get out of bed . . . wake up to it . . . go to school, it's still on, come home it's still on, go to bed, it's still on . . . on for about three weeks until my mum says, 'Turn it off!'

In part, Margaret is doing 'being interviewed' and putting herself in an imaginary position of (adult) control: 'if I'm driving a car' – though, at 15, she doesn't drive! Despite the self-correction, the construction of autonomy persists. Her self-descriptions suggested a mode of life in which musical sound saturates almost all her time not in school. In her account, the particular identity of the music seemed subordinate to a continuity of sound which moves with her, moulding her perceptions of time and distance, her moods and her relation to school work. Indeed, in the group discussion she commented that:

> When I'm doing my homework I always listen to acid ... it makes me work ... [*CR*: Why's that?] I dunno it just does and it makes me laugh as well when they can't get it together, you know they're all moaning on about you know they can't get it together and I'm sitting there doing my homework and they can't get it together.

Though developing a detailed account of Margaret's integration of music into her everyday being-in-the-world was not my aim, it is of some importance to at least suggest its significance. It is useful, again, to turn to the geographical metaphors offered by Harvey (1989). There is some basis for representing Margaret's use of music as a matter of control over the physical space through which she moves, music enabling her to carry a sense of place across movement from one space to another and, with some interruption, through the differentiated time phases of the day. Harvey, in a discussion of the postmodern experience of space and time, suggests this:

> Spaces of very different worlds seem to collapse upon each other, much as the world's commodities are assembled in the supermarket and all manner of sub-cultures get juxtaposed in the contemporary city ... and all the divergent spaces of the world are assembled nightly as a collage of images upon the television screen. There seem to be two divergent sociological effects of all of this in daily thought and action. The first suggests taking advantage of all of the divergent possibilities ... the opposite reaction ... can best be summed up as the search for personal or collective identity, the search for secure moorings in a shifting world. Place-identity, in this collage of superimposed spatial images that implode in upon us, becomes an important issue, because everyone occupies a space of individuation (a body, a room, a home, a shaping community, a nation), and how we individuate ourselves shapes identity (Harvey, 1989: 301–2).

I would not see some combination of these two 'divergent sociological effects' as at all improbable within the daily strategies of any one individual. But it is the second, and the concept of 'place-identity', which is of particular relevance here. Margaret's account located her within the audio-space of the music: the radio at home, a personal stereo wherever she goes. It is thus through the physical presence of music that she appears to construct a 'place-identity' which is as mobile as her own body but, for her, extends beyond such strictly personal boundaries to imbue times and spaces, what is external and other, with the musical sound in which she locates herself. School regulations interrupt this continuity, enforcing an order of regulated talk and silence, and thus proscribe this fantasy of self-reflecting autonomy. But of course Margaret, and many others, would surreptitiously reconnect themselves to their personal stereos and thus at least attempt to keep their identities in place.

A further dimension of this self-location, and self-encapsulation, through a physical and emotional immersion in music, is evident in Margaret's identification with music as an occasion for dance:

> . . . the Inspiral Carpets' concert was good . . . everyone that was there was sort of my age . . . jumping around getting excited.

> Ragga's more fast, faster . . . you can dance to it [Speaking of *Do the Right Thing*] . . . the girl at the beginning couldn't dance . . . she had no rhythm . . . I swear I could've done better.

> . . . if I'm at a party or a club I want music I can dance to.

> There's no point in playing acid if you're not going to dance to it.

Dance is often prominent in the self-presentation of girls (see Frith, 1983; McRobbie, 1991; 1994; Richards, 1995; Thomas, 1993; Thornton, 1995) and, in this case, there was an insistent element of self-assertion in the way that Margaret invoked dance as a crucial intensification of her relation to music. The pleasure of the bodily self is made central but it should be recognized that there is also some degree of self-categorization in age terms and, within her age and gender domain, a measure of competitive vehemence. Thus, though the meanings and forms of dance have been elaborated considerably since Simon Frith wrote *The Sociology of Rock* (1978), it is still well worth noting, however briefly, the tendency of his widely influential analysis. Writing of working-class 'girl culture', he argues:

> The problem is to find a husband – hence the significance for girl culture of dancing. In Britain, more young brides, of all classes, still meet their husbands at dances than in any other way; and the most dramatic change in female leisure is the abruptness with which women give up dancing once they are wed. The point . . . is that if marriage is a girl's career, then her leisure before marriage is her work, is the setting for the start of her career, the attraction of a man suitable for marriage (Frith, 1983: 228–9).

Despite the slightly weird anachronism of this passage, it does serve as a warning that dance is by no means a pleasure to be celebrated simply as a 'liberatory moment'. Of course, there's a danger of being reductive here, of implying that the essence of dance is a competitive pursuit of success in a heterosexual scenario. My broader argument is, however, that if dance is still, as Margaret appears to suggest, enmeshed in rivalry between girls, dancing is also enjoyed in other ways, and understood to have different meanings, by many participants in its various forms. For Margaret dance is also, clearly, about an enjoyment of her own body and thus overlaps with the narcissistic use of her personal stereo (Du Gay *et al.*, 1997).

Despite the importance attached to music in Margaret's remarks, whenever the question of buying cassettes and CDs was raised with her she was quick to point out that music was available without spending money, money which was reserved for other matters – from food to make-up (see Frith, 1983; Thornton, 1995). For example, she claimed to be content to listen to other people's music:

> . . . I see it as a waste of money anyway, buying music when all you have to do is turn on the radio or tape it off someone else – it's just as good. I listen to my brother's music . . . I like it and it's played loud but my mum plays Irish music loud, so if it's a choice between that and John's music, I prefer to listen to John's music . . . I like some Irish music, I like a bit of everything . . .

Margaret thus made possessing music marginal and made no strong personal claim to any particular genre. However, music appeared in her account as intrinsic to her social world, and to inhere in her relationships with others. It emerged as an element in her negotiation of social distance and proximity: a qualified preference for ragga over Irish music, for example, and for disconnection through use of her personal stereo.

Research into the uses of reading and of television in domestic settings (see Morley, 1992) has suggested that relationships with others are partly negotiated through particular styles of consumption; reading novels as a strategy for securing personal time or, to the contrary, watching television with others to reconstitute a sense of familial belonging are perhaps familiar instances. The variety of modes of listening to music in both domestic and public space are of comparable complexity and importance. The music over which Margaret represented herself as having some control was that of the radio in her room and the cassettes played in her personal stereo. In her account, neither appeared to intrude significantly on others in the family. By contrast, her brother, John and her mother are presented as asserting their music, their taste, even if the source, in John's case, was within his own room. The meaning of particular practices may vary. For example, playing music loudly in a domestic context may oscillate between, or combine, elements of self-presentation and the wish to exclude, or distance, other members of the family. Margaret's elder sister, by contrast, appeared to have no place in the domestic sphere and to be associated with being out: '. . . I know she goes out, she goes to clubs like the Dome and they play, they play indie.' As I have suggested, there is great scope for research centred more in the domestic context and not, as here, based in classroom discussion with school students. Equally, further research could look more closely at sibling relations and friendship networks in the formation of taste. Nevertheless, there was, in the way that Margaret represented her family, a significant outline of her negotiation of identity in her relationship-through-music-to-others. Margaret's comments suggested a complicated interface between musical cultures, inflected by class and gender, within a single household.

In the individual interview, I was eager to hear of some more definite attachment to a particular music, despite her reluctance to be identified with any one genre. She responded in this way:

Well, I'm attached to popular music, when I say popular music, I don't mean like classical music, that's alright, when I'm in the mood it relaxes me ... when I say popular music, I dunno, songs that make you, I dunno, cry or something, something nice, popular music that you can sing along to and get into but that can be, that can be by anyone, that can be by Madonna or Dire Straits or anyone ...

CR: So you like songs ...

Margaret: Mm, I like songs, I like songs that I can sing along to when I'm at home, or with just a few people ... but if I'm at a party or a club I want music I can dance to ...

CR: Right, right ... but I mean if you're listening to songs I mean does it matter what they're about?

Margaret: Yeah, if I'm listening to them it does ... if it's songs like 'yeah I'm gonna go nigger bashing' I'm not gonna like it even if it does sound good ...

CR: What kind of songs are like that?

Margaret: Oh I dunno, anything like, I dunno, if there is a song like that then I don't think I would like it

CR: Right

Margaret: Yeah it has to have lyrical content, I don't just like the music, I like the words ...

The emphasis on the emotional quality of the music, on a participatory response, and the sense of intimacy it might provide can be compared with accounts given by girls in Chapter 7. Both bring into play a popular motif of 'responsive emotionality' (see Shepherd, with Giles-Davis, 1991). But, in this educational setting, it is important to note that her responses constitute her as a *moral* self, competent to discriminate among and within risky cultural products – even if there is some equivocation in the suggestion that she may listen without listening to the words: '*If* I'm listening to them it does ...' The implicit criteria here seem derived from a view of words, certainly as emotionally expressive, but also as carrying the burden of moral integrity in a medium where musical sound can be a source of excitement and of pleasure but might otherwise be without moral value.[4] Alan tended to locate his version of this in authorship, but Margaret was perhaps more careful to leave the matter of differentiation more open: so that, in effect, her choices could be construed as demonstrating her own individual moral and aesthetic responsibility. Indeed, in this respect, Margaret was well positioned to enter the continuing discourse of moral discrimination towards which English and some versions of media studies have aspired (see Chapter 1). And, though transposed from the religious to the secular discourse of English, the desired state of 'critical discrimination' still carries connotations of spiritual 'ascent' (see Eagleton, 1983).

As I argue in both Chapters 5 and 6, Margaret was the most adept in combining self-positioning as both a moral, educated self with an autonomy from any particular musical culture or associated youth cultural category. She spoke easily of immediate others in terms of social and cultural categories:[5] her brother had always been a 'ragga' and was 'working-class' (if also a student at Sussex University); her sister was assigned to the category 'middle-class'; and yet, of herself, she said:

> I ain't one or the other really . . . I'm not anything really . . . I dunno, most people are probably like me . . . most people are probably more like me than one or the other, they'll listen to anything and they'll do anything, they can't be classified . . . I can be friends with anyone, don't matter . . . whatever you turn on the radio you can get into it . . .

Here, her autonomy is carefully defended, not least by claiming almost to represent 'most people' and through that displacement into the third person, 'they'll listen . . .', 'they can't . . .' reasserting her own eclectic mobility. It is striking that here she speaks in more strongly working-class idioms than on other occasions within the same interview – 'I ain't . . . I dunno . . . don't matter' – as if assuming a less middle-class cultural identity than that deployed elsewhere, notably in her writing (see Chapter 6 and Richard's comment in the introduction to this chapter). However, she does classify both her brother and her sister, thus both drawing upon a discourse of social categorization and refusing, primarily for herself, the tendency to fix and delimit subcultural styles characteristic of both popular and academic discourses around youth. This tendency to refuse self-categorization has been carefully analysed by Widdicombe and Wooffitt (1995) and, though they somewhat neglect the structural features of social contexts, their comments are suggestive of how unstable identities can appear as speakers (identified by their clothing as members of subcultures) shift tactics:

> By examining the subtle procedures through which identities are occasioned, resisted, and negotiated in interaction we begin to appreciate social identities as utterly fluid, variable and context-specific. This is partly because the very meaning, content and form of identities are made contextually relevant to address contingent interpersonal concerns. And attending to sequences of talk as forms of social action necessarily engenders a dynamic conception of self and social identity (Widdicombe and Wooffitt 1995: 108).

In my own research, there is comparable evidence of the variability they identify, though within the institutional context of a school classroom where participants enact continuing identities, to describe students' self-identifications as 'utterly fluid' would be a considerable exaggeration. In an earlier study Buckingham suggests a similar, but more contextually framed, approach:

> What it means to be male or female, working-class or middle-class, black or white, an adult or a child, is not given or predetermined. These 'subject positions' are, at least to some extent, relative terms: they define each other, but their mutual relationships are far from fixed and unchangeable. On the contrary . . . they can be asserted or disclaimed for different purposes in different social contexts (Buckingham, 1993a: 268–9).

In considering my data, to read either assertions or disclaimers as evidence of fixed identities would be misleading. For example, Stephen, like the others, never identified himself in terms of the categories to which he assigned others. Thus, as I have noted, though he said that he listened to ragga, he did not claim *to be* one and actually mocked their dress style and spoke of them always as somewhat other to himself. The variety of black music he referenced gave him considerable room for manoeuvre. Alan offered only limited acknowledgment of any connection between music and identity for himself but was able to represent those who listen to acid as drug users. Margaret, in the group interview, most obviously drew on a kind of sociological discourse and thus displayed some confidence in making the connections around which others hesitated:

> Yeah but the thing is music is a very powerful medium . . . the music someone listens to . . . it makes them, sort of behave the way they behave . . . 'cause a lot of people who listen to ragga become raggas and become sort of . . . some of them do, some of them don't . . . sort of violent and like that and people, a lot of people who listen to like hardcore go out to raves, take loadsa drugs, it just depends, it just depends on what they're into . . .

The social determinism here, qualified in this setting, though unlikely to be turned back upon herself, is consistent with her unwillingness to be placed too exclusively within one genre. It is as if too much of one genre might transform her into a youth cultural clone, compromising both her moral self-positioning and her indeterminate presence relative to the closure which self-categorization may imply. In this respect, Margaret is closer to the first of those 'divergent sociological effects' suggested by Harvey: a degree of elusive and easy mutability is presented as an ordinary everyday way of being (see Bourdieu, 1986). In many ways, Margaret's stance seemed often to approximate that of being 'hip'. If Alan adopted a craft version of musical aesthetics, and Stephen voiced its black variant, Margaret, more than the others, tended towards the hip tactics characterized by Ross (1989):

> To be hip . . . always involves *outhipping* others with similar claims to make about taste. Hip is the site of a chain reaction of taste, generating minute distinctions which negate and transcend each other at an intuitive rate of fission that is virtually impossible to record. It is entirely inconsistent with the idea of a settled or enduring commitment to a fixed set of choices (Ross, 1989: 96).

I don't want to exaggerate this correspondence but, as will be apparent in the next two chapters, Margaret did tend to operate in this way – with perhaps a tacit understanding of how doing so made her appear 'in the know' (see Ross, 1989: 81) and thus able to 'make (cultural) capital' out of her position, whatever her actual knowledge about music.

By contrast, Asiye emerged at the very end of the group session as having a broad interest in pop. She volunteered little more than that she listened to Capital

Radio. It was very difficult to elicit much more substantial comment from her though, on a later occasion, she became a little more involved in a group discussion involving several girls but no boys. So Asiye does figure in both of the next two chapters, though the detail of ethnically differentiated relations to popular music remains undeveloped in this book, to be considered in further research.

There are a variety of explanations for the emergent pattern of indeterminacy which can be suggested here. First of all, it is fairly clear that the way these 15-year-old students positioned themselves was motivated by a desire to distance themselves from childhood and, further, to locate themselves in the liminality and indeterminacy of adolescence, between childhood and the supposedly settled fixity of identities in adult life. To some extent therefore, as I suggested in Chapter 2, there is always the possibility of a mixing and blurring of the categories associated with race and ethnicity, class and gender. Indeed, it may be that claims to indeterminacy are themselves tactical – responses to being positioned as risky and troublesome by the regulatory discourse of adolescence. If adolescence is lived by some young people as defiantly indeterminate, this may contribute to some degree of cultural fusion and exchange. There is some evidence of mobility across cultural boundaries in several studies of urban youth, each placing some emphasis on the scope for both cultural hybridity and for movement between ethnically inflected identities (see Hebdige, 1979; 1987; Hewitt, 1986; Jones, S., 1988). The resources for such cultural mobility are variously located in the particular ethnic composition of some inner city areas, in friendship networks and in the proliferation of popular cultural forms, especially music. However, there is also evidence that beyond the relative indeterminacy of adolescence, on entry into adulthood, more bounded identities are established and the social basis of cultural mixing is perhaps only rarely sustained (Hewitt, 1986).

At this point, it is worth emphasizing again that the evidence I've been discussing was produced in a context where school students were being addressed by a kind of teacher. Positioned as adolescent, their responses were perhaps wary of censorious judgements, at other times, defiantly assertive. Margaret, and the others, tended to refuse the kind of single essentializing interpellation implied by asking questions with the form of 'What does your liking for music x say about you?' Inescapably, indeterminacy was also of some tactical value, given the institutional overdetermination of the social relations of the interview situation. Margaret, more than the others, also positioned herself as a competent and articulate student and, in Chapter 6, I will show how this self-positioning was enacted in the production of a written assignment.

It is important to note that this indeterminacy must also be attributed to their specific lack of social and economic power: at 15 they are relatively dependent upon their parents. In the individual interviews all three referred to their mothers buying records or CDs on their behalf: Stephen commented that he would 'ask my mum to buy me . . .'; Alan, that 'if I like a CD, I'll ask my mum to get it for me like on a Saturday'; and Margaret, 'if I want music really badly and no one else has got it for me to tape off them, if no one else has got it, me mum'll get it for me.' Of course, the boys kept their mums out of the group interview and, given such strategies of self-presentation, it is worth recalling earlier tendencies in youth research to collude with participants' claims to a male street culture independent of its domestic anchorage. But, at this age, their lives organized between family and school, they had very limited social and economic power to establish substantially differentiated lifestyles and construct more securely autonomous identities. Their power is more appropriately conceived as semiotic: with meagre material resources they remake their cultural identities in minor ways, constrained financially within patterns of transient consumption. Their quite limited collections of CDs and cassettes, the details of their clothing, of make-up or of jewellery, are examples of the small things to which I referred, briefly, in Chapter 2.

Despite these various reflections on the need to interpret this material with some caution, I do want to reaffirm the relevance of the geographical perspective to an understanding of the cultural tactics of identity. I particularly want to stress that Harvey's analysis of postmodernity is essential to an understanding of the compressed and complex world in which these adolescents find the resources for 'borrowing, mixing and fusion' (Johnson, in CCCS Education Group II, 1991: 71) and, however constrained, appropriate them in the process of trying out the sense of themselves – thus, often, both mixing and demarcating in the same moment of self-positioning. Some reflections on the earlier history of this tendency are sketched by Andrew Ross:

> Just as the music industry cannot fully anticipate how its products will be received, so too, a fixed socio-economic analysis cannot fully account for the popular taste of consumer groups, many of whom 'misbehave' in the choice of their musical tastes, a delinquent practice that surfaced most visibly with the appearance, in the mid-fifties, of a 'youth culture' whose generational identity was organized around its willingness to cut across class-coded and color-coded musical tastes (Ross, 1989: 77).

The communicational possibilities and pressures of postmodernity are not, then, peculiar to only the past decade or so but are features of a longer history of cultural change within which youth has been a crucial site of combination and consequent remaking (see Kress, 1995).

For the students discussed in this chapter, their choices were not in any way final or definite. But neither were they just free-floating or arbitrary: they each have their own histories within particular families, within a particular locality and a particular school. Their musical preferences, and especially their relationship to pop, cannot be explained *simply* as the effects of the music industry's power to manipulate taste. Where they are located, and the sense they make of their locations, informs their relationship to the field of music and makes the vision of *mass* culture, a market driven homogeneity, somewhat implausible. It needs to be acknowledged, however, that the particular cultural resources available to young people are always also *of some specific kind* and are clearly formed, in part, in contexts of production to which they do not have access. The importance of the institutional domain of cultural production should not be underestimated (see Goodwin, 1993). Indeed, there is a case for teaching young people about precisely those domains of which, from their restricted vantage points, they can have only slight knowledge (see the discussion in Chapter 8).

The youthful experience of popular music may be formative and may persist in the making of adult identities but, as adults, these young people will doubtless continue to reinterpret their own youth and their musical tastes. In the research for this book, it wasn't possible to develop a longitudinal study and thus to explore the duration and reconstruction of knowledge about, and tastes in, music over a lengthy period of time. Nevertheless, between the immediacy and transience of their present involvement with popular music and their futures, teaching can engage with, and invite some reflection on the positions they adopt. The following chapters continue to tease out the terms in which they represent their tastes in music, but also begin to address more directly the question of how teachers might work with their students' experience of popular music in classroom practice.

Notes

1   Richard had also remarked, 'I do feel slightly odd as . . . whether I like to admit it or not, a kind of middle-aged man who in some ways has interests which kind of go outside my stereotyped education and age and so on . . . I do feel slightly at sea culturally . . . I'm allowing myself to proceed into something which is fundamentally for younger people . . .'
2   There is an interesting discussion of what groups do, with particular reference to class, in Jordin and Brunt (1988); see especially pp. 240–7.
3   Ironically, as Simply Red is substantially preoccupied with reworking aspects of black music.
4   Susan McClary comments: 'The political folksong is the Left's version of the Calvinist hymn: words foregrounded to control "the meaning", music effaced to the status of vehicle, all untoward appeals to the body eliminated' (McClary in Rose and Ross, 1994: 31).
5   In Hey's (1997) study working-class girls did not employ an explicit language of class. Here, Margaret is closer to the middle-class girls also discussed by Hey:

> . . . Suzy becomes her own semiotician, decoding how 'they' located her image in the classic terms of a subcultural commentary . . . The conceptual language of class was a structured absence from the lives of working-class girls. The nearest they came to class discourse was in the submerged forms: 'snobs', 'boffins' and 'swots'. The all-stars conversely produced themselves through professing classed taste and classed understandings (1997: 118).

Chapter Five

Transient, Tactical Knowledge

CR: Right so there's not one kind of music that you decide you're gonna stick to?

Jamie: No 'cause you can say 'Oh well Alan likes the Housemartins' (much laughter) but then there might be a song that he don't like

Paul: . . . and then he doesn't like the Housemartins

Introduction

This chapter presents extracts from further conversations with both the students already represented in Chapter 4 and with others from the same media studies class. It documents another attempt to talk about music but with a particular phase of classroom work as a focus. The chapter is thus, in part, a reflection on the particular aspect of teaching in which I was involved. Towards the end of the period in which the class worked through a pop music assignment, I extracted four girls and four boys, and conducted separate discussions with them. The sessions took place in the English department's office.

The inter-related questions of adolescence, identity and musical taste are located here through a central contrast between the positions taken up by boys and girls. The degree of gendered division within this class emerged more strongly in this material than in the earlier interviews. The discussions were set up in terms consistent with their self-organization in the classroom: almost invariably in distinct groups, girls on one side, boys on the other. Furthermore, the discussions were events of an unrepeatable kind, internal to the particular process of teaching and evaluation through which I was able to form a working relationship with the students. In short, they were not autonomous research events but were embedded in their continuing work for their GCSE in media studies.

It is important to visualize the discussions – with me present as a teacher and with a tape recorder placed centrally amongst us. One of the group held the microphone and, to some extent, took up a mediating position between me and the others.

Certainly this helped to give the groups some sense of a discussion among themselves, but the questions and their sequence were still my responsibility and I acted very much as a teacher, intent upon sustaining discussion. Despite this, and especially with the boys, the form of the event was often conversational, frequently departing from or elaborating around the prepared questions. These are discussions of a very particular kind and must be read as offering only partial and provisional evidence of the students' knowledge of music. As in the preceding chapter, their knowledge was elusive and seemed mostly a transient phenomenon, tactically orientated to the circumstances of the discussion. At times, I felt that the meanings of music for the students could not be recorded through responses in which conscious elaboration had much place (see Thomas, 1993: 78). Sometimes, the significance of musical references was registered in silences and refusals or in moments of derision and laughter. I argue, therefore, that in the practice of media teaching, there is a need to explore a wide variety of ways of engaging with popular musical knowledge rather than assume that talk, of the kind typically involved in group evaluations, will enable students to articulate what they know. In common with recent arguments for 'practical work' in media education (Buckingham, Grahame and Sefton-Green, 1995; Buckingham and Sefton-Green, 1994), I see discussions of the kind represented here as just one moment in a necessarily more diverse practice.

It has been argued that, often, 'adolescents are over-impressed by the inquisitive attention of adults such as researchers and like to be seen to have "opinions" and to debate as adults have opinions and debate' (Hewitt, 1986: 7). To some extent, this tendency is apparent in the extracts discussed below (see, especially, Margaret's contributions), but their self-presentation was framed by a model of evaluation and their negotiation of my involvement as a teacher rather than a researcher. On the whole, they didn't aspire to (middle-class) models of adult debate and, to the contrary, took up various positions as adolescents, pupils, gendered and classed subjects and participants in youth culture.

There was a tension between the formality of the event, an evaluation, and, for them, the immediate social currency of musical reference. What the occasion and my questions required was a reflection on the classroom work they had been doing but, clearly, to speak of popular music could not be separated from its tactical significance in positioning themselves among their peers. The precarious division of private social relations from the public context of the classroom could not be sustained. The girls spoke to each other of their parents or families or of specific friends in common, and thus some sense of how music was implicated in their lived social relations became more present in the discussion. But this did not involve any more elaborated description, any more explicit referencing of the music. On the contrary, music was referred to that much more implicitly and entirely within the terms of the particular social relations within which it seemed embedded. This, though marked by a greater display of levity, was also evident among the boys. What they could tell me, and what emerged in their discussions, was never 'of music' abstracted from the continuing negotiation of the immediate social context.

It follows from these observations that the voicing of tastes in these sessions was, to some degree, a matter of tactical positioning within the specific form of the event (see Widdicombe and Wooffitt, 1995). Tastes, often understood to be fixed, natural and discrete, are indeed peculiar and puzzling, not easy to explain in any terms. It is no surprise that tastes are exceptionally difficult to disentangle from the lived social reality and the lived sense of self in which they are embedded. Despite this, a social theory of tastes, one which challenges their apparent idiosyncrasy, can provide ways of grasping at least one of their dimensions – the logic of tastes in particular social fields. The work of Pierre Bourdieu, notably *Distinction* (1986), provides the most elaborated theory of *taste* as a matter of location within relations between classes and class fractions and thus constantly undercuts any claim that preferences are purely personal. To the contrary, in Bourdieu's terms, to express a taste is to situate the self in a particular, socially differentiated, field of relations. In my own borrowing of Bourdieu's argument, discussed in more detail in Chapter 7, the identities staked out through the expression of tastes need to be understood as socially tactical; particular claims to 'fixity' or 'naturalness' might thus serve relational purposes. In what follows, tastes are implicated in marking boundaries but, in other ways, they contribute to allegiance, to the experience of subjectivity as a shared domain, rather than as individual, quirky, isolating. Tastes in music are perhaps peculiarly powerful, constructed as one of the more emotive means through which, in the transitions from child to adult, relations to others are negotiated and redefined (see McClary, 1991). In these discussions, therefore, the expression of tastes is not taken to be simply a truth about the speaker but is seen as, at least in part, a negotiation of possible positions within the particular social dynamics of the event, within the microcultural politics of adolescent gender relations.

To conclude this introduction, I want to emphasize that without access to specific forms of music education, talk about music can appear simplistic, descriptively vague in the sense that the experience of form and sound will be allocated to a limited set of categories, often presented as binary opposites: bass or treble, fast or slow. It is still the case that where formal vocabularies are available, they are closely associated with reading music and with instruction in serious music and therefore will be unlikely to enter discourse around popular music (but see, for example, the innovative work of McClary, 1991, on Madonna). But whatever ways of speaking about music are regarded as legitimate in the formal context of education, the informal domain does not require a discourse about music which might represent it and secure its place at that level of 'official' cultural legitimation. Furthermore, in informal contexts, between knowing participants in the culture, description is largely redundant, the detail of difference left implicit in the vocabulary of generic distinctions. Here, the students' words are mostly those of popular discourses, borrowed and reinflected in exchanges between them. Sometimes, seemingly orientated more towards my presence, they repeat the words through which I have asked the question or the words they have heard from other teachers and by which they can position themselves as 'good' (or not) (see Bakhtin, 1988; 1994).

A Music-Audience Assignment

It was my intention to explore their engagement with music through the teaching of a unit of work based on producing publicity materials for a new artist. In the process, I hoped that they would gain a more explicit understanding of the knowledge which they had already acquired in informal contexts. The unit of work began with a brief exploratory task through which they could find out something of their fellow students' musical tastes. It was followed by the presentation of several images gleaned from fashion magazines though subsequently cropped and photocopied to somewhat disguise their source. In fact, in much of the work that I did with them, these images became the principal object of their fascination and of our discussion. Their immediate presence as a classroom text, and the students' previous learning of a media studies vocabulary orientated towards the description and analysis of the visual, made discussion appear easy and secure. As I argue in the next chapter, in media studies such discussions are likely to be centred in the now familiar, if not unproblematic, practice of *image-analysis* (see Barthes, 1972; 1977; Buckingham, 1990; Gauthier, undated). It was of some importance to them to appear competent in this practice, but to speak of music was not what they had been taught to do. In Green's (1988) terms, we were thus all more at ease with a focus on *delineated* rather than *inherent* meanings.

The unit of work served two main purposes. It was necessary to devise something which would resemble the work with which they were familiar. It was essential that assessable outcomes be available at the completion of the assignment; these were the students' last few months in school and their GCSE exams were a significant preoccupation. In fact, the unit was closely based on one already devised by a new teacher in the department, a former English and media PGCE student at the Institute of Education. What I planned was thus intended to emulate current practice in media education; it was not a research tactic conceived discretely for the 'elicitation of data'. Initially, I asked the students to read a set of questions around the use of popular music and, after some rewriting, to interview other students around the school to answer them. The questions were adopted by the group with few modifications. Some did emphasize particular questions, adding one or two significant new enquiries: 'Is there a type of music which you find offensive?' and 'Do you ever use drugs to enhance music?' In this instance, the students' own strongly linked preoccupations with dress, dance, drugs and music informed an intensity of interest in the issue of music and cultural identity which was, if anything, somewhat frustrated by the particular form of the assignment demanded of the group.

The presentation of the initial assignment outline took the following form:

GCSE Media Studies – Spring Term 1993

Year 11: A Music-Audience Assignment

This assignment has two main stages. The first involves finding out what you can about the people that might buy a record by a new artist. The second involves producing the publicity materials through which the new artist is to be promoted. So what you have to do is this:

First: read through the survey questionnaire. It was written by teachers interested in finding out more about the music that their pupils listen to. Your job is to rewrite and redesign it as a survey which you can carry out with people of your own age. Your aim is to get information that will help you decide how best to launch a new artist.

Each of you will need to interview five people. Responses to your questions will be shared and discussed within your group.

Second: You have to choose one artist from the images provided. You need to think how to present and publicize this artist for an audience of people in the age band from 15 up to, say 20. You will have already considered the most popular sources of information for new music and how best to place an artist so that he or she is heard and seen by the right age group.

Here you have to produce the following materials:

1   A title for a new single and a design for the sleeve.
2   An advert for the artist's forthcoming album, video and tour.
3   A review of the album for a well known publication.
4   A storyboard for a promotional video.

In addition, you will have to complete an evaluative essay which will show how you researched and produced your project and will include comment on the success of your completed materials.

Questionnaire (to be rewritten)

1   What are the main ways in which you listen to music? [Tape – CD – Record – Radio – TV]
2   How do you find out about new music? [TV – magazines – music papers – friends – relations]
3   To which radio stations do you listen?
4   Do these stations play music that is new to you? [If so, what?]
5   Do you have your own radio at home?
6   Is it possible for you to listen to what you want when you're at home?
7   Are there any kinds of music that you really dislike? [If so, what?]
8   Is there a particular kind of music that you identify with?
9   Do you ever go to hear music live?
10 If you go to clubs, or to hear music live, how would you decide what to wear?
11 Pick out and group together the kinds of music that you listen to most often:

reggae	rap
hip hop	ragga
dub	ambient
soul	blues
retro	techno
acid	house
jazz	hardcore
heavy metal	junglism
slam rock	indie
funk	swingbeat
rave	grunge
[add on any not listed . . .]	

12   To which of these, if any, do you dance?

The questions included a list of genres (see above), some picked out from earlier conversations with members of the class, others gleaned from music magazines. These questions, and particularly the list of supposed musical genres, provoked some bewilderment and mild derision. To the list of genres many added: pop, classical, punk, garage, thrash, psychedelic and bhangra. Several of the genres identified in my list were rejected as inappropriately named: rave and retro for example. Other generic titles were seen as obscure and unknown, except, perhaps, to Margaret: swingbeat, slam rock, and grunge were not familiar to them in early January 1993. No one recognized the term *ambient*. Margaret was quick to ask 'What are these? Don't you know?' Claire pointed out that they, and others, may well listen to music belonging to these genres without knowing such a repertoire of generic terms. Though some of the terms were used by the students in earlier interviews, those few which came from the more adult discourses of music journalism (*i-D*, for example) were not a part of their everyday repertoire. But it was partly because of the genre list's imperfect relation to their more familiar set of terms that its presentation became a productive basis for clarification. Moreover, it thus became apparent that the way they divided the current field of music into particular genres would depend not just on what the music *sounded like* but on what particular discourses around music they encountered in reading teenage magazines, watching TV and listening to radio.

In their responses to the assignment, despite diversity of ethnic identity and some degree of class difference within the group, the most marked differences in the routes they took through the work and the subsequent evaluation were those displayed between the girls and the boys (see Richards, 1990). Margaret, in particular, was keen to construct the field in terms of gender difference and, though she was clearly keen to position herself as my 'special' informant, her account was also quite persuasive. My experience of the whole group as participants in the classroom was that the girls tended to work more consistently and with some, if not unvarying, commitment; the boys adopted a slow and indifferent, leisurely and distanced relation to the work. The girls were individually more willing to discuss their progress through the assignment; the boys tended to form a more closed group, resistant to 'teacherly' interventions. But such differences were also, in part, evidence of their negotiation of my presence, and the meanings that might be attributed to their involvement with me. What it meant to them to be chosen, and what they might allow it to mean, had to be carefully managed. For the boys, to be selected out individually, and to be seen to respond with interest, in this adolescent male culture, could risk taunts of 'sucking up' and other homophobic allegations (see Sennett and Cobb, 1972: 82). For the girls, to be chosen and to secure my attention carried no comparable risk and, whatever their perception of my age and appearance, could probably be enjoyed as reflecting their success in attracting the interest of a male visitor, thus confirming themselves in 'the hegemonic masculine gaze' (see Hey, 1997).

Talking to the Girls

In the session with the girls (Sara, Margaret, Gemma, Asiye) there was an attentiveness to the questions I posed which, in marked contrast with the boys, suggested some degree of interest in taking up and sustaining the position of student in relation to my presence as teacher. Initially, there was an almost disconcerting formality in the way that they placed themselves physically. They looked as if they were engaged in an event which, in its recording, would be the basis of judgement upon them. They tended to reply to my questions cautiously, replaying the terms of the question as I had asked it (see Widdicombe and Wooffitt, 1995: 97). Once the main body of assessment orientated questions had been asked, more informal utterances, expressions of exasperation and amusement or comments between friends did occur. But still, the tension between formality and a less constrained conversational banter did persist.

Given this brief account of the situation, I want to consider some of the detail of what they could say. Take my initial recorded question and the response:

CR: The point is, in the process of doing a unit of work like that, what do you think you're learning about, are you actually finding out more about music or are you just using the knowledge of music that you already have?

Margaret: Well, I didn't actually learn anything about music from it, I just like demonstrated the knowledge I already had . . . How about you Sara . . . ?

Here the response is contained safely within the boundaries of the polarity I presented in my question; further, the term *demonstrated* is one which locates her response within the assessment rhetoric presented to GCSE students. Uncomfortable with the question, but also assigned the responsibility of holding the microphone, Margaret turned to pass the question to Sara, thus turning her responsibility to her own advantage. Margaret occupied a key position throughout the discussion, presenting herself as always, if not infallibly, knowledgeable. For example, in response to my repeated attempts to elicit more explicit definitions of the musical genres with which they shared a familiarity, and to which I had no easy access, Margaret was adept in handling the difficulty they all encountered – that of there being no elaborated discourse of musical description available to them – by transposing the problem to the level of a philosophical conundrum:

Sara:	Well you know about it [music] but you've asked me several million times now to define hardcore to you
Margaret:	Yeah he's asked me that as well . . .
CR:	Yeah so what're the problems in explaining it, why is it so difficult?
Sara:	'Cause there're so many different types of music
Margaret:	You've got to hear it for yourself yeah
Sara:	We know what it is
Margaret:	It's like asking, it's like asking someone to define I and then if you say me, they say define me . . . you can't just define something like that, if it's something you know . . .
CR:	Yeah OK, but I mean is it because in a way you're all so used to the fact that you all know what you're talking about?
All:	Yeah
Margaret:	You don't meet young people who say 'So what's hardcore then?'
CR:	No, well, exactly
Margaret:	Everyone knows what it is . . .

This moment illustrates both Margaret's position of relative power and precisely identifies the peculiarity of making explicit what is known and familiar to participants in an informal cultural practice. Her strategy was effective in enabling her to justify what, in this formal context, might be judged a linguistic inadequacy in terms which counter that implication with a display of rhetorical skill. In effect, she turned age-relations to my disadvantage, leaving my question exposed as an act of cultural incompetence, and, in this instance, positioning herself as an adolescent insider to an adolescent culture. At other points in the discussion, Margaret took on the role of restating some of my more rambling and discontinuous questions:

Margaret:	Instead of using the pictures he means wouldn't it be better to listen to the music . . .

She thus mediated between myself and the group. As I have suggested, she seemed to position herself as a respondent more privileged than the others. However, all of the girls were more interested respondents than the boys and this was apparent in their more focused attempts to engage with whatever questions I asked. Similarly, though they did voice criticisms, their comments on the work that they were asked to do were more positive than those offered by the boys:

CR:	What did you enjoy most in actually doing that unit of work, if anything?
Margaret:	I enjoyed designing the record sleeve
Sara:	It's something we wanted to do more than something we had to do, I suppose you could put it like that
CR:	Why, why did you want to do it?
Sara:	'Cause it was an interesting type of topic, it's not something you can get to do in all your lessons [Yeah – Margaret] . . . something different, totally different
Gemma:	I enjoyed designing the sleeve as well

Whatever the degree of their actual enjoyment, here, once again the girls take up the question, repeating the word 'enjoy' and, through Sara, elaborating in response to its invitation, position themselves as 'good' (*really* interested) students: 'something we wanted to do', 'interesting', 'different'. Enjoyment, however, should not be assumed to correspond directly to any formal measure of success. It seemed, more loosely, that 'enjoyment' was accepted as an element in their tacit understanding of femininity as at least partially confirmed within the settings that education constructs (though see Hey, 1997, for some detailed differentiations). Perhaps for them, to please a (male?) teacher, confirmed their self-positioning as feminine within heterosexual discourse (see Richards, 1990; Wolpe, 1988). Being a good student and being a girl, in this context, did seem more likely to involve convergent performances. By contrast, for the boys, pleasing teachers required some more awkward effort of reconciliation between contradictory versions of the gendered self. This is discussed further in my account of the parallel session with the boys, below.

At this point, I want to expand upon the girls' relation to music through further extracts from the transcript:

CR:	. . . I mean what I'm getting at is how important is it to you to be able to buy music on record or CD or tape?
Margaret:	I don't, I never buy music . . .
Sara:	It has to be . . . really, really good that I really really like
Margaret:	I don't, I can't remember the last time that I've bought music 'cause if I like something [get it?] . . . off other people . . . yeah, well I just, dunno, dunno, one of my sisters or my brother'll get it probably so I just tape it off them
CR:	So do none of you actually collect tapes or records?
All:	No
CR:	Not really . . .
Gemma:	My mum goes out and buys tapes, stuff that I like, she goes out and buys it for herself
CR:	So where, I mean if you dance to music where do you actually get to dance to it?
Margaret:	Oh loads of places

CR:	Like?
Margaret:	Clubs, raves, parties but I don't really, I don't really dance at parties
CR:	Where do you dance, at clubs?
Margaret:	. . . and raves
CR:	Right, is that the case for everybody or . . . ?
Gemma:	Not really
Sara:	I don't really go to raves, I've never been to a rave . . . I've been to parties and danced there, I always dance at parties
Margaret:	I don't
CR:	But you never actually, would you actually . . .
Margaret:	It's my reputation
CR:	Is it?
Margaret:	I sit there and go 'I never dance at parties' unless I'm really drunk and then I don't dance to hardcore
Sara:	You didn't dance at Julian's, did you?
Margaret:	No (laughs)
CR:	If you heard something at a party or a rave or whatever, that you were dancing to, would you ever actually try to
Margaret:	Buy it?
CR:	. . . buy it?
Margaret:	No, but I know lots of people who do, like my friends who're like into mixing and stuff . . . they buy records to mix in with their other records
CR:	Are they . . . girls?
Margaret:	Boys
CR:	Right
Margaret:	Girls don't really do that so much
CR:	I know, I wonder about that . . . why, I mean it doesn't seem to be the case that girls collect records or tapes or CDs at all really or not to any significant extent, I wonder why not?
Margaret:	I think it's a bit of a waste of money, I wouldn't bother wasting my money on that 'cause I can spend it on better things

To some extent, Margaret is doing 'being interviewed' again, appearing to claim a first-hand knowledge of activities associated with older youth (her sister?) and beyond the experience of the other girls present.

Bearing in mind, again, the tactical purposes of these responses, there are a variety of themes to follow through here. The self-identification as dancers, though neither common to all four nor uncomplicated for any of them, was nevertheless an important point of difference relative to the boys' comments on music and dancing. *Buying* and *collecting* music was, on the whole, less evident in the girls' self-accounts than in those of the boys. This is a contentious point. Wider evidence, derived from statistical survey data for example, is not especially sensitive to gender differentiated patterns of consumption and use.[1] The scope of my own research did not extend to those contexts of consumption where other kinds of data might have been produced. My argument is limited to the terms in which the students represented themselves and, therefore, I don't intend any conclusive claim about the gendered division of young people's engagement with music. But this issue should be one of continuing importance for media teachers seeking to involve their students in exploratory investigations of young people's uses of music. Moreover, my speculative claim that strong self-positioning through the possession of music might be associated with a more separated and delimited version of the self, is one which should inform the conduct of such investigations: a matter for self-reflection and for small-scale enquiry by students themselves. In my research, this emphasis on *possession*, for young people between 15 and 17, was less marked in the girls' self-accounts discussed here and in Chapter 7. As I noted earlier, their relative lack of money constrained any significant spending, and they tended to deny that the money they did have was spent on music. For Margaret, with her personal stereo, the economy of home-taping gave her sufficient access to the music she wanted to hear. On the whole, music was to be heard and perhaps to be danced to, the pre-condition for pleasurable activities and not a set of objects to be accumulated.

By contrast with buying and accumulation, dancing is assumed to be an activity central to the lives of adolescent girls (see Chapter 4).[2] As it happens, in this particular session, two of the girls made no claim upon it – Asiye did not speak, Gemma evaded the question with 'Not really'. These girls were all still living at home with parents and, at 15, their lives were regulated and limited in ways which made occasions for dancing relatively infrequent. However, the girls' preoccupation with dancing as the preeminent mode of involvement with music was more evident in the assignments on which they were working and which I discuss in the next chapter. Moreover, dance music, among the larger group of girls in the class, was significantly more popular than other forms. In this session, Sara acknowledged more involvement, though it was restricted to parties, a forum which Margaret disowned as a place to dance unless 'drunk' and thus implicitly less responsible for compromising the social identity she wished to sustain. Between the girls here, Margaret positioned herself as somewhat more hip than Sara, implicitly locating parties as beneath both clubs and raves in her cultural hierarchy. The reputation Margaret wishes to sustain is not, it seems, primarily to do with risks to her sexual status, but is mostly a matter of maintaining her particular sense of subcultural distinction (Thornton, 1995). Margaret was keen to make these distinctions, taking space in the discussion to claim a degree of cultural authority. At the same time, she also most effectively portrayed herself, constituting herself as having, or being, an *image* and thus someone to be looked at, by myself as the only man present, and by the other girls. She represented herself as more completely composed than they, as yet, could claim to be – and this was achieved both by her words and by her attention to details of dress and make-up.

Another dimension of the way in which these girls placed themselves, explicitly contrasting the mode of their enjoyment with that of boys, emerged in a discussion of ragga:

CR:	Do girls listen to ragga very much . . . as much as boys?
Margaret:	Yeah . . . boys take it in more . . . I mean generally boys are more listening to the messages of the song . . .
CR:	Which are what?
Margaret:	It's like 'Oh yeah girls pum pum went did this shot a man blah blah blah girl's a bitch' all that but boys, boys listen to that more than girls and think of it like more 'this is serious, this is the way I feel blah blah blah' more than girls do
CR:	I mean I've not heard much ragga . . .
Margaret:	Girls like the music, I like the music, I don't like some of the messages that it's putting across to young boys . . . when I say young boys I'm not trying to sound like a grown up, they're more my age but . . . influenced by it
Gemma:	There's one, there's one ragga song that puts across a message about gambling and having to go out and shoot all of them and I don't think that's a very nice thing to be putting across
Margaret:	Raggas are really anti-gay . . . [Yeah . . .] and like no respect for girls really . . . no respect for any woman except for their mums really (laughter) . . . it's fashionable to respect their mum but no one else, it's true

Margaret was marking out quite a complicated position here. She differentiated between two modes of listening, one attentive to the sonic qualities of ragga, the other engaging with and entering into the meaning of what is spoken or sung (see Goodwin, 1993: 94). She tended, on this occasion, to attribute the latter to boys alone, those others who, in that common strategy of displacement, are influenced by the message and 'take it in'. This apparent vulnerability, or willingness, to ingest ragga meanings – to take them into the self – is what, in the discourse of media 'effects', adults might ascribe to children and adolescents. Here, Margaret almost locates herself as an adult, 'grown-up', but, given her position as an adolescent herself, shifts more definitely towards voicing her critique as a girl, implicitly drawing upon the sedimented common sense that girls mature earlier than boys. By these means, she thus locates herself as able to explain, and distance herself from, boys' enjoyment of ragga. Moreover, as I suggested in Chapter 3, she also achieves a position in an educationally legitimated feminist discourse – if simultaneously submitting herself for approval by myself as a (male?) teacher.

In these moments, Margaret positioned herself as capable of a somewhat distanced, rational and self-aware enjoyment and a discrimination between elements of a single piece of music. She thus enabled herself to adopt some mobility between positions allowing both enjoyment of the music and condemnation of ragga machismo, which she mocked with considerable wit, thus further securing her self-representation as the most 'hip' among this group of girls. Whatever one might think of ragga, her tactical belittling of aspirations to adult masculinity among both the young male audience and the ragga performers themselves – on the one hand 'little boys', on the other, only able to 'respect their mums' – was entirely successful here. It made me laugh, it made the other girls laugh, and she got herself quoted both here and in an earlier version of this chapter.[3] She voiced 'the right words', but also as if they were entirely her own (see Bakhtin, 1994), to secure approval and amusement both in the immediate context and in publication. As I will argue in the next chapter, Margaret was able to position herself within a discourse of critical rationalism which gave her the opportunity to be both *hip* and *educated* – and thus to secure *subcultural* and *educational* capital in the same moment (Bourdieu, 1986; Bourdieu and Passeron, 1977; Ross, 1989; Thornton, 1995).

Meanwhile, Gemma's more muted criticisms tended in the same direction but largely echoed Margaret's formulations. When I moved the discussion towards rap, it faltered because of their relative lack of interest in, or knowledge of, this music. But, following a question about Queen Latifah, Margaret, once again, took up a distinctive position, in this case approving of the sound of male rappers, and thus sustaining her self-representation as able to differentiate between ideological meanings and the sonic qualities of music (see Green, 1988):

Margaret:	I dunno I don't really like women rappers, nothing against them, it's just like, I don't know . . .
Gemma:	. . . sounds different
Margaret:	A man's voice sounds better doing it, I think, it's just 'cause what I'm used to really . . . I like De La Soul, I used to like De La Soul
Gemma(?):	My mum liked them
Margaret:	Everyone liked 'em . . . Arrested Development are good

In this case, however, it is apparent that Gemma's comments are perhaps a little problematic for Margaret. She has to elaborate quickly around Gemma's 'sounds different' and also dilute the possible blow to her prestige contained in the remark that 'my mum liked' De La Soul. Thus, she renders 'liking De La Soul' an instance of their universal popularity rather than indicative of some quality she shares with another girl's mother and quickly moves on to initiate a brief exchange about Arrested Development, at the time a much more recent innovation associated with rap.

In the next extract from the discussion, Asiye set off a debate in contention with her observation that there was no strong connection between dress style and musical taste:

Asiye:	I mean you can't really tell what a person listens to just by looking at them
Gemma:	Yeah you can
Asiye:	I can't
Margaret:	'Course you can if you see like say take someone for example, take Pauline for example someone dressed like a ragga, you don't think 'Oh they must be into classical' do you? You think 'Oh they're into ragga' and if you see other people, if you see

	Peter —, then you think, you don't know who Peter is do you? [I do —] yeah you know if you look at Peter and you think 'Oh he's into hardcore' . . . [section omitted] . . . It's dress, it's the way people dress that makes you
Gemma:	Yeah but look at me, you wouldn't think I listen to ragga would you?
Asiye:	Maybe it's the, just
Margaret:	You wouldn't think you didn't listen to ragga
Gemma:	No but you wouldn't exactly say
Sara:	'Cause she listens to it most of the time
—⁴:	Oh you'd look at you and think you could listen to anything
Gemma:	True, which I do
Sara:	What about — what would you say they were into?
Gemma:	Teeny bop music (laughter) Take That
Sara:	Geena (?) had that thing on, what's it called . . . New Kids on the Block, do you remember?
CR:	You don't like Take That?
All:	No
CR:	What's wrong with Take That?
—:	What's right with 'em?
Margaret:	They're little, they're little boys [section omitted]
Margaret:	I don't hate them . . . I'm not really bothered by them . . . there's gotta be, there's gotta be that kind of music for some people, it's just not for me . . . if I see girls who're into Take That I'm a bit sort of like . . . I don't have any respect for them or anything (laughing) I don't have an . . . [section omitted]
CR:	What do you think of the girls who like Take That?
—:	. . . waste of time . . .
Margaret:	The girls who like Take That are just so immature and stupid . . . they're just childish and like . . .
Asiye:	You wouldn't think they were interested in the music, they just fancy the person, the people 'cause if they were ugly I doubt if anybody would really take any interest in them . . .

In the discussion considered in Chapter 4, Asiye was much more reticent, saying little more than that she listened to London's mainstream pop radio station (Capital). But she was interested in being present and volunteered herself for the smaller group discussions on both occasions. In this case, her comment raised another kind of question about relative degrees of knowledge among the group and involved further positional negotiations. Asiye's apparent uncertainty in reading dress codes in relation to musical tastes was not entirely dismissed by the others and could be read as another instance of that tactical refusal to be categorized that was sometimes adopted by others in this study. Gemma, and to some extent Sara, took up a mediating position, between Asiye and Margaret, by suggesting a degree of indeterminacy in the relation between public self-presentation and musical preference. Margaret, to the contrary, and in this context without reference to herself, seemed to regard such a view as a consequence of a lack of knowledge, knowledge to which she positioned herself as having access. Once again, Margaret seemed to invoke a hierarchy of cultural competence within which she could claim the hip stance and, in this case, voice the informed opinion she had encountered elsewhere in educational discourse.

In the exchanges which followed, they negotiated the division which emerged between them, in part through a shared unwillingness to accept rigid correspondences between appearance and taste when they might be referred to themselves (see Widdecombe and Wooffitt, 1995: Chapter 5) and, more powerfully, by taking up a collective self-positioning as older and more sophisticated in relation to Take That, the 'teeny bop scene'. In deriding *teeny bop*, they located themselves as a group along an implicit axis of age. In this respect, dividing themselves from younger girls was somewhat more urgent than differentiating themselves from boys, with whom they would not expect to be confused in any case (see Hey, 1997). Thus, despite the fact that the audience for Take That must have been composed largely of girls between the ages of 9 and 13, here these 15- and 16-year-olds acknowledged little sense of connection with, or prior involvement in, the 'teeny bop scene'. Again, the educational setting is important: here girls are grouped together within a narrow age band (one year) and in the presence of a male adult. To like Take That would be to (re)locate themselves in middle childhood – immature, 'stupid', 'childish' – a condition of relative powerlessness from which they are concerned to distance themselves. Furthermore, they implicitly refuse the act of (female) subjection to (male) stars commonly attributed to fans. To some extent, they claim maturity and the power it implies, by inscribing themselves both in a more dispassionate aesthetic (music, not bodies) and in a discourse of adult heterosexuality (big, not little, girls/bodies). It is far more important for them, therefore, to position themselves as growing beyond, if still within, adolescence, rather than to affiliate themselves to any one genre of music; and on this even Margaret and Asiye, momentarily, agree.

Talking to the Boys

A group of four boys, one black (Stephen), the others white (Paul, Jamie, Alan), agreed to be recorded discussing their work. The session was marked by a buoyant refusal of seriousness. They grinned and giggled, fell and jostled against each other and spread themselves on the chairs, softer than those available in the classroom. They made the discussion an occasion for having a laugh, dismissive of the work but animated by just 30 minutes away from the classroom. In fact it was a much easier, informal and relatively conversational, event than the session with the girls. Thus there was, throughout, a mood of relaxed amusement, despite negative and critical comments like this:

> *CR*: What did you enjoy most, if anything, in actually doing this unit of work?
>
> *Stephen*: Erm . . . Not doing it would have been the best thing I reckon . . . I didn't feel it was worth it . . .
>
> *Jamie*: This has been the best bit really
>
> *Stephen*: I reckon it was worth us doing it . . . maybe to do up the work . . . I didn't really enjoy doing it, that's the reason why . . . well I'm not writing no . . .
>
> *CR*: What did you think of it, did you enjoy any of it?
>
> *Jamie*: This bit

'This bit' was full of wind-ups, mockery and laughter. There was much less of that effort to cooperate, of serious engagement with the questions, which characterized much of the discussion with the girls. In one respect, this can be explained in terms of their somewhat defensive lack of investment in educational success. For example, reflecting on the dissipation of classroom time, but without gravity, Jamie commented '. . . this time [next year] we'll be regretting it probably'. For them, as I observed during many lessons, time in school passed, conversations hung, hardly audible, between boys leaning away from their work, waiting for the lesson to end (see Willis, 1977). But the context of the discussion also provided them with an opportunity to enact, or perform, 'being boys'. In the classroom, they were often wary of being singled out, keeping a distance from the teacher and the dialogue that might threaten to separate one from another. However, together as a group in the English department's office, they were less at risk, less vulnerable to the inquisitive intimacy of a one-to-one dialogue with myself as a teacher. Somewhat free of that mix of anxieties – the sexual and intellectual threat of being singled out by a male teacher – they could negotiate my questions from within the security they constructed for themselves-as-a-group. The discussion was a layered and complex event. Their utterances, voiced publicly for each other, were inflected by actions, looks and laughter. Stephen also made much of his control of the microphone, frequently inserting his own whispered but, as recorded, highly audible comments. But the others also often seemed to manipulate the volume of their remarks, or their proximity in relation to the microphone. In effect, then, they made the event an occasion over which they could exercise some degree of precarious, and mutually contested, control.

Given this description of the session, I want now to select out some particular strands in their discussion. In many ways, Stephen, despite his negative comments, also spoke as someone with a case to make, sometimes as if on behalf of the group. He was the only one to suggest the mode of teacher engagement which, together in the classroom, they made so difficult – arguing for more individual help from teachers. He was also a little more inclined towards a broad view of education as informing him in relation to a future beyond the school and beyond a narrow understanding of the *local*. To some extent, this was consistent with his self-location in the black Atlantic diaspora (Gilroy, 1993) which emerged in the earlier interviews. Then, it was apparent that his significant range of reference allowed a sense of international connection, and that what was local, a black pirate radio station for example, also embodied a transnational culture. By contrast, Alan, on this occasion, was somewhat dismissive of Stephen's call for knowledge of other countries: 'a country like El Salvador, you ain't exactly going to go over there are you'. Thus by comparison, Alan anchored himself in a much more bounded space than that implied by Stephen's black cultural geography.

It was Stephen who made the one distinctive suggestion about what an engagement with music in media studies could be like:

> *Stephen*: If you took us to the studio where they like . . . and showed us
> what they do there, maybe that would help us more understand
> some more things or something

This wish to know more of the conditions of production, of the work process through which the music they know is made, is one that should inform any practice of teaching and identifies a domain of productive knowledge from which school, for him, was frustratingly remote. In one way, this illuminates his comment that he would do the work if he was interested in it. What a meagrely resourced classroom could provide was, in this case, not enough to make working worthwhile. I want to expand upon the importance of work-related contexts for learning in later chapters but here it is worth noting that his critical responses are by no means of school as such but are really quite specific and, despite their lack of elaboration, productive.

In developing an argument around this discussion with the boys there is a tendency to assume a consistent degree of contrast with what the girls had to say. However, while noting differences, it is important to avoid any exaggerated polarization. For example, they did listen to much the same range of music and, on the whole, the differences lay in the way they spoke of their modes of engagement. Thus, though the girls seemed largely uninterested in spending their money on music, and accumulating a collection, the boys did claim to collect, if not always buy, tapes and, in some cases, CDs. I raised this issue with them:

> *CR*: . . . do you all buy records and CDs?
> *Stephen*: (very close to the microphone) Nah, nah only buy records or
> tapes what I'm interested in . . . if they just . . . I like music . . .
> I wouldn't buy it, copy it off of someone . . .
> *CR*: Do you collect music on tape
> *Stephen*: Yeah
> *CR*: I mean do you tape . . . what you tape from other people's
> records?
> *Alan*: Yeah from other people or someone at home whatever
> *CR*: And you buy CDs . . . How many have you got to by now?
> *Alan*: 37
> *CR*: 37!
> *Stephen*: From last August
> *CR*: What about you?
> *Paul*: Well I buy 'em, I record 'em off me brother, friends, depends if
> I like it or not I buy it

In fact, home-taping seemed to be quite widespread among both boys and girls but here, given money, the boys would spend it on records and CDs. Furthermore, the quick and exact quantification of Alan's CDs (a fact seemingly already known to Stephen) suggested a pride in achieving an individuated and quantifiable embodiment of musical tastes. Such pride is characterized as distinctively masculine, and with some humour, in Sarah Thornton's comment that 'The size of a *man's* record collection has long been a measure of his subcultural capital!' (Thornton, 1995: 118; and for a fictional treatment, see Hornby, 1995). The fact of possessing a collection of 37 CDs seemed to constitute Alan's main claim to distinction among these boys. His literally remarkable, and perhaps envied, collection was also an indication of money earned, and thus of a masculine maturity achieved, in a context where most of the boys, lacking any income, seemed to borrow or tape from brothers and other relatives. Indeed, in the earlier interview with Alan I was drawn into a conversation which seemed propelled by a similarly masculine concern with money and the technology, the system it could buy.[5] This hints at the argument I resume in Chapter 7, where I suggest a relation between the achievement of male identities and the assembly of objects – objects which serve to make visible, and to demarcate, the precarious autonomy of such identities. Though I make this case with reference to Chodorow's (1978) account of 'separation' in the formation of masculine identities, it is important not to neglect either the boys' dependence upon other family members for both money and recordings or, as will become apparent in Chapter 7, the greater financial power to collect suggested by those more middle-class students.

A further, and similarly contentious, point of difference between the girls' self-representations and those of the boys lay in their responses to my questions about dance:

> *CR*: . . . one of the things I asked a moment ago was about whether or not you buy records but I mean the thing, I s'pose – when I talked to the girls, or three or four of the girls, on Friday – that they said more was that dancing seemed to be important and that the music that they talked about was generally music that they danced to . . . I mean is that important to you? Does dancing come into [inaudible] to any extent at all?
>
> *Stephen*: Nah
>
> *Others*: No
>
> *CR*: No? So you wouldn't buy something because you think it's good to dance to, you wouldn't tape it because you think it's good to dance to?
>
> *Jamie*: . . . all that matters is whether you like it . . . it doesn't have to make you wanna dance

My conversational approach, introducing the topic by reporting to them something of the girls' earlier comments, can be criticized for eliciting precisely the response I received. But I had to inject such information to keep the discussion going.

Retrospectively, I realized that it is a methodological tactic given some support by Bourdieu:

> [P]eople could place themselves not in relation to a question to which they must invent both an answer as well as [a] problematic, but in relation to problematics and responses which have already been prepared. In other words, the opinion survey would be closer to reality if it totally violated the rules of objectivity and gave people the means to situate themselves as they really do in real practice in relation to already formulated opinions.[6]

Furthermore, it would have been a bit strange to pretend that these boys do not already know that 'girls are into dancing'. I wonder, too, if dance is still an activity from which boys might want, necessarily, to dissociate themselves. Dancing was actually acknowledged, but not in response to a direct question, elsewhere in the session – by Jamie, for example, 'it makes you wanna move more than say 60s.' Even in tactical terms among the four boys, there seemed little to be gained by a complete denial of interest in dance. Whether or not these boys did dance, it is certainly the case that they did not make dancing a central feature of their self-presentation. There are risks in dancing, perhaps even in speaking of an interest in dancing: to dance can attract the look of others, putting the body on display, open to desire, to admiration and to ridicule (see McClary, 1991). But, equally, for boys to lay no claim to competence in dancing at all might just as easily invite mockery – of inadequacy in contexts where they do actually meet up with girls outside school. Furthermore, forms of dance are now quite diverse and, especially since the innovations of punk and the more recent formation of club cultures (McRobbie, 1994; Redhead, 1993; Thornton, 1995), can include relatively anonymous actions of improbable interest to onlookers. What does emerge more definitely here, and later in the session, is that they tend to represent choices in buying or taping music as somewhat autonomous, and again with some hint at separation from others: 'all that matters is whether you like it'. Thus, though brothers and friends are acknowledged (and may be significant sources), choices tend to be located more in individuated tastes than in their participation in social activities such as dancing.

The boys were sometimes resistant, evasive and mocking in their responses to my questions. While they were willing to offer explanations of the music I asked about, they also exercised some care in representing how they individually, and sometimes as a group, wanted to be positioned in terms of musical taste. For example, Stephen, at the same time as offering some more public responses, also resorted to close asides to the microphone, marking himself off from the others somewhat and distancing himself from genres of music for which he presented himself as having little respect. In the following extract, as in the earlier interviews, he positioned himself within the terms of a black cultural domain. To some extent, he continued to situate himself at a vantage point somewhat apart from that adopted by the others. This phase of the session began with a question about 'hardcore':

Jamie:	It's the hard bit of an apple
Stephen:	(close to the microphone) I reckon it's a loada, a loada drum beats
Jamie:	No it depends, some of it's good, some of it ain't good, some people've put more interest into it, more money into it, make better records
Stephen:	(still close to the microphone) You could do it at home really with a couple a pots and pans and a organ
CR:	(addressing Jamie) Could you describe it then?
Jamie:	You can't . . . it's very difficult
Stephen:	I reckon it's, it's quite a lota bass
Jamie:	Yeah that's it . . . it makes you wanna move more than say 60s . . . it's more for like . . . some people might take drugs with it like
CR:	But it's dance music
Stephen:	Yeah energy, energy rock . . .
CR:	With the record that's number one at the moment, would that be hardcore, 2 unlimited
—:	That's techno
Stephen:	Nah, that's techno . . . I reckon they're all the same but they just give 'em different names when they feel like it
CR:	It sounds similar?
Jamie:	. . . more synthesizer
CR:	What, techno's more synthesized? So you know there's a difference even though you couldn't describe it
Jamie:	There's a difference [section omitted]
CR:	If you say something's hardcore rap, what do you mean by that? When you say it's hardcore . . .
Stephen:	Well you can hear if . . . it's probably . . . just got . . . you could hear mostly . . . steal things if you understand . . . that's all they do . . . they just sampling . . . so if you hear a bit of rap you probably say it's hardcore rap or whatever
CR:	Right . . . what's the difference between rap and hardcore rap?
Stephen:	There's not a difference I don't . . . they're just tiefing [thieving], that's just putting some cruddy [crappy] beat behind it . . . change it for themselves

The main dialogue here is initially between myself and Jamie, with Stephen alternating between audible interjections and more 'subversive', semi-whispered, comments close to the microphone. Both *hardcore* and *techno* are, if not entirely endorsed, given some considered attention by Jamie – one of those boys who did indicate some interest in dance music. Stephen's comments mock such music seemingly on the grounds that it requires little musical skill and, in this respect, his comments are not unlike those Alan made with respect to acid and rap. Thus, though Alan and Stephen have different musical preferences, to some extent they do both draw upon a common discourse of musical value. Stephen's response to my question about hardcore rap confirms this. He takes the question to refer not to a particular category of rap, hardcore as adjectival, but to a mix, implying a conjunction of hardcore and rap. In effect, he describes a sampling of rap mixed with a dance track – 'just tiefing, that's just putting some cruddy beat behind it'. Given his marked black pronunciation of 'thieving', it's reasonable to suggest that here he speaks very much from a black cultural position. Indeed, it was as if, in this context, to allow hardcore to describe rap, a music he did endorse, might contaminate it with that which he did not. Ironically, the accusation of stealing is made in much the same way that Alan belittled rap by contrast with the authenticity of musicianship and self-expression he located in Simply Red.[7] Thus, to reiterate, they render the music they reject as other by means of broadly similar criteria of musical value perhaps sharing a history in a discourse of (male?) musicianship as a craft, with its proper sites of production: in a studio, and not at home, in the domestic domain, with 'a couple a pots and pans and a organ'.

Jamie, an elusive student only very occasionally present in class, could confidently refuse being positioned by my questions and imply some competence in discrimination within genres – 'it's just whether or not I like it.' He introduced the term taste, explicitly, into the discussion. But even without it, much of the teasing and provocation, which continued through most of the interview, involved implicit allegations of bad or laughable taste. If Stephen was able to classify himself through an endorsement of the taste categories associated with black music, the others were sometimes a little more vulnerable – to each other, not to my questions. The following discussion took place towards the end of the session, in response to a suggestion that they present and explain the music they like:

Jamie: You can't explain why you like it
CR: Well you could try, well you can . . .
Jamie: It's taste innit . . . different taste
CR: OK, so what's taste?
Jamie: I dunno . . . taste's not something that's really definable
CR: What . . . what do other people think, is taste hard to define?
Stephen: No, not really . . . yeah
CR: I mean is taste just to do with the particular person you are?
Jamie: Well it varies all around [I reckon – *Stephen*] it ain't, there might be coincidence in tastes and similar tastes but no one's gonna be exactly the same [You probably just have – Stephen] some people like more bits than other on a record [section omitted]
Stephen: I reckon it's ages and things like that and what you get from friends and stuff . . . you get . . . get like . . .
CR: Yeah go on Alan, if you've got something to say, say it, come on
Stephen: Ah shit . . . you get ideas from your friends, what they listen to, if you like it, sometimes you just, they give you an idea of the music . . . he likes Simply Red and Erasure (laughter, derision)
Alan: (protesting)

Stephen:	Julian Clary
Jamie:	. . . live in a time warp
Stephen:	. . . and things like Julian Clary and Boy George . . . I don't like a couple a dem I wouldn't like look at but like some, some their songs on what's it called er, Undercover, I would find some of them alright, not all of 'em, like Arrested Development, that's the kinda music I like . . . if he listens to it, when we do erm music lessons, we just listen to music from everybody, what they like so
CR:	(To Alan) Do you like Arrested Development?
Alan:	. . . bit, I sort of like two songs . . . [Mr. Wendell]s'alright . . . Revolution's alright
Stephen:	He prefers what's 'is name, Julian 'n' Clary
CR:	I mean what kind of music is Arrested Development anyway?
Stephen:	I reckon it's funk rap
CR:	Funk rap . . . yeah
Stephen:	It's got like y'know funk beats or . . . they just rap and some other jazz and stuff, they just mix it . . . southern kind of rap, southern rap [brief section omitted]
CR:	(To Jamie) What do you listen to?
Jamie:	All kinds of music . . . it could be a bit of music from anything . . . if I hear it and I like it, I listen to it
Stephen:	. . . that was from Freddie Mercury
Jamie:	I didn't mind the first song, but I like all things, reggae or it could be pop music, anything, anything in pop music, it's just whether or not I like it
CR:	Right
Stephen:	Same here and for everybody
CR:	Right so there's not one kind of music that you decide you're gonna stick to?
Jamie:	No 'cause you can say 'Oh well Alan likes the Housemartins' (much laughter) but then there might be a song that he don't like
Paul:	. . . and then he doesn't like the Housemartins
CR:	What's so funny about the Housemartins?
Paul:	What ain't funny about 'em?
Stephen:	They're just a funky band . . . they're not really . . . they're just dry really
Jamie:	The Flying Pickets . . . Remember the Flying Pickets
CR:	What about you Paul, is there one particular kind of music you like more than others?
—:	(on Paul's behalf) Morrissey (laughter)
CR:	What's that?
Jamie:	Morrissey
Paul:	No, hardcore

The transcript cannot adequately represent the layering of comment and counter-comment and the continuity of laughter and derision. Nevertheless, it should be apparent that, as the question of taste gained a faltering momentum in the discussion, the efforts they made to satisfy the insistence of my questions were increasingly mixed with provocative attributions of taste to others. Certainly such attributions produced anxiety and could not be left unchallenged, but no one was unduly disconcerted by any particular attribution and indeed what took place was, it seemed, normal for this group and for the wider male culture in which they participate (see Buckingham in Buckingham 1993b; Mac an Ghaill, 1994). Of course, that 'normality' is one which heavily prescribes heterosexual identification and routinely ridicules any ambiguity in male self-presentation. Here, these boys draw upon a homophobic discourse, implicitly feminizing each other by asserting their taste for acts defined as gay, cross-dressing or wimpish – Erasure, Boy George, Julian Clary.[8] However, within this group, on this occasion, the potential for division or exclusion was not realized. It was particularly striking that, despite Stephen's teasing of Alan and others, he did nevertheless re-identify himself with the group in terms of the general argument about taste: 'Same here and for everybody' and, moreover, drew on a more social account of taste thus somewhat undermining the threat involved in isolating individuals in their tastes: 'I reckon it's ages and things like that and what you get from friends and stuff . . .'

Nevertheless, Stephen also tended to initiate, and was himself exempt from, the various 'less-than-heterosexual' taste attributions. The vulnerability of the others, partly contingent on power relations within the group, could also be magnified by remaining reticent. Not to state tastes, and thus position themselves, was to risk being positioned by others and this, in this context, seemed to have a sexual connotation. Perhaps for Paul to state, bluntly, hardcore was more than to fix himself through a single generic affiliation. Given the connotations of hardcore in the wider context of media culture, referring invariably to the most visually explicit pornography, it is not surprising that the term, even though unequivocally denoting a musical genre in this context, can also be inflected in an especially masculine way. At the very least, hardcore implies hard as in tough, hard as in erect as well as hard as in hardcore pornography. Paul, who was physically the slightest among those boys present, has to respond to Jamie's taunt without hesitation. To like Morrissey, and accept not only sexual ambiguity but association with a figure long out of fashion, at least in the south, is clearly to be made ridiculous. Along with other bands, The Housemartins or The Flying Pickets[9] for example, the meanings of these attributions are seemingly self-evident among these boys and their force requires no elaboration, except marginally for my benefit. In this larger context then, hardcore also has the weight of authenticity – because it is not 'techno' or in the charts and is constructed as subcultural – and can therefore be an extremely economical means to freeze that play with their positions implicit in having others declare their tastes for them.

But I do not want to suggest that claiming a fixed taste identification in this way is always the tactical preference. It is Paul, after all, who remarks that a taste is ephemeral: 'and then he doesn't like the Housemartins'. Indeed, they all retained a degree of taste mobility and just as, at one moment, hardcore was the secure option so, at another, was representing the self as floating free from any particular affiliations at all. But what does unite these tactical options is that in adopting either of them, it seemed to matter to the boys not to be taste-classified by others. In this respect, then, they were using a repertoire of performers to entice each other into risky object choices and, in effect, to reassert the boundaries of their version of masculinity. To play this game demands both the specific cultural knowledge they largely share – Arrested Development are safe, Erasure are not – and the determination not to accept the position in which someone else places them. Within these terms it is clearly inconceivable, and would immediately disrupt the security of the game, to either simply accept an attribution or to lay claim to an act regarded as other than heterosexual.

It should be recalled that the girls were by no means indifferent to this sort of tactical positioning through taste. For example, none of the group considered earlier would want to be identified with a taste for Take That. For them, it was of some importance to position themselves in terms of a later age phase and thus to refuse 'childish' immaturity. Their self-positioning was orientated towards adult futures if also drawing upon knowledge they represented as particular to young people – thus turning being adolescent to their advantage in relation to myself as an adult. But, in the group, they did not taunt each other with problematic tastes but attributed such tastes to others not present. Thus, though they too, like the boys, are positioned as adolescent and do not welcome being positioned by others, they did not so obviously challenge each other with the risks of attraction to inappropriate performers. Of course, that potential was there and for any one of them to claim to be a fan of Take That would be unwise in the context of that group. However, for the boys it was a more insistent part of their practice to wind each other up and thus both to intensify and police the anxieties associated with masculinity. Their practice – repeatedly reenacting being boys – combines the uncertainties of adolescent positioning with a somewhat higher level of vulnerability to allegations of insufficient (hetero)sexuality than that evident, on this occasion, among the girls.

Implications for Practice

In this and the preceding chapter it has been important to engage with what students say about popular music and the contexts in which they say it. To engage with such talk, and to enable some reflection on its socially tactical meanings, should be a continuing concern in teaching about popular music. However, what constitutes knowledge about music is so variable, both across and within generations, that it is impossible to eliminate uncertainty and disjunction in such talk. The 'object of enquiry' – knowledge about music – cannot be separated from the particular social relations of the groups gathered to discuss it. As I have argued, the talk that has provided the data for this chapter should not be read, just sociologically, as evidence of gender differences among the students (though in combination with other kinds of data it has that potential). The primary concern has been to consider how knowledge about music is constituted within the context of group evaluations – and how within these events the students have positioned themselves in relation to each other, to myself as their teacher and to the assessment task required of them.

To varying degrees, all of these students were unwilling to invest in any fixed position and, to the contrary, sustained some degree of mobility among possible positions and the identities they might imply. For them, the priority appeared to be that of negotiating self-positions within the double context of an evaluation and a gender-exclusive peer group. With the complicated exception of Margaret, they seemed much less interested in proving themselves to be capable of mature debate, thus orientated to middle-class adult forms of exchange, than concerned to be effective participants, survivors perhaps, in a performance where knowledge about music is transient and tactical. For them, the primary urgency of the context, despite their implicit acknowledgement of its formality as an evaluation, was located in the social relations of the group. This is, as I have suggested, marked by some degree of gender differentiation in practices of self-representation, but across both groups knowledge of popular music is somewhat ephemeral, framed by the occasion and by their uncertain or abbreviated educational trajectories.

I felt dissatisfied with these discussions. The students' knowledge remained elusive; the scope of their commentary on the assignment seemed limited. I still hoped that, with less immediate, face-to-face modes of self-representation, these students might bring into my view rather more of what they knew. But again, in retrospect, I could see that what I conceived of as knowledge did not correspond to the transient and socially embedded forms of knowledge in circulation among these students. The logic of my frustration, for teaching, was to focus more minutely on other forms of articulation – as I do in the next chapter – and to consider other, further, alternatives to discussion-based attempts to talk about popular music. This logic, and its implications for practice, are followed in the remaining chapters of this book.

Notes

1   See, for example, the Mintel 'Market News' reports.
2   See Brennan, and Bennett, in Brackenridge (1993); Frith (1983); McRobbie (1991; 1994); Mungham, in Mungham and Pearson (1976); Roman, in Roman and Christian-Smith (1988); see also Thornton (1995).
3   See Richards, (1994).
4   Speakers unidentified.
5   It is of some interest that 'During September 1994, Mintel commissioned exclusive consumer research from BRMB on aspects of audio-visual products in order to obtain up to date information on the ownership of these products across the demographic spectrum.' On the basis of the data, it is suggested that 'men are more likely to be attracted by up

to date technology than women, whereas the women are, perhaps, more likely to suffer (sic) from technophobia and tend to be more concerned with ease of use'; and, further, 'men are more impressed than their (sic) womenfolk by the number of functions an audio-visual item possesses, and they are more likely to accept the recommendations of a consumer magazine in making a purchase.' CDBRMB/Mintel Market News (1994): Product: Audio-Visual Review – The Consumer.

6   Bourdieu, P. (1979) Public opinion does not Exist, in Mattelart, A. and Siegelaub, S. (Eds), *Communication and Class Struggle*, **1**, New York: International General, 124–30. Quoted in Mander (1987): 127–8.

7   Alan may have attempted to diminish the cultural prestige of black music by his comments on sampling and mixing (see Chapter 4).

8   Erasure seem to be read as (ambiguously?) gay and, among these boys, as inadequately masculine (wimpish). Boy George, most popular in the early 1980s, has a similarly ambiguous gay/bisexual image and is recalled as representing a particular fashion for cross-dressing. Julian Clary is, in Britain, a successful, openly gay, TV presenter and comedian. He is also known for, sometimes spectacular, cross-dressing.

9   The Flying Pickets does seem an obscure reference here but perhaps the link with The Housemartins has something to do with a cappella singing. Such singing, by men without instruments, might be considered effeminate (see Green, 1997).

Chapter Six

Classroom Subjects

Introduction

In this chapter, I want to turn to the written assignments produced by the Hackney students in the Spring Term of 1993. In reading their assignments I have drawn on the discussion of school genres offered by Hodge and Kress (1988) and, particularly, have focused on how signs belonging to non-school, popular and commercial genres, have been appropriated and reinflected in texts produced for assessment. An example discussed by Hodge and Kress is worth outlining here, however briefly. They refer to a primary school project, in this case on the topic of *supermarkets*, and argue that:

> The project, as a genre, demands that children attend to sets of relevance constructed by a powerful other, the teacher (although the teacher functions as mediator for the classifications of a larger 'discipline'). The project demands the assemblage of a text that brings together the relevant materials in the relevant order . . . (Hodge and Kress, 1988: 249).

In discussion of pages from one girl's project, representing commodities sold in the supermarket, they point to the incorporation of actual food labels into her text, a process they call 'quotation':

> This metaphor of 'quotation' may serve to illustrate the child's relation to semiotic systems generally. On the one hand the child is always in the position of taking existing signs from semiotic systems and 'quoting' them in her own semiotic uses; on the other hand, she is therefore also in the position of 'reproducing' signs when she uses them in their 'own' text . . .
>
> . . . for the child . . . these signs are at a great 'distance' from her own semiotic experience. The mode of production of these labels/signs is remote from her in every way; it is a process known to those who have power. At the same time therefore the use of these ready-made signs promises to confer power to her text. Bringing signs of that complexity into her text

promises both some control and power for her text. That is of course quite like the use of powerful indexical words in certain domains in the speech or writing of those who wish to gain power by indicating their membership of particular groups (Hodge and Kress, 1988: 251).

A key aspect of my argument in this chapter is that varying degrees of power are recognized, by the students, in the genres available to them. Faced with a school-based task – producing an assignment for assessment – but simultaneously invited to emulate specific commercial genres associated with the music business, how do these students negotiate these demands? In what ways do they position themselves through the forms available to them and what forms of power are claimed from those positions? A part of the answer to these questions can be formulated by approaching their media studies assignment as, like the *supermarkets* primary school project, a genre in which the disparity between different domains of power – the school and the music industry – can be explored and manipulated by school students.

The class had been asked to produce a variety of items publicizing and packaging a new, previously unknown, artist.[1] The starting point was an array of photocopied and cropped images of young women and just one man – images drawn from fashion magazines and intended to be both anonymous but generically close to 'pop iconography'. We did not listen to any music and my intention was rather that they adapt the images to represent music of interest to them. They were also asked to do some very small scale investigation into the listening habits of people of their own age and, on the basis of their findings, to plan a promotion of their new artist addressed to the later teenage market. All of this was familiar for them and for me: a way of working with popular cultural material in a context where visual dimensions have been emphasized and where the wish to teach about institutional power is realized through varying degrees of simulation. In a sense they were set up to model their work on that of professional marketing and, appropriately, they judged both the task, and their own efforts, somewhat in terms of what they perceived effective promotion to involve. Within the history of media studies in schools, teachers have tended to favour explanations for this approach which stress its capacity to sharpen the students' awareness of the ways in which they are addressed by the media. They have not, on the whole, thought of themselves as teaching their students to be good at these commercial practices. As I have argued elsewhere (Richards, 1997), the separation of 'culture' from 'commerce' in English teaching, and its traces in the related development of media studies, is a continuing and powerful force in teachers' understanding of themselves and their intentions.

Such a division can produce some especially marked disjunctions between teachers' valuations of students' work and the students' own interest in what they produce. As will be apparent in the assignments which are discussed in this chapter, school students may articulate claims to subjective identity and a kind of 'cultural authenticity' in commercial forms read by teachers as completely incapable of carrying such meanings. For example, the production of forms of black music may involve simultaneous claims to both commercial power and cultural identity which still, in school, might be regarded as contradictory. In the early 1970s, David Morse defended

Motown (Morse, 1971) against the accusations that commercialization produced cultural 'inauthenticity' – and thus, by the way, as my favourite tutor in American literature, undermined my continuing adolescent division of black music between the opposed poles of folk and commercial. More recently, Andrew Ross (1989) has made a similar case:

> I will . . . call attention to the fragments of another, less idealized history, one that is linked to the capacity of popular music to transmit, disseminate, and render visible 'black' meanings, *precisely because of*, and not in spite of, its industrial forms of production, distribution, and consumption. These commercial forms, whether on record or in performance, were, after all, the actual historical channels through which 'black' meanings were made widely available, and were received and used by a popular audience, even a black audience. There is little comfort in this other history for purists, but then the cultural and social changes that are mediated by shifts in popular taste are always messy, and never pure; as a result, they are seldom canonized as decisive, and more usually regarded as epiphenomena of *real* changes, which always take place elsewhere (Ross, 1989: 71, italics in original).

The readings I want to offer in this chapter, particularly Cheryl's assignment, depend upon a challenge to 'purism' and, as I argue in the concluding chapter of this book, involve a degree of reflexive self-critique for teachers formed, like myself, in the academic literary culture of the 1960s and 1970s. Ross's argument is one which raises crucial questions for teachers considering what kind of history of popular music might be constructed in taking students beyond the immediacy of their own present tastes. The tendency to order such a history in terms of folk origins and commercial appropriation is, whatever the coherence of academic critiques (see Middleton, 1990), one which the teachers I talked to might still find difficult to resist.

It should be emphasized that this tension is not only an issue in the work of black students in the group. Alan's self anchorage in consumption (37 CDs) or Margaret's self encapsulation in music radio have already been cited in relation to Harvey's (1989) analysis of 'time-space compression' in Chapter 4. Their assignments, discussed later in the chapter, will offer further illustration and complication of this issue. But, in provisional summary, I want to reiterate that teachers may tend to operate with an overarching binary division between commerce and culture whereas most of their students are preoccupied with marking distinctions between the authentic and the inauthentic *within* commercial popular culture itself (see Frith, 1983; Thornton, 1995).

I want to turn now to say a little more about questions of sexuality and of gender. These dimensions reappear here both in the students' relation to classroom work and in their generic preferences, aspects of which are evident in the assignment material. Of course I selected the images with which I wanted them to work – I too am implicated in this. To some extent, media studies has interested me just because it appeared to engage with cultural forms otherwise excluded from, and regarded as disruptive of, the formal school curriculum and its contribution to a power/knowledge relation in which young people are positioned as 'juvenile' (see Mac an Ghaill, 1994). Media studies, perhaps in common with drama, continues to render more permeable the boundary between school identity as *pupils* and the range of social identities either claimed by, or available to, young people elsewhere. Allowing such permeability can be regarded as teacher recognition of sexuality as a domain of which students are entitled to speak, not one only known to, and thus controlled by, adults and into which supposedly pre-sexual subjects are introduced. But this also has a regulatory dimension as, through such permeability, teachers are able to know more about those they teach. However, there is a case for suggesting that, if sexuality intrudes more fully into classroom discourse with the turn in attention to popular culture, it can thus compel teachers to address students less as children than as, like themselves, participants in a culture which, as Foucault (1976) has argued, speaks endlessly of sex (see Mac an Ghaill, 1994; McRobbie, 1991; Richards, 1990; Wolpe, 1988). In media studies then, the knowledge called into play so often includes a sexual component that it is hard to see how teachers could continue to sustain a clear division between themselves as 'knowing' and their students as 'innocent'.

Sara

These issues can now be given a more particular focus through some examples from the students' work. Sara described the images I offered in this way:

> Photograph 1 – This photograph is of a white man, who's middle aged but fit looking hes standing between two men dressed in dark clothes they both have cloth like turbans on there head, They look like there from the middle East probably Muselim.
>
> One of the men is pointing out something to the white man who's looking very concearned. My guess is he's a Journalist or reporter of some sort.
>
> This photograph would not make the cover of any record.

> Photograph 2 – This is a picture of a young white woman. The photograph shows only her head and shoulders. She's dressed in a black laceie top with holes in it underneath is bare skin. Her hair is piled on top of her head with wind blowing to give an effect this photograph looks like she's a model posing for a clean make-up advert.
>
> This photograph could be the cover of a record, something like Gloria Estefan the style of music would be South American/Cuban beat some type of pop music.

> Photograph 3 – This is a photograph of a young black woman. The photograph is of her body down to her thighs. Shes wearing black collotes with

a gold chain belt, she has a white shirt with large bottons only one of which is done up, the rest are undone which means we can see the beginning of one of her breasts. She also has on a black short jaguet one hand is in her pocket and the other is out streatched in front of her. She's in a side pose. This could make the cover of a record for a soul single.

Photograph 4 – This is the same woman as above. She's in a front pose. She's wearing a white shirt, which looks like a wrap over the photograph has been taken just as she's swang round so her top is open so we can see one of her breasts. Her mouth is open and she's looking stright at the camera.
    This photograph could be used on the front of a single for a pop song.

Photograph 5 – This photograph is the top half a black woman. She's standing with her hands at her sides facing foward. She has a wild hairstyle which is all different lengths and in all different directions. She's wearing a sleeveless leather top which looks rock hard.
    This photograph could be used on a single for a hardcore tune.

Photograph 6 – This photograph is something of a Demi Moore look. Theres a young woman with short hair sitting down with her back hunched foward. She's wearing a white tee-shirt and white trousers, over her shoulders, she has a white blanket which gives the impression her heads sticking out of a wall. Her arms are resting on her knees and in her hands shes holding a cup. This photograph could be used on a single, to portray a clean softie girl next door pop image (sort of Kylie Monogue when she first started in the pop world).

Photograph 7 – This photograph is the top half of a young woman, she's standing facing foward with her arms lifted behind her head, she's wearing gloves and a bra so her arms and stomach are bare. Just below her belly botton is a belt then theres a gap of bare skin then another article of clothing which we can't see. Her head is slightly tilted and her eyes are closed. Her hair is just below shoulder length and the style looks like bones or dents of some sort. She would make the ideal cover for a hard core single – its the one I chose.

This quite lengthy set of descriptions needs to be placed within both the social relations of the classroom and the various genres she negotiates. In her description of the images there is a kind of dutiful and efficient replication of the dispassionate dissection often encouraged in media studies but, in her dismissal of one image and decisive placing of others, there is also an implicit self-positioning as a knowledgeable participant in popular music culture. Her self-presentation as a motivated student, competent to produce the forms of writing required, is thus held in some tension with the lack of explicitness in her criteria for assigning images to musical genres. To be explicit, and thus to seek legitimation in the school context, is not, in this moment, conceded; the rhetorical authority of her judgements is achieved through their brevity and implicit self-assurance. She writes from within a culture to which she can assume teachers do not belong. She is thus able to occupy a position of some relative power in which the balance of forces determining the production of her writing tilts, in one moment, her way, in another, back to the teacher. Indeed, in concluding her study she added an unrequested glossary, explaining terms such as *hardcore* and *rave* and thus placing her addressee as the recipient of knowledge over which she has some control and, at the same time, placing herself as a capable classroom subject – both subject to, and subject/agent of, this act of formal explanation.

To frame a further reading of her assignment, it is worth pausing to comment on her cover. The cover sheet was handwritten, carefully, but on a descending, slightly erratic, diagonal: 'Media Studies . . . Music-Audience Assignment . . . By Sara . . .' To the left of the diagonal, in the bottom half of the A4 sheet, she pasted a photoreduction of her chosen image, tilted so that a line bisecting the figure – through the face vertically and down beyond the navel – would run approximately parallel to the diagonal axis of her title.

This is an assignment embedded in a transaction between myself as a male teacher and mostly working-class girls drawing upon a discourse of adolescent sexuality (see McRobbie, 1991) and, in a majority of cases, quoting images which I provided and thus legitimated in the classroom context. As I have argued in the preceding chapter, and as others have suggested (see, for example, Wolpe, 1988), it is of some importance to girls positioned in adolescence to be seen by male teachers as rather closer to being adult women than to school children. How does this inform my reading of her work? Most of what the school genre assignment requires as formal identification and differentiation is present on the cover but it is controlled by the image. Indeed the raised arms provide an axis which crosses the parallel diagonals to direct the reader's look to the title 'Media-Audience-Assignment'. This suggests a balancing of compliance as a student with the power of a quoted image, strongly emblematic of a particular female sexuality. It is also possible to read this as, therefore, a double compliance: an acceptance of both pedagogic and hetero-sexual positioning. Thus the power achieved through quotation is circumscribed, limited to inscription within feminine heterosexuality (recall, though, that she has been asked to produce something which will sell an artist).

Without undermining this reading, which I think is persuasive, I do also want to suggest that, given her position as a school student, her use of the image is also an assertion which disturbs the educational frame in which her knowledge and her school identity are supposedly contained. Like many of the girls involved, she appeared to enjoy some aspects of the work or to want to say so in a particular way:

> This assignment was the best we've ever done in media studies. It was fun to do and easy to get research material because its what the children in school are 'in to' (the latest craze). Doing the questionnaire was the most fun it wasn't like work, it was just like talking to your friends about their music interests . . . The hardest part was chosing the artist and finding a name for her, the group and the song. I settled for Hardcore Erotica as the group name and Kiss as the name of the artist and single.

In this, 'fun', if accompanying rather than displacing work, appears to register an experience of herself as more legitimately social, as more involved with others, than is usual within school. At the same time, she moves, with no acknowledged contradiction, from appearing to be one of the children ˙in school to the choice of 'Hardcore Erotica' and 'Kiss' as names for her group, and her artist and single. I have already discussed the connotations of 'hardcore' and here the most sexual meanings are privileged by its conjunction with 'erotica'. However, the images she accords a place in her map of music culture are all representations of female sexuality and the sole photograph of a man was dismissed, implicitly, for belonging to an inappropriate genre – journalism. 'Hardcore Erotica' is, in her work, given a distinctively female inflection.

Her chosen image was incorporated into a collage – for the cover of a CD single – which she described, in a simulated review for *Just Seventeen*,[2] thus: 'This single has a wicked front cover with Kiss in more clothes than usual reading between the lines its gonna be a fast seller.' Here, she writes as someone addressing the audience to which she would define herself as belonging – teenage girls – and adopts what appears to be a self-consciously coded style, implying the sexual intent of the collage in a way which suggests a strongly shared understanding between writer and reader but, equally, a mutually recognized need to be oblique – as if to deflect the attention of adults, in the mode of address common to the problem pages of teenage magazines. Such a repositioning of herself somewhat beyond her location within the social relations of the classroom contains more than an expression of adolescent sexuality – which might be dismissed as both familiar and predictable. There is a claim to knowledge here and to the power that might imply. In this respect, such knowledge, which includes a knowledge of sexuality, can suggest how differently people of 15 and 16 might be placed within media studies – relative to other areas of the curriculum.

Sara's CD collage is an exercise in redundancy and saturation, layering together elements convergent in meaning. The hardcore figure is this time angled along an axis descending from top left to bottom right but is significantly fragmented and concealed by glossy female lips to the lower left, a large X to the upper right, and the word KISS tilted from mid-abdomen and down into the bottom right hand corner. The word LOVE is placed at the top of the frame immediately above the dancer and, directly below, at the bottom of the frame, another glossy female mouth. Other components, forming a background, include the old His Master's Voice logo and an expressively drawn image of Madonna with jutting breast cones (and the words 'Protect Your Assets – Madonna Does'). Despite, or more probably because of, the singular intent here, the collage, framed approximately as a CD cover, is effective in its obsessive visual design – the X (kiss/forbidden) is replicated in the larger composition so that the converging diagonals of the dancer's raised arms combine with the diagonals formed by the white ground of the word KISS, and thus the whole frame is organized by a large X.

Within media studies, and perhaps in art, the collage has become a familiar vehicle for the 'quotation' of bodily, and other sexually significant, imagery. In the marketing of music and other commodities, variants of collage also have wide currency – combining familiar generic signifiers or star images with other often dissonant elements. Her collage is therefore both imitation of a commercial strategy and fulfilment of an already familiar school task. In this case the reproduction of preformed images in her text enables her, simultaneously, to meet the demands of a school and a commercial genre. But, whatever her success in meeting such requirements, this collage might be construed as *only* further acquiescence in the positioning of women as sexual objects. Her own comments, in her evaluation, seem to confirm this:

> Kiss (my artist) was the only one out of the photographs we were given that could be used on a hardcore single, it might have been something to do with the sterotype for hard-core singers. The pose she's in surgests 'look at me' her eyes are closed so we don't have the idea that she's looking at us but that we're looking at her. She's showing a lot of her body, her arms are open behind her head representing a pose such as 'take me'.

This is exactly the analysis one would expect a GCSE media studies student, carefully taught to deconstruct advertising and magazine images from a kind of feminist position, to offer in writing – as proof of her competence in the discipline. The woman's body as object of (male) desire, arranged to satisfy such a (male) gaze, is, in those terms, adequately described. But what else might it mean to her and in what sense has she enjoyed 'appropriating' this image?

> I'm not a great artist so I never wanted to draw the front cover that's when I came up with the idea of cutting pictures out of magazines. I could see it in my head as being really bright but that never happen. The cut out pictures all came from *Just Seventeen* and the photograph of my artist was reduced on the photocopier. The front cover isn't just a load of cut out pictures there was some thought (it had to attract the right audience) in it especially with the lips and the word kiss. I also thought the X would symbolise a kiss but not many people understood that and it had to be explained . . . (I'm very proud of my front cover).

I want to argue that her CD cover, the collage, in combination with her evaluative commentary, enables her to occupy mutually contradictory positions. She holds firmly to her position as a competent student of media studies, thus to be approved by her (male) teachers: 'there was some thought (it had to attract the right audience)'. But she also suggests that she is more sexually knowing than many others, and therefore also places herself as, implicitly, more mature, more adult: 'I also thought the X would symbolise a kiss but not many people understood that and it had to be explained . . .' For girls, to 'please' male teachers in this way need not involve any intractable conflict (however, see McRobbie, 1991). The sense of division in Sara's self-presentation is more apparent in her selection and manipulation of the hardcore image. If as a student she is critical of the image – a stereotype – she did choose it and her comments suggest fascination, a pleasure in the image as a kind of narcissistic ideal, not what she is but the body she might wish to inhabit.

Elsewhere, in a discussion of the popularity of *The Little Mermaid* and of a current iconography of dance, I have suggested that images of this kind are incorporated into young girls' play and might be taken up as a fantasy of the embodied self-in-control (Richards, 1995). Sara's account might usefully be juxtaposed with my own. First, Sara:

> ... her arms lifted behind her head, she's wearing gloves and a bra so her arms and stomach are bare. Just below her belly botton is a belt then theres a gap of bare skin then another article of clothing which we can't see ... the ideal cover for a hard core single – its the one I chose.

And my own comments:

> Dancing to Madonna is about projecting the self into, taking the form of, her body. To achieve this seems to depend upon reorganising the child's body to mark out the place of breasts and the nakedness of the belly ...

> Arms raised above the head to display the breasts and belly, even if encased in mock armour or underwear, represent the crucial stance ... Perhaps, despite the patriarchal structure in which dancing is located ... for girls there is a visible proof of bodily autonomy and self-control implicit in being seen to dance, to present a body enacting intention (Richards, 1995: 147).

Of course, my analysis is speculative but, in the larger context of debates around the meanings of dance for women and girls, it is reasonable to suggest here that Sara's choice of the image implies *both* some complicity with positioning as a sexual object and some degree of more reflexive pleasure in the embodied (female) self.

I want to move on now to discuss, with varying degrees of detail, each of the girls' assignments in turn. It's important to note, before doing so, that not only were these assignments addressed to male teachers, but they were also quite public within the context of the classroom and could be read by others as evidence of 'tastes'. The reading of each others' work among the groups of girls was a common activity and there was thus some conversation within and between groups of girls – conversations which, if they seemed to be mutually supportive of each others' efforts, were also therefore a significant context in which they could expect their work to be judged (see Hey, 1997).

Asiye

Asiye, often present, but rather silent, in my earlier investigations, produced a thoughtful and meticulous assembly of materials. Asiye was unhappy with the images offered to her and chose her own. Her image was eventually selected to represent an apparent preoccupation with *love songs*:

> The name I have decided to give my singer is Isabella Marell.
>
> The reasons for this is because of the way she looks, the name suits her and blends with the type of song I have chosen for her to sing.
>
> I chose several song titles for her to sing but decided in the end on 'I look into your eyes'.
>
> Other song titles I thought of include 'I look into your face', 'Remembering you', 'Look at me' and 'Can I love you'.
>
> The reasons for choosing these song titles are because they are all to do with love and the theme for her song is love songs. Isabella looks the type to sing love song rather than other types of music like raggae, acid, rave funk, hardcore, etc. I chose her because of the type of song she is most likely to sing. I had decided on love songs before I had seen her so I thought she fitted best with the type of song chosen for her.

Sara chose the image of a woman with her eyes closed and much of her body displayed to an implied onlooker. Asiye's image connotes a look which is inter-subjective, rather than a look at the body (either from the vantage point of an other or in reflection). She included no less than 14 copies of the image – with only the addition or subtraction of the name Isabella. Her assignment thus repeats the image of the face, without variation, though implicitly reiterating her song-titles: 'I look into your eyes', 'I look into your face', 'Remembering you', 'Look at me' and 'Can I love you'. These are all strongly relational, in marked contrast to the disembedded 'Kiss'. In fact, the image she chose was more like that found in, or on the cover of, magazines addressed to adult women. In this respect, she appropriated an image which is at an even greater distance from teenage culture than those I supplied to them. Thus, though it is possible to argue that she too lays claim to an image of adult sexuality, her choice is one which suggests a different relation to images of women in popular culture. Another reading of this image, in combination with the song titles (especially 'Look at me'), which also places it at some distance from adolescence, could be pursued through Lacanian categories, acknowledged earlier, but not substantially integrated into my analysis. It may be that here the fascination with looking and being looked at can be located in early infancy, the *mirror-stage*, and thus the looking is less overtly sexual than ontological, seeking to contain anxieties on that level: What do I look like? Do you like looking at me? Do you see me as I see myself? Can I see myself in your looking at me?[3]

Unlike Sara, whose endorsement of hardcore was common among white mono-lingual students, Asiye seemed to locate herself in a popular music to which many of the other girls would claim no connection. But not because, like Take That, it was associated with younger girls. It may be that, from a more marginalized ethnic position than many of the other girls, Asiye was unable, because she lacked the more detailed knowledge, to differentiate herself through endorsement of an 'off-centre' genre. Though, in earlier discussions, she identified herself as listening to one of London's most popular pop radio stations (Capital), here she chose an image which, in her presentation of it, would be far closer to the genre of light romantic songs promoted by the Euro-Vision Song Contest.

For a majority of the class, both girls and boys, there was some degree of coincidence between sexual identifications and musical genres. In selecting a genre, therefore, judgements were made which also entailed a representation of a sexual self to others. And as Weeks (1981) has suggested, after Foucault, 'sexuality' has been constructed, historically, as the 'truth of ourselves'. In an interview with an English and media studies teacher, which I discuss more fully in both Chapter 8 and the postscript, some particularly salient observations on this point were made:

> . . . it's a very sensitive area because it's so personal and I know how I feel about . . . I mean I put up a display of my own album covers and I know how I feel about people coming in and making fun of them . . . I feel, I sort of, I take it personally because they're mine and like I think, that's, see, the Wham! video is a useful thing to study because actually the kids do quite like George Michael but nobody is a really big fan of his any more so nobody feels hurt if people criticize it, on the other hand they sneak- ingly quite like it because it's got good dance routines and they don't mind saying 'Oh I quite like that' rather like if you were watching an old black and white movie, somebody might say 'Oh you know that bit's good' and so it is quite good to study things that are a bit more distant from every- body, that nobody's got a big kind of investment in . . . [section omitted] . . . the Madonna unit was actually quite, it's interesting but it's quite problematic because of the sort of, y'know it brings out a lot of different opinions and people aren't respectful towards each other like . . . many of the girls have gone off her or say they've gone off her, don't want to be associated with her but used to like her and so it's sort of, it's a delicate area really because it's involved with, it's sort of y'know, because it's involved with teenage sexuality in a way isn't it really . . . if you think back to our own teenage days, music was so much part of the scene you were on . . .

There is quite a lot of discomfort here. The teacher, Alison, was by no means new to teaching and had been at the Hackney comprehensive for several years. She was extremely wary of teaching which might produce highly disruptive emotional responses among her students and a lingering difficulty for herself as a teacher (see Richards, 1990; Williamson, 1981/82). In fact, she never did allow me to enter her classroom and it was not her class with which I was allowed to work. Her sense of self-exposure in displaying a collection of album covers, in revealing a liking for what others might reject was, even for her as a teacher, painful. For adolescents, in the public space of a classroom, the risks are undoubtedly considerable. It is quite possible, then, that for Asiye, it was just safe to do romantic pop, even if she had no particular attachment to it.

Claire

Claire, a white working-class girl, also chose her own image. Among the girls, she was probably the least strongly orientated towards the assignment genre, appearing to enjoy the opportunity to 'do music', without too much concern for self-positioning as a conscientious student. Her cover sheet declared, in large handwritten letters set against an angular, explosively graphic, background – POWER OF MUSIC. Below, in smaller capital letters, she placed her name and, immediately below that, in a smaller, plain, handwriting – media studies. She wrote no evaluation and there was virtually no commentary or explanation relating to the various elements which she did complete. Without the range of items assembled in the other assignments (by the girls at least), I've found her work much more difficult to comment on than that of any other student in the group.

In fact, for Claire, I doubt that the assessment of her work by her teachers was of much importance relative to her interest in music. For example, she positioned herself through music in ways which teachers normally regard as disruptive. She was one of several students who, from time to time, attempted to listen to music in the classroom, usually with a personal stereo. On one occasion, Claire drew me, with somewhat hushed confidentiality, into listening to some rap (Ice-Cube taped from Kiss FM) and, on another occasion, lent me a cassette she had been given as a Christmas present:

> hard fax 2 – twice the vice! 28 clubscene floorfillers featuring: rotterdam termination source – bizarre inc. – rage – wag ya tail – messiah – altern-8 – sunscreem – liberation – the shamen – franke – urban hype – the aloof – plus . . . (*hard fax 2*, various artists, Columbia – 1992 Sony Music Entertainment (UK) Ltd.).

She didn't name this music generically and it is important to recall that it was Claire who had pointed out that the generic terms used in current music journalism could be both unknown to her and refer to music to which she does listen. It was apparent, therefore, that how audiences name and define the boundaries of musical genres would vary in accord with the combination of other media discourses with which they might be familiar (see Thornton, 1995). It is also possible that Claire was 'doing music as subculture', implying that the music she was into might be elusive and unnameable – or as yet unnamed by the particular sector of music journalism to which I had access. Going somewhat beyond those others who argued that 'you can't describe it, you have to listen to it', she seemed more inclined to locate her identity in listening to music and outside classroom discourse. Unlike Margaret, she did not represent herself in terms of a middle-class inflection of 'hip' and seemed unimpressed by pressure to reformulate her experience in appropriately educational terms. Thus, read from the perspective offered by Kress, it is possible to see Claire as uninterested in being 'repositioned':

The education process is about the processes of classification, repositioning individuals with respect to potent social/cultural classificatory systems, re-ordering the classificatory systems of those who are the learners. Power is involved at every point in that process, in the struggle over particular terms, over whose classificatory systems are to prevail, whose are to be valued and whose are to be dismissed (Kress, 1985: 63).

Her stance could be characterized as 'resistant' but, to be honest about this, I think that she just didn't see any need, or want to bother, to project herself into a position from which to reclassify her informal enjoyment of music.

I want to turn now, if somewhat briefly, to the visual material she did complete. She chose an image of a young black woman, apparently dancing, framed from around the thighs upwards, turned, as if caught in motion, towards the onlooker, smiling fully, hair loose, a chain and pendant resting between her breasts, defined by a long dark jacket. She wrote, in various styles suggestive of display poster conventions – 'Jessica on Tour From April 28th . . . The new album "Money can't buy Love" on video out now' – and thus placed the image as satisfying the requirement to produce a publicity poster for a tour and a related album release.

Her CD cover makes no use of this image. It is, probably, a parodic montage: the central motif is composed of three images – a young woman alone, unsmiling; a couple beginning to embrace; a close-up of the same couple kissing. This central image is surrounded by grotesque cartoon figures, reminiscent of medieval gargoyles, each signifying – necessarily, given their exclusion – various caricatured emotions of envy, frustration and voyeuristic excitement. There are, additionally, two saintly fig-ures displaying astonishment and disapproval. Superimposed are the words 'Money!' and 'buy Love'. Music is signified by a cartoon radio and by the words '20 Lurv Songs'. The central image looks as if it came from a teenage magazine and repro-duces the heterosexual scenario once familiar in their photostories (see McRobbie, 1994). Is this a somewhat distanced, parodic, comment on romantic love songs? How does this connect with 'Jessica' and the song 'Money can't buy Love'?

Claire also produced a storyboard for a promotional video. The setting is a dancehall. 'Money can't buy Love' fills the opening frame, to be followed by a frame in which the 'two lovers' are at the centre of a dance floor, and behind them a large heart. The third frame repeats the 'two lovers' but with Jessica singing on stage in the immediate background. The fourth and fifth frames are captioned: 'they are getting on rell well'; 'some of his friends come over to them'. There is then a 'flashback' to the first frame: 'Money can't buy Love'. The following eight frames are captioned thus:

7   back to the lovers/his mates says something to him and leve the girl out
8   his friends leve
9   they finish their dance
10   he tells her that he loves her and he's got to go
11   he gives her a kiss and some money
12   he leves her holding the money in her hand

13 she is in the middel of the dance and all the lovers dancing around her
14 back to Jessica finnishing one song
15 flashback – Money can't buy love

There is a significant and familiar tension here: between heterosexual coupling and the power of male friendship groups to reclaim the girl's partner. One reading of this narrative would argue that the girl is left alone, with a manipulative gift of money and the implicit message that the humiliation is public and visible. It might follow that recognition and empathy is offered by Jessica and the knowing song she sings. The image of Jessica used for the tour poster could be read, therefore, as a fantasy of the self, less vulnerable to, and uncompromised by, desire for a male other. But in the final frame the word 'can't' is unclear, as if 'can' has been written over it. This would imply a cynical twist to the narrative and displace an empathetic relation between Jessica and the girl with an ironic disparity. This would be confirmed by the apparent omission of the word 'can't' from her CD cover. These ambiguities must remain unresolved and, as I have suggested, were perhaps characteristic of Claire's relative lack of interest in completing the task within its prescribed terms. Whatever the case, it is important to conclude this account of her work by emphasizing that, though her assignment shows some fluency in the manipulation of 'teen romance', what she has produced is also uncertain and puzzling, not just because that was the way she wanted to represent herself but also because she was constrained, no doubt, by the resources that happened to be available to her.

Cheryl

Cheryl, a black girl, seemed far more inclined to seek an educational future beyond compulsory schooling than Claire (see Mac an Ghaill, 1994: 150). She produced work which was striking in that it combined a very strong self-presentation as a student determined to appropriate the task on her terms. She presented her assignment with a simple computer graphic – Media Studies Assignment by Cheryl . . . – and, unusually, placed her evaluation at the beginning. She thus orientated the reader – her teachers – at the outset and gave considered, rather dispassionate, reasons for what she had done. However, she made no use of the images provided and selected instead a variety of shots of, apparently, the same young black woman to whom she gave the name 'Riazz'. Riazz, on her CD cover dressed in white shorts, white halter and white peaked cap, is presented smiling with her hands shoved in her pockets, the single title perhaps also describing her presence: 'Fresh 'n' Funky'. In her evaluation, she located Riazz thus:

> I chose soul with a twist of other elements of music for my character to specialise in because I believed that she isn't the kind of person to sing pop i.e. Kylie and Jason, plus she looked like the kind of person who could sing the style of En Vogue or Mary J. Blige . . .

The distinctions she makes are between both genres and identities: she adds that 'the first person I chose didn't go well with the music I wanted to match her with . . .' and, in her effort to align image and music, she appears to be attributing an ontology to her character and thus to imply an expressive authenticity in the relation between performer and song. Her review of Riazz's album *Speechless*, authored by 'David Samson' for *Smash Hits*,[4] elaborates her identity and her musical provenance in a variety of black musical genres:

Riazz: the woman who gave soul a new name has now produced an album which includes the smash hit, 'Fresh 'n' Funky'.

The lp includes, the slow and sensual 'You're breaking my heart' and the velvety but more up beat song 'Love don't make the world go round'.

Guest stars such as Salt 'n' Pepa, Bobby Brown and Jamacan star Buju Banton appear on the album accompanying her by rapping, M. Cing and singing like you've never heared them before.

If you like Hip hop, Ragga, Swing beat and Soul, this album is definitley for you, it is entertainable, up beat aswell as slushy and most importantly it is danceable.

Overall if I had to rate it out of ten I would give it an eight.

Riazz has definitly got alot of potential for 1993.

In this generic mix, elements of British, Caribbean and American black musical cultures are assembled around a figure whose name is itself a kind of hybrid, blurring cultural differences but within familiar black pop conventions (for example, Yazz, Jazzie B., or Yo-Yo). Like Stephen, Cheryl clearly positions herself within the culture of the black Atlantic diaspora (Gilroy, 1993).

As I have suggested in the introduction to this chapter, the combination of market oriented contrivance and claims to subjective depth may be read as paradoxical from the vantage point of teachers formed in the discipline of literary criticism. To the contrary, I want to suggest that in Cheryl's work, the authenticity of a black identity is a condition of the coherence of her 'market representations' and her reproduction of those representations is, recursively, a confirmation of the cultural power of such an identity. For example, the reverse side of her CD single cover is remarkable in its careful, graphically precise, reproduction of packaging rhetoric:

Side A 'Fresh 'n' Funky' Side B 'You're Breaking My Heart'
Produced and Arranged by Ashley Banks.
Excutive producers Vibe Entertainment + Diva Sparks. Programming by Chanel Parkinson.
Engineered by Rahim at N.Y Studio's.
Assistant Engineer Scott 'Racoon' Canton.
Mastered at Westside Mastering Labs Inc.
Management Vibe Entertainment
Management in Association with Ella Shiffon. GOYE

This text is accompanied by three small images of Riazz. The reproduction of a set of signifiers borrowed from an attractive commodity is itself a claim to an authenticity which, in this media studies assignment, is more intensely valued by the students than the reproduction of the formal features of the specific school genre. Here, therefore, the presentation of these market features is, in the display of such a particular knowledge, to assert the cultural power of specifically black commodities. This is a more politically inflected instance of the power implicit in 'quotation' of supermarket/commodity labels discussed earlier (Kress and Hodge, 1988). The identity of the student is allied with, and distinguished through, a position within that other, non-educational, domain – the black commercial culture of music – a domain in which the favoured image is again that of an 'uncoupled' but sexually mature woman.

Cheryl's storyboard for the 'Fresh 'n' Funky' video begins with a girl falling asleep in bed. In the second frame 'she wakes up on a hot tropical island' (numerous palm trees in the background); in the third, the 'camera rotates and pans clockwise. Girl spins round'; in the fourth, the words 'Fresh 'n' Funky' appear like graffiti on a wall ('close shot of big wall with scribbled graffiti'). The fifth frame is a 'close shot of a man clicking his fingers. Music starts'. The sixth, 'Girl falls in front of the graffitied wall and discovers two cartoon characters standing next to her'. The seventh, 'All three of them start dancing'. In the eighth frame, 'She touches both of them and the cartoon characters turn human.' In the ninth, 'She finishes dancing then walks off. The two boys keep dancing'. The four remaining frames introduce a new setting: tenth frame, 'Shot of children playing'; eleventh frame, 'She plays double dutch with some girls'; twelfth frame, 'It's time for her to go, she waves goodbye to the children'; thirteenth frame, 'She wakes from her dream back in her bed'. This is a familiar scenario in pop videos.[5] The use of dreamlike dislocations of space and time and the mixing and transformation of human and cartoon characters is, of course, quite commonplace (see Goodwin, 1993: 76–7). However, it is, like Claire's storyboard, a narrative in which a girl dances but ends, once again, alone.

There are problems, as I noted in discussing Claire's work, in 'reading' material of this kind. But, to the extent that it is the girl's dream, it can be argued that it therefore privileges her subjectivity: her presence determines transitions from one setting to another; her music and her touch seemingly transform the cartoon animals into boys. Nevertheless, she leaves them, to reappear in a playground where she engages in a game with a group of girls. If the girl is Riazz, the tropical island and the graffitied wall are consistent with the signification of black cultural geography; but the locations are not strongly specified and tend to overlap each other. The narrative is ambivalent in that it appears to move towards a heterosexual romance scenario but, midway, abandons any continuation of dancing with the boys to return to something more like a childhood scene. It is, like Claire's narrative, a generically familiar negotiation of the boundary between childhood (being with friends) and the achievement of heterosexuality (being coupled). The girl seems to exercise both power in dancing and freedom in withdrawing and walking away. It is, then, a narrative which, from the position of an adolescent girl, in between childhood and adulthood, can be read as a tentative engagement in a sexualized world, an engagement which is articulated through the discontinuities of pop video rather than the linear inevitability of teen romance.

Gemma

I want to look at the work of three more girls before discussing the boys' involvement in the production of these assignments. Gemma, Margaret and Abby are all white. Gemma produced an assignment centred on the same figure chosen by Sara – that of the hardcore dancer with her arms raised above her head. In Gemma's case the title for both band and single was 'Into Oblivion' – a familiar motif in rave/club culture (McRobbie, 1994; Thornton, 1995). Gemma often worked at the same table as Sara and, to some extent, their approach appears similar. However, Gemma seemed to write more within the constraints of her position as a student and to have been less interested in reproducing the media forms available to others. Her review, for example, was presented more as a piece of school work than something to be read in a magazine: she did not offer a media format, location or author. Her writing is uneven in tone, veering between an approximate use of journalistic idioms and a more formal, distanced classroom discourse:

> Into Oblivion are a fab new band. They have just brought out a single. Its called into oblivion and its really good. This band will probably go a long way they will also go to number one.
> The young lady who sings is a very talented girl and she has a great voice, she's another Annie Lennox. She also has a great future ahead of her.

The uncertainty in her mode of address, compounded by the lack of an invented authorial stance, suggests her difficulty in moving outside the immediate educational setting and the teacher–student relationships within which her writing is conceived. By contrast with Cheryl, for example, the discursive resources to which she has access, at least as represented in her writing, seem to confine her largely to a school student identity. Her evaluation is similarly marked by a greater acceptance of the prescriptive authority of teachers:

> When we first *got given* this project and what to do, we *got given* a questionaire on music. *We had to ask* our friends different questions such as when they listen to music . . . Then we were given some pictures . . . and *we had to choose* one . . . *we had to make* a cover and a name for a new bands album this was not easy . . . Then *we had to write* a review . . . This project was very interesting because music is. something that most teenagers are interested in. I think my end result is quite good [My italics].

This review, with some slight emphasis added by my editing, is largely devoted to representing herself as carrying out instructions given to her by her teachers; she appears dutiful, almost polite, and her evaluative comments relate to her own efforts, not to the nature of the task. Somewhat at odds with most of her comments, she adds that it was 'very interesting' – as if it is a part of being a good student, and perhaps a 'good' girl, to reassure the (male) teacher. At the same time, she confirms her willingness to be addressed as a teenager, again by contrast with others who claim a more adult identity.

Margaret

Margaret and Abby also did what they were told, or asked, to do. But their tactical negotiations of the task demonstrate a more middle-class array of cultural resources – resources of a kind probably less available to those other students discussed so far (for example, the 'aggressively hip' students in Frith, 1983). Margaret took the sole image of a man offered to the class and worked in a desultory, rather dissatisfied, way towards completion of each of the tasks they 'had to do'. I want to quote at length from her critical evaluative essay:

> The first thing we had to do for this project was ask 15 to 20 year olds about their taste in music. We were given a questionaire and told to re-write it. I thought that there should have been a question referring to drugs as I know lots of young people take drugs to enhance music. For example, hardcore ravers take speed and ecstacy. People into indie drink a lot and take acid trips. All young sub-cultures smoke cannibas. Therefore a question relating to drugs was very relevant to this topic. Also the question about what people wear was also very relevant and I think deserved exploring. So I asked the interviewees if what they wore reflected the music they were into. I also asked if there was any kind of music which people found offensive. Quite a few people found Ragga and Heavy Metal offensive regarding their views on women. I also thought the questionnaire needed a question referring to whether people buy records, tapes or CDs.

This is her first substantial comment. It makes clear that she has a knowledge which she feels enables her to identify inadequacies in the range of questions presented by her teachers. Thus despite the often repeated reference to the compulsory demands made by the assignment, and her self-positioning as a somewhat long-suffering student, she moves to adopt a position of some authority, rivalling that of the teachers and enabling her to record a degree of agency in her subsequent development of the project. She is concerned to differentiate herself individually and to adopt a position as a somewhat distanced mediator between the cultures of youth and the quizzical ignorance of teachers; she does not, *in her writing*, implicate herself in what she describes, and her knowledge, given the conventions of educational discourse, is thus enhanced by its removal from the taint of immediate personal experience. She knows, better than most in this group, exactly how to produce the kind of writing that is valued – because it is taken as evidence of the emergent, autonomously critical and reflective subject. A striking example of this occurs somewhat later in her essay: 'Before I did the review of the album for a magazine I skim [crossed out] researched a bit by looking through music publications . . .' The self-correction here indicates the process of representing her self in the written mode; the more rational, purposive and educated subject does not just skim even if that is what it looks like.

These are her comments on her choice of image:

> We were offered a fairly limited choice of images. They were all women except for one man. I noticed that everyone else was choosing women, so I chose the man to be different and also because it seemed a bit challenging. The man was white and middle aged. I think in the original picture he was meant to be a journalist or something because he has a bag slung across his shoulder. He had lots of people around him, but I cut him out and put clouds behind. I decided from the first time I saw him that he would be Spanish American rock musician so, with a little help from sir I came up with the name Pedro Escobar. I took a particularly long time to choose a title for the single because I wanted something really convincing to go with the image. I decided on 'On my Way' because the man is looking ahead in a way that suggests he has a destination to reach.

Of course she very explicitly states her wish to differentiate herself individually here but, more substantially, she offers an account of her work which places her in a position of some power: she takes a challenging image and transforms it, constructing meanings which were not immediately available in the raw material. To work with a given image, rather than select her own, declares her skill in the practice of the particular discipline – media studies – and might thus be assessed as a more convincing demonstration of her understanding than those assignments in which an image from another source was substituted. So the individualism she appears to claim could also be construed as a kind of conformity. At the same time, she works at the image and the related tasks with a degree of detachment; despite her strong interest in music and her earlier self-presentation as a knowledgeable participant in popular music culture, there is little attempt here to either represent the music she likes or to explore versions of sexuality – though choosing a man and rendering him *exotic* (Pedro Escobar) could be seen as sustaining her 'hip' stance. Still, there is a greater separation between the regions of personal identity and that of public knowledge in Margaret's production of written work for assessment than in the work of the other girls. However, in talk, Margaret was somewhat more inclined to move back and forth across the boundary between personal and scholastic self-presentation and, indeed, was therefore seemingly less middle-class than 'in' her writing. There is thus a degree of variability in the particular class attributions which can be made, dependent upon the type of material in question – Margaret appears in a variety of positions across a range of representational contexts.

Some of the other girls, and certainly the boys, were not so inclined to represent themselves either 'as' or 'in' writing. But though there is some indicative relationship between writing and a particular kind of class relation to education, it is inappropriate to use writing as if it could be an especially reliable key to the true identity of the students. As I suggested in Chapter 3, it is more plausible to see classroom writing as one among a number of representational forms in which, in different ways, students act to produce possible, not necessarily mutually consistent, positions – this writing might thus be considered, like talk, as a situationally specific event within a set of social and institutional relationships. As I have argued in earlier chapters, rather than read this material for testimonies of the self, I am concerned to interpret their writing in terms of tactical self-positioning in the context of its production.

Beyond the conformity of Margaret's critical-evaluative discourse, there is also a more antagonistic tendency: the terms of the pretence which the assignment invited students to accept are more directly questioned. The assignment suggested an imaginary self-positioning in another domain, that of the music industry, and thus offered an invitation to play: let's pretend, even though what is to be produced will be largely handwritten on lined paper in the school classroom. This pretence is in contradiction with the more powerful fact of positioning as a student – everyone knows this is just a game played in school. Further, the invitation to play is not welcome to those leaving childhood and seeking to enter a more adult oriented phase of youth. Margaret concluded her evaluation thus:

> With the facilities I had to use I think my CD cover was reasonably successful. It is the only piece of work I am really satisfied with. The poster was unsuccessful because it looks really unproffesional. I would have prefered it in colour, but we don't have a colour photocopier. The review of the album was fairly good, but too short. I couldn't think of much more to write and the reviews in magazines are always short, so I based it on them. The storyboard was my least successful part of the assignment because I found it really hard to draw the pictures well. Also the video wasn't very imaginative and would need more variation of scene in reality.
>
> This unit didn't exactly help me to find out more about music, just reinforced what I already knew. During this unit of work I have learnt just how difficult it is to design record sleeves and videos, before doing this work I thought it would just be easy, and fun. But although it was enjoyable it was also hard work. If I could change anything with my work I would make it more profesional looking.

The dissatisfaction here suggests that the whole assignment is 'only playing' and that, as such, it is not for young people who are no longer children. There are important issues to emphasize here: it suggests, yet again, the unsatisfactory way in which schooling sustains some aspects of adult–child relations beyond the age at which most children are happy to leave childhood; it points to the way in which schools, and subjects like English in particular, have long sustained too great a distance from the practices and sites of work and particularly work regarded as commercial and industrial rather than continuous with academic culture. It also implies the problematic subordination of practical production to tasks defined by the anachronistic imperatives of examinations (see Donald, 1992; Jones, 1989). In Margaret's wish to make what she produced a more fully realized example of a commercial genre she implies a desire to go beyond the context-tied value of school genres to achieve something which has a more pervasive presence and power throughout contemporary market culture. But in doing so, she is not refusing school and her position as a student as such; it is more credible to suggest that the critique implied is of the particular constraints, resources and social relations of schooling as it is presently constituted.

Abby

There are some continuities here in looking at the last of the girls' assignments. Abby also aspires to achieve the authenticity of the commercial genres simulated in the assignment. She rejected the images offered to the class and chose her own set of images of dark haired young women (being a dark haired young woman herself); like Margaret, she was attracted by a Hispanic name – Guadalupe Lopez:

> My friend decided to do an unusual singer who was from Central America which gave me the idea to do a North American Hispanic singer.
> So I went through the magazines looking for a Hispanic model, I soon found the model I wanted and tried her picture out on the background. It looked good so I decided to use that picture.

As she progresses through her evaluation, there is a recurrent use of *real* and *realistic* to designate the degree of correspondence between her own artifacts (poster, review, CD cover) and the products they simulate. Reality is here constituted through attention to details of language, style, design and graphics:

> I then had to design a tour poster. I chose a picture of a woman who looked a lot like the model in the front cover, only she had short hair. I decided to make it more real by having a support act. I had to keep the design basic as when I've studied the magazines for ideas the ads are always small and plain. I put the poster in a design for a magazine and labled the words like they would be on a real tour ad. I then had to make a review for the artist. I looked at magazines and wrote in the style, putting my one sided view across as I felt I was actually supporting a real artist.

I decided to make my own magazine review page and also reviewed some other real artists work on it. I used pictures of an actor as the DJ who reviews the page and a picture of Tom Jones to make it more realistic.

The 'reality-effect' is conferred by a genre which is not, like those particular to school, an artifice within which to acquire marks; by including names, pictures and references to real artists Abby limits, but also compounds, the masquerade. The claim to inhabit non-school genres is a claim to a degree of power for her work but it is made just because her position, and the status of what she actually produces, is no more than material for assessment. For her work to really have a use-value beyond the relation of student to examination, a different set of relationships between schooling and the public domain of media artifacts would need to be constituted (see Avis, in CCCS Education Group II, 1991). In a sense, she is up against the boundary of her identity as a school student and, given the still strong division of that identity from those with more of the power and responsibility of adulthood and with some productive agency, what she makes of the task is inescapably contradictory. The majority of what students do in school does not invite this play with forms of non-school production and it can be seen that in media studies, if not exclusively there, the practices involved do focus and register tensions in the experience of being schooled. Abby's CD cover was among the most meticulously attentive to detail, even including a computer bar-code and an array of carefully drawn logos. The allure of a West Coast corporate address – 1299 Ocean Avenue, Suite 800 Santa Monica, CA 90102 – is also suggestive of the wish to locate her text as originating precisely where she is not, beyond the immediate reality of a classroom in Hackney. Thus, though what she produces may attract a relatively high valuation by teachers, her texts are also marked by their non-school, media authenticity – they gesture towards a domain of textual production remote from the constraints of the school classroom.

Stephen and Alan

The very few boys who produced any kind of assignment at all were clearly similarly orientated towards this other scene of production and, being less concerned to sustain student identities than most girls, actually produced remarkably little. There were almost as many boys in regular attendance at this class as there were girls; but only two completed the music assignment and, in both cases, their work was less substantial and less elaborate than that of the girls. Stephen, who commented that the work was not worth doing – because it was classroom based and remote from actual production – did produce a roughly sketched CD cover: a side view of an American football helmet with a large letter 'G' logo and captioned George and The PACKERS. The choice of such a helmet does call upon the imagery of a highly masculinized sport and the name 'George' was given to an image of a young white woman selected from the initial set. Furthermore, a further image, its purpose unclear, was a carefully controlled computer graphic displaying the biological symbols for male and female touching – above, the name George, and below, 'A Challenge'. No explanatory notes and no evaluation accompanied these or the other items he presented. Despite his interest in black music, this material seems to represent aspects of music marketing more associated with the dance music of which, elsewhere, he was quite dismissive. However, within the school context, it seems likely that images originating in sport and in computer generation connect the little work that he did do with quite strongly masculinized features of the curriculum.

In some respects, Alan's work is similar: in this case a black model is also given an ambiguously male name 'Sunny D.' if more explicitly identified with a pop repertoire. Alan's listing of songs is a plausible set of romantic pop songs – 'Please', 'Belive Me', 'Live It Free', 'Come To Me', 'Call Home Sometime', 'Your Mine', 'I Need You, Now', 'Hearts can be Broken'. Though an interest in lyrics which explore love and relationships was acknowledged by Alan in an earlier interview, here the particular music genre is not one with which he otherwise appears especially concerned – except as 'covered' by Mick Hucknall/Simply Red. There is no cover sheet, no evaluation and no explanatory comment. The image of the black model is cropped in incorporating it into his CD cover – LIVE IT FREE! – and is used much as it was received for his album/concert poster – 'ALL I WANT IS?' (CD, Tape, Vinyl) / Live at Wembley. Again, like Stephen, the products have been made, the task fulfilled, but there is a lack of detail in the replication of media forms and a kind of roughness to their presentation, consistent with much of their other work. This could be indicative of a lazy indifference to schoolwork in general, but, equally, it hints at their relation to the play-like nature of the tasks. To some extent, their work suggests a lack of interest in the pretence involved in simulation. They decline to minimize or conceal the material character of a school-based assignment and are thus, as boys at 16, unwilling either to be enthusiastic children or to pretend that their products are other than the outcome of work with scissors and glue, pencil and paper.

Alan's review was, at first, surprising in its presence and its quantity. Though written, and on lined school paper, it is more like a script to be spoken:

The great New debut ALBUM FROM SUNNY DAVIES IS TOPPING THE ALBUM CHARTS ALL OVER THE WORLD AND HAS MADE HISTORY by Realeasing TWO Songs FROM, ALL I WANT IS, Reaching Number 1 WITH BOTH OF THEM AND AT THE SAME TIME THE GREAT ALBUM HAS STAYED AT NUMBER 1 FOR 7 WEEKS.

The TWO Songs reached Number One IN, First JUNE 94 WITH 'LIVE IT FREE' AND STAYED IN THE CHARTS UNTIL MID JULY.

THE NEXT SONG to REACH THE TOP SPOT WAS 'HEARTS CAN BE BROKEN' WHEN IT KNOCKED 'US 3 R 2' of the TOP IN AUGUST 3RD AND STAYED THERE UNTIL SEPTEMBER 28.

THE FIRST SONG (LIVE IT FREE) ALSO REACHED NUMBER 1 IN 3 OTHER COUNTRIES.

AND 'HEARTS CAN BE BROKEN' REACHED NUMBER 1 IN A
.MASSIVE 6 different COUNTRIES.

SHE HAS JUST Realeased ANOTHER SONG FROM HER ALBUM
CALLED 'COME TO ME' AND IS AT A HANDSOME POSIOTION IN
THE CHARTS AT 22, WHO KNOWS maybe SUNNY WILL MAKE
FURTHER HISTORY BY MAKING IT 3 NUMBER ONES ON THE
TROT.

HER ALBUM IS STILL SELLING WELL AND WE HAVE JUST
BEEN INFORMED THAT SUNNY WILL BE APPEARING AT WEM-
BLEY ON THE 15 16 + 20th OF OCTOBER AND YOUR Faverite pop
MAGAZINE will be giving away 3 pairs of TICKETS TO SEE SUNNY
DAVIS only if you can answer THIS EASY Question.

"WHO WAS THE LAST PERSON/S TO Reach Number One IN
boTH Album and singles CHARTS?

WAS IT = BRUCE + TRIGGER

ANNIE ARMITAGE

or WAS IT

Kenny Joansom.

If you THINK ITS YOUR lucky day just phone THIS HOTLINE
0898=7989.

Soming up SUNNY DAVIES ALBUM I would Deffinatly Recom-
mend you buying this.

C–D. = £13.99p
L.P.   = £9.99p
TAPE = £7.99p

Review Completed by DAVID CLARK.

It is difficult to adequately represent the shifts between upper and lower case
writing here and, often, the formation of his script seems to hover indeterminately
between the two. To some extent there may be some correspondence between these
shifts and the way that he conceives the speaking voice which, clearly, is intended
to utter these words – 'we have just been informed'. In fact, the idioms he adopts
suggest a high degree of familiarity with television and radio pop reviewing styles
and a considerable awkwardness in attempting to represent these within the notional
form of a magazine review crossed with a school genre. He wrote his full name at
the top of the page, his form 5MT, and the date 10-2-93. His work is constrained
by the customary privileging of written material in school; here, there is no reasonable
basis for the writing demand and its effect is to impede the more fluent assumption
of the speaking voice he strives towards (see Kress, 1994). It is, again, a matter of
the task positioning him as a school student rather than as a more adult student-
producer located within the domain the assignment gestures towards. There is
some basis therefore for suggesting that the task was probably experienced as
consistent with the usual order of schooling and its regulation of the forms of
representation and subjectivity. For Alan, it was neither an opportunity for making

very much of what he already knew nor for learning more of the variety of actual media practices.

Unlike several of the girls, the boys were relatively uninterested in taking up positions which might recognize some value in the exchange of effort now for an educationally formed identity later. Thus, even though the focus here was in the popular domain and even though the tasks were not, on the whole, strictly bounded by conventional school genres, the mode of engagement was conditional upon the investments that students made in being particular kinds of people (see Avis, and Carspecken, in CCCS Education Group II, 1991). The class orientation of some of the girls (a combination of where they understand themselves to be placed and where they aspire to be) was formed and represented in common terms with many of the boys. However, for the boys, the persistence of some particular features of an older working-class masculinity did seem to make it that much more of a compromise to appear as someone good at school-work (Mac an Ghaill, 1994; Willis, 1977). This male working-class habitus seemed tightly bounded and thus not easily contaminated with forms of presentation, implicitly of themselves, involving 'neatness', 'attention to detail', 'thoroughness' and 'efficiency' (see Kress, 1995: 92). As I've noted, most of the boys did not present any work for assessment at all and their character- istic classroom presence was, in terms of what 'we-as-teachers' perceived as appro- priate and worthwhile, distracted and disengaged.

There is more to this, however. Stephen's computer graphics and Alan's review might also, if more tentatively, be read as evidence of some reconfiguring of working- class masculinities – they appear to appropriate, if as somewhat masculine, modes of representation associated with the media and computer technologies and previously regarded as feminine (see Connell, 1995; Mac an Ghaill, 1994). As I suggested in Chapter 5, Stephen, in that instance taking a more traditional male working-class position, pointed to the actual production context of music – the studio – as a worth- while place to visit because there, rather than in the classroom, useful learning might take place. So, though the privileging of access to high technology is a familiar feature of masculine fantasies of power and control, it is also an entirely justifiable challenge to the inadequacy and anachronism of a media studies constrained by a school classroom no more equipped than it may have been 30 years ago. Access to computers, though by no means a guaranteed agent of magical transformation in the social relations of schooling, does nevertheless make possible some degree of repositioning as a student–producer in a more credible relation to the domains of adulthood and work (see Jones, 1995: 239).[6] Such access is consistent with the stress on taking up a more adult position, beyond the teacher–pupil/student relation, which for both the boys and the girls was a persistent concern.

In anticipation of arguments made in Chapter 8 (and see Richards 1996b; 1997), I want to mention here that teachers who have a knowledge of a vocational practice and its associated technologies are often more likely to be regarded as 'legitimate authorities' by the working-class students – both boys and girls – discussed in this and the preceding chapters. Teachers, like myself, preoccupied with what students already know, and with access to forms of knowledge sometimes hard to represent as 'useful', are not likely to be perceived as anything more than 'just teachers' (see

Carspecken, in CCCS Education Group II, 1991). An additional adult identity, perhaps a continuing history of involvement in another practice, might enable teachers to offer and sustain an experience of school as more integrally connected to other socially and economically productive settings. In the context of this argument, there is also a need to question the very powerful authority of writing and the assumption that the knowledge and reflection we aim to develop always has to be relayed through its forms. Other practices – of a dominantly oral or visual kind, for example – need to be recognized and the identities they anchor given more than the status of marginal and transient curiosities. Whatever the difficulties in reconstituting the relation of adolescents and teachers to schooling, there is significant scope for development in forms of teaching which do not take the conventional classroom and its particular culture of literacy as central.

Conclusion

The teaching strategy reported here, like the interviews and discussions examined in Chapters 4 and 5, was deliberately contained by the pattern of existing practice in GCSE media studies. The constraints which such an approach imposed – image work and minimal resources – were productive: their assignments provided valuable evidence of how the students negotiated, and sometimes ignored, the form of the demands made upon them. The reading I have offered, drawing initially upon Hodge and Kress (1988), has foregrounded the question of power in transactions between students and the formal demands of the curriculum.

In this school setting, the working-class boys were particularly uncomfortable with the demands of writing and, by contrast with their involvement in the group evaluation discussed in Chapter 5, they showed little enthusiasm for such work (see Willis, 1977). The earlier oral discussion, between boys and with me as a male teacher, had allowed a performance of masculinity which could be enjoyed and in which everyone could participate with some satisfaction. In writing, such opportunities for performance seemed largely unavailable to them, and their interest in the images was, apparently, satisfied elsewhere. Indeed, the disappearance of the images from their folders was itself a matter of some amused mutual accusation – the images, destined for inclusion in their GCSE assignments, had been diverted, they alleged, to their various bedroom walls, thus, implicitly, relocated as objects of masturbatory rather than scholarly pleasure. The masculine identities the boys were interested in sustaining were in an uneasy tension with the central need to write in order to complete the assignment. However, for a majority of the girls writing appeared to present an occasion for some confirmation of their skills as young women (see Kress, 1995: 92–3) and, though with widely varying degrees of fluency across modes of formality and informality, and with the partial exception of Claire, they did strive to complete the written components of the assignment. Certainly, for Margaret and Abby, writing was a resource which they could use to construct a more middle-class public persona than, on the whole, they could achieve through talk – especially in contexts shared with their fellow students. Nevertheless, for girls in this mostly working-class group, even for Margaret and Abby, and more obviously for the others, their investment in the power of such middle-class identities, through writing, was still somewhat equivocal. At 16, at the end of compulsory schooling, they had not, it seemed, settled how they might project their public identities beyond the threshold of GCSEs and into the immediate future that lay beyond their completion of Year 11.

My reading of the assignments in this chapter was first formulated about a year after I taught these students. But the emphasis of my reading shifted, and the chapter was thus somewhat rewritten after I extended my research into a selective school and the work of media studies students in Year 12. In the next chapter I present, by contrast, examples of a more settled and more resolute investment in the construction of self-identity in writing, specifically through discussion of autobiographies framed, initially, by the fantasy of participating in *Desert Island Discs* – or something very like it.

Notes

1   As I noted in Chapter 5, this initiative replicated work done with another class by a recently qualified English and media studies teacher.
2   A British magazine addressed to teenage girls, on the whole somewhat younger than 17.
3   I owe this potential reading and this way of elaborating the questions to Joe Tobin of the University of Hawaii.
4   A British chart-pop magazine addressed to young teenagers and pre-teens.
5   For some detailed analyses of rap videos by women (MC Lyte, Salt 'n' Pepa) see Rose, 1994: Chapter 5.
6   See also Hatcher, R. and Jones, K. (1996).

Chapter Seven

Live Through This . . .[1]

Introduction

There are two main intentions guiding the discussion to be presented in this chapter. First of all, I want to return to the concept of taste and to pursue the argument that taste is more than an expression of an individual's objective location in systems of social classification and difference. This emphasis has been foreshadowed in previous chapters, of course, and clearly informs my discussion of the material in Chapters 4 and 5. Here, I want to develop a more critical discussion of the work of Bourdieu. Though I have derived fundamental aspects of my understanding of taste from his work, and will clarify these in the following discussion, I want to argue for more emphasis on agency in the formation of taste. The second intention is to further the examination of forms of school-based writing in the representation of popular cultural experience. In the research for this chapter, I explored a more autobiographically orientated mode of writing with Year 12 students in Edmonton.[2] In the discussion which follows, I want to refer back to the material considered in Chapter 6 and to suggest how differences in the class composition of the group and in the nature of the educational setting have informed the production of self-accounts.

It was not until January 1995, two years after I carried out the taught unit with Year 11 students in Hackney, that I initiated a new phase of work with a group of A level media studies students. The earlier interviews and discussions were productive of tactical self-representations but the written assignments had offered more specific evidence of how school students position themselves simultaneously in the popular and school-based discourses available to them. So, to extend this more specific concern with the contradictory discursive orders of popular and school culture, I adopted a mode of enquiry which again involved the production of writing. In this case, the emphasis on an autobiographical form was intended also to elicit more evidence of how adolescents represent themselves, to themselves and to others. Furthermore, to call upon them to draw on music, as a symbolic resource in their autobiographical self-accounts, required some plausible model of self-representation. The BBC Radio 4 programme, *Desert Island Discs*, provided a starting point.[3]

Some preliminary attempts to determine a viable approach to music biographies were made in the context of a media research seminar involving me and a number of teachers of media studies in secondary, further and higher education. The form in which members of the seminar were asked to report on their musical tastes replicated the flattery and the fantasy of being invited to select favoured records to play on *Desert Island Discs*. Though I do not intend to comment on the self-reports offered in the seminar, at least not in any detail, the session was interestingly unnerving, personally revealing and, to some extent, uncomfortable. Thus, even among consenting adults of similar educational background, already quite well known to each other, self-presentation through musical tastes was perceived to be more risky than a discussion in which selections of books, films, television programmes and even clothes might be the main concern. Indeed, if I look back to Chapter 1, and my own autobiographical disclosure of musical tastes, I'm aware of how careful I have been, eliminating reference to all sorts of things I once owned but subsequently had to expel, along with unwanted identities.[4]

These biographical games suggested several possibilities. Taste in music appears to be constructed as revealing 'interiority' – because music is culturally positioned as a distinctively expressive and affective medium. Moreover, there is a broad, though culturally circumscribed, reading of the physical characteristics of music as mysterious: a medium which, because it cannot be seen, can be felt but not touched, and which may be experienced as both filling the external space around us and penetrating the boundaries of the body as well, might thus be equated with religious concepts of spirituality and of inter-subjective communion. The histories of both European classical and of African-American music are significantly entwined with traditions of religious assembly and of the various configurations of inter-subjectivity which they have aspired to achieve. For example, Jazzie B's 'Soul-II-Soul', though seemingly an entirely secular concept, nevertheless recovers the religious connotations of soul music.[5] Of course, the religious modalities of inter-subjectivity inscribed in soul performance are always also constantly reappropriated as metaphors of sexual experience. This is perhaps further confirmation of the way in which translation between the domains of religious, sexual and musical experience is characterized by some convergence around concepts of disconnection from the everyday and a dissolution of the enclosing boundaries of the subject (see Bourdieu, 1986: 79–80).

In this context, taste, while being a matter of locating the self in a social classification, can also be understood as an element in the discursive construction of relations between subjects. Thus, subjects may position themselves in relations with others through a mapping of such relations onto the allegiances and divisions available in discursively constructed taste categories: friends might, for example, register friendship through a common liking for rap and not pop. Equally, the negotiation of boundaries may be, in fantasy, strictly around a singular self, or may locate the self with numerous others (fans, perhaps) or, of course, may be dyadic – in the sharing of tastes, as a signifier of intimacy. Such boundaries can also be exclusions, sometimes vigorously insisted upon – by people for whom the inter-subjective taste relation is more sharply defined by refusing to include others.

There are emotional dynamics involved in the formation of tastes and taste allegiances which, though no doubt informing responses which can be read in terms of public social self-positioning, are not thus exhausted by such a reading. Bourdieu's methodology (in this case large scale social surveys and questionnaires) provides the means for mapping relations between cultural choices, objective social positions, and the distances between classes and class fractions within a national culture. The statistical production of such a map has a provisional validity – it allows plausible hypotheses about relations between culture and class on a macro-sociological scale. However, it does not address questions of biographical specificity or, in thus neglecting such questions, conceive of social subjects as divided and complexly formed through many more social categories than class and as continuing to reform themselves in more fluid and variable sets of relations with others. To suggest how Bourdieu might inform teaching, I need to complement his own approach by attending to the subject-ive negotiation of the meanings given to tastes by people themselves. But before I do that, I want to show how Bourdieu's analysis frames my own concerns.

A Social Critique of the Judgement of Taste: Some Distinctions

In the midst of Bourdieu's grand social survey of French cultural distinctions, he calls for something more than his primary methods can provide. He suggests that:

> Bourgeois culture and the bourgeois relation to culture owe their inimit-able character to the fact that, like popular religion as seen by Groethuysen, they are acquired, pre-verbally, by early immersion in a world of cultivated people, practices and objects. When the child grows up in a household in which music is not only listened to (on hi-fi or radio nowadays) but also per-formed (the 'musical mother' of bourgeois autobiography), and a fortiori when the child is introduced at an early age to a 'noble' instrument – espe-cially the piano – the effect is at least to produce a more familiar relationship to music, which differs from the always somewhat distant, contemplative and often verbose relation of those who have come to music through con-certs or even only through records . . . (Bourdieu, 1986: 75).

In this, Bourdieu argues that the formation of taste is located in early routine incul-cation, prior to any possible self-reflective consciousness. Thus, by contrast with Willis *et al.*'s (1990) view of youth as the critical phase in which 'symbolic moulds' shape adult identities, he implies the scope for other, more fully biographical, modes of research into the formation of the 'habitus'. Bourdieu writes of 'an immediate adherence, at the deepest level of the habitus, to the tastes and distastes, sympathies and aversions, fantasies and phobias which, more than declared opinions, forge the unconscious unity of a class' (Bourdieu, 1986: 77). Alluding to the child in D.H. Lawrence's story 'The Rocking-Horse Winner' – 'who hears throughout the house and even in his bedroom, full of expensive toys, an incessant whispering: "There must be more money"' – Bourdieu thus argues for a kind of 'social psychoanalysis':

> . . . to grasp the logic whereby the social relations objectified in things and also, of course, in people are insensibly internalized, taking their place in a lasting relation to the world and to others, which manifests itself, for example, in thresholds of tolerance of the natural and social world, of noise, overcrowding, physical or verbal violence – and of which the mode of appropriation of cultural goods is one dimension (Bourdieu, 1986: 77).

Here, the relationship between subjective formation and social difference is more than merely a matter of subject positions within discourses. The formation of a 'habitus' encompasses all the dimensions of becoming, and sustaining, a differentiated social being (Bourdieu, 1986: 170–2).

However, despite the potential for further research which Bourdieu's concept of the habitus suggests, in *Distinction*, the complexity and uncertainty of identity (see Rose, 1984: 18) remains proportionately insignificant in the context of a macrosociological model of social relationships and their reproduction. Though Bourdieu's data is sometimes complemented by more sustained forms of interviewing and observation and by photographic evidence (Bourdieu, 1986: 503–12), individual subjects, their biographies, and the familial histories which partly form them do not figure in the text, other than as occasional illustration of the structural order within which their tastes are located. As I have suggested, teaching requires a more situated knowledge, informing and illuminating the more particular details of classroom exchanges, wary of larger, sometimes schematic, generalities. In fact, the practice of teaching demands more attention to agency and to the complexity of individual subjects' choices and self-understanding than the practice of macrosociological theory. I am certainly not arguing that Bourdieu's analysis is wrong but that its level and purpose cannot adequately inform the practice to which my own account relates (see Bourdieu, 1992).

Bourdieu does not eliminate agency from his theoretical system but he does quite carefully qualify what it might mean:

> Without subscribing to the interactionist – and typically petit-bourgeois – idealism which conceives the social world as will and representation, it would nevertheless be absurd to exclude from social reality the representation which agents form of that reality. The reality of the social world is in fact partly determined by the struggles between agents over the representation of their position in the social world and, consequently, of that world (Bourdieu, 1986: 253).

With this in mind, it is useful to turn to what Bourdieu has to say about youth:

> The 'young' can accept the definition that their elders offer them, take advantage of the temporary license they are allowed in many societies ('Youth must have its fling'), do what is assigned to them, revel in the 'specific virtues' of youth, *virtu*, virility, enthusiasm, and get on with their own business – knight-errantry for the scions of the mediaeval aristocracy,

love and violence for the youth of Renaissance Florence, and every form of regulated, ludic wildness (sport, rock, etc.) for contemporary adolescents – in short, allow themselves to be kept in the state of 'youth', that is, irresponsibility, enjoying the freedom of irresponsible behaviour in return for renouncing responsibility (Bourdieu, 1986: 477–8).

In some respects this corresponds to the argument which I proposed in Chapter 2 – that youth and adolescence are institutionally powerful categories to which young people are subject but which they also draw upon in contesting the social relations, particularly of schools, in which they are positioned. However, Bourdieu's reference to 'struggles between agents over the representation of their position' should also qualify his suggestion that the young 'allow themselves to be kept in the state of "youth"'. For though this is one plausible reading of the social position accepted by young people, many other meanings and consequences of irresponsibility need to be considered. Otherwise, there is a risk of acquiescing in Bourdieu's construction of an historically enduring deception in which the differing possibilities of youth are blurred together. To the contrary, I want to emphasize that if tastes in youth are less constrained to fit into the prevailing order of (good) taste, then they can be less conforming to cultural boundaries, both those of 'official' culture and of popular culture. They might be more promiscuous, more (dis)located and more unpredictable than Bourdieu appears to accept (see Bourdieu, 1986: 466–7). 'Youthful irresponsibility', however much a deferral of social power and responsible adult agency, can be productive of significant cultural innovation and not least through the mixing of perhaps otherwise disparate cultural elements which, confined to the young, are thus brought into relation with each other. For example, schools, because they bring together disparate groups on the basis of their youth, provide one kind of context for such mixing (see Hewitt, 1986: 154). Thus while reconfirming the subordination of the young, they also contribute to the preconditions of cultural recombination.

The limitations of Bourdieu's descriptions, particularly when faced with historical specificity and change, with expanding cultural diversity and with questions of political action and ethical choice, have been noted by many critics.[6] Despite this, the account developed in the rest of this chapter continues to engage with his approach to the logic of taste. My own emphasis, however, is upon taste both as public social category (which might therefore be the object of extensive discursive analysis) and, for social actors, a continuing relational strategy, drawing upon historically particular cultural repertoires, always provisionally fulfilling a variety of purposes in the lives of particular individuals. Some of these purposes I would expect to be available to subjects as strategies of which they can be conscious, and of which they can give accounts, if the need arises; other purposes are undoubtedly of the kind mapped into Bourdieu's elaboration of habitus. Still others may well be more intractably unconscious, in the psychoanalytic sense, and are thus, strictly speaking, beyond the scope of my research.

However, it is of some importance, at this point, to turn, if only briefly, to the psychoanalytically informed approach adopted by Cohen:

> ... the family romance in all its forms ... potentially connects the child to
> sites of social aspiration outside both family *and* school ... [working-class
> youth] construct out of materials to hand (friends, work-mates, the neigh-
> bourhood) those territories of desire (Freud's 'other scenes') which make
> the oppressive circumstances of working-class life and labour seem just
> about bearable (Cohen, in Bates *et al.*, 1984: 148–9).

He argues that the resources of popular media culture are incorporated into the fantasies constructed both within families and in the gender divided self-presentations
of adolescent peers. Thus, in delineating the family romance, he focuses on:

> ... those normative structures of projective identification through which
> parents and children, usually of the same sex, misrecognise in each other
> the social embodiment of developmental ideals constructed by the dominant
> culture ... [thus] TV, or movie stars, rock stars, sporting personalities ...
> furnish the models for 'supermum' or 'superdad' against which actual par-
> ents are often compared invidiously. They also provide all those 'famous'
> first names (e.g. Elvis, Marilyn) whose symbolic function is to inscribe the
> child's history in a certain genealogy of parental desire (Cohen, in Bates
> *et al.*, 1984: 148).

Such fantastic transformations of the immediate facts of family relations and identities are not, of course, peculiar only to the working-class subjects of Cohen's
research. The students discussed here are also caught up in transitions explored, in
part, in terms of other places, other selves and a sexuality somewhat disembedded
from real relations with others.

Autobiographies: Live Through This ...

The following discussion centres on the way in which 22 Year 12 students represented themselves in response to a request which I recorded, for myself, in the
following terms:

> I would like everyone to work out a way of selecting six track titles which
> might be used to represent yourself – using music to structure a condensed
> autobiography – to other people. It is up to you to decide on the kind of
> audience you want to address and what the context might be; equally, the
> context might well suggest a particular persona. You could, for example,
> imagine a scenario in which you have been invited onto a radio programme
> to talk about yourself and the music that you like. So, in whatever terms you
> choose, you need to suggest why your tracks matter to you, when they did
> so, and what you can say about them now.

I had prepared this in advance of my meeting with the students but I neither read it to them in this form, nor gave it to them on paper. As it happened they were together with one teacher,[7] watching a lengthy compilation of pop videos, in preparation for subsequent work on the recording industry. I simply took the opportunity to speak to them when their attention seemed to waver and it was thus appropriate to break from continuous viewing. I spoke to them briefly, elaborating on the text I had prepared. Certainly my identity as an Institute of Education lecturer interested in research was more distinctly defined for them than it was for the students at the Hackney comprehensive. To some extent, their response to the task might be judged as informed by a degree of respectful acquiescence and relative familiarity with the manner and interests of academics. These students, all studying for A levels in a selective school, were organizing their present in terms of a future in and beyond study at university level. Nevertheless, I did not offer any extended explanation of my motives other than noting that I was interested in questions of taste. I did suggest that, if they wished, they should bring along taped compilations of their chosen tracks to accompany their written response. Two weeks later, when I returned for a discussion with them and to collect their writing, several did offer tapes and one or two played selections and talked around them.

By contrast with the assignments discussed in Chapter 6, the written material produced in this context, though closely related to a current A Level media studies topic, was not obviously 'to be assessed'. To some extent, this made their writing a little less constrained by the need to produce the appropriate conventional forms. Whereas the Hackney students' writing mostly corresponded to a familiar, subject-specific form of organization, I found the 'autobiographies' more difficult to read in terms of any generic form. I had suggested that they might frame what they wrote in the terms of a publicly broadcast form where their lives and their interests in music might be of central interest. I had also mentioned that, if they wished, they could write as someone other than themselves and thus adopt a temporary media persona. In fact, in their responses, they seemingly wrote as themselves though, as will become apparent, the degree of personal differentiation which that implies must be judged against the common repertoires of self-representation upon which they drew.

Twenty-two students, virtually everyone present, gave me writing samples. What remained unsaid was whether they should expect to see it returned to them and, if so, for what further purpose. The teacher responsible for the A Level course seemed to speak as if their writing was 'for me', to be given without any expectation that it be returned. This identified what they had done as more of a response to a research enquiry than a necessary piece of coursework. That I expected their cooperation on this basis was itself indicative of assumptions which I did not make with the GCSE students in Hackney. The Hackney students would not work to satisfy the needs of academic research. However, the A Level students were willing, capable and familiar both with forms of writing about themselves and with requests to work for teachers. My presence and my requests were accepted because of such pre-existing expectations, shared by students and teachers alike. In effect, I assumed both the outcome of their particular experience of schooling and their complicity in the continuation of its demands even beyond the limit of compulsory attendance. Indeed, to write about themselves, in some detail, must have seemed quite natural for students accustomed to believing their words and their thoughts to be of value. To be asked to provide writing for research, beyond the requirements of teachers, perhaps seemed further confirmation of what they 'knew' about themselves. Despite this, there were a few students whose writing subsequently suggested some ambivalence; I will discuss these examples in the course of this chapter.

A further significant contrast between the classroom relationships evident in Hackney and those which appeared to prevail in Edmonton also emerged in the discussions surrounding the completion of their writing. Both the A Level media studies teachers also volunteered to represent their own life-histories in terms of their involvement in popular music and to do so in addressing the assembled group of between 25 and 30 students. There was far more security for these teachers in relocating themselves 'in adolescence', and in representing both past and present tastes in music, than was possible in Hackney. There, for teachers to reveal personal aspects of themselves would risk some mockery, animated by a class coded antagonism. As Alison, the Hackney teacher quoted in the preceding chapter, recalled, displaying her own tastes in music had allowed some unwelcome ridicule; in such a predominantly working-class school, class differences between students and teachers must inevitably divide any attempt to construct a common experience of youth. In Edmonton, the teachers appeared more at ease, as if addressing younger versions of themselves, safe within the assumption of shared continuities between school identities and future adult positions. Indeed, I had been slightly apologetic in requesting autobiographical writing, and had suggested a fictional persona as one way of deflecting anticipated challenges to the intrusive aspect of the request. But there was very little overt resistance to such autobiographical display, despite the fact that I was a stranger to them.

Autobiography, as a classroom genre, is typically introduced by teachers as a means to recover early childhood experience and clearly also entails the prescription of subject positions distinct from, because enabling reflection upon, those located 'in childhood' (see James, 1993). These students were very much accustomed to teachers seeing them as mature, distanced and reflective (see Moss, 1989). In fact, they were all likely to be very competent in this particular social practice of remembering and to have access to a variety of discursive forms in judging how to represent themselves on this particular occasion (see Middleton and Edwards, 1990).

Here, I suspect that I had invited a piece of writing with far more popular precedents than *Desert Island Discs*. In the wider cultural organization of long-term memory, popular music radio constantly orders the past through the recovery of chart music, differentiating seasons and years and decades. Alongside such practices as photography, particularly in combination with holidays, music has been constructed as one of the primary means of recovering memories, of 'liminal moments' and particularly their associated emotions. As I suggested in Chapter 4, with reference to Harvey (1989), the construction of self-continuity, in the context of 'time–space compression', draws upon the resources provided by commercial popular music.[8] The task thus invited them to use a cultural resource with which, in these more general terms, all would be familiar. This may well be a further explanation for what was, on the whole, a relative subordination of school orientated features in their writing. The discursive forms on which they drew in producing their notionally self-representational texts appeared mostly to derive from a popular rather than a scholastic repertoire.

On the particular occasion when I requested their writing, the group was composed of white students only, of whom perhaps two or three were Jewish. By comparison with the Hackney class, they were a much more middle-class and culturally homogeneous group. Furthermore, the past trajectories of these students were strongly convergent. At the age of 11, they had been selected from a large number of applicants by competitive examination and were therefore likely to be characterized by a significant commitment to educational achievement. The school has also favoured those students who are accomplished in the performance of classical music and many were, in those terms, musically literate.

In their writing, the range of musical references and the modes of self-representation suggest, to some extent, shared repertoires. Indeed, there is some evidence of 'tastes', in Bourdieu's sense, which might be connected with their class and educational locations. However, it is important also to read these pieces of writing as self-representational in their forms of organization, rather than simply in terms of explicit evidence of musical preferences. Taste, as a feature of social position, does not disappear from my analysis but it is clearly more than an objectifiable quality of subjects and is more appropriately examined as a trope in the contextually variable discursive construction of the self.

As in the preceding chapter, I want to examine the writing in some detail, with attention to its modes of presentation (see Kress, 1993a) and to the educational context of its production. There were too many individual cases to discuss them all here but I have selected a significant, and representative, range for discussion.

David

In response to a brief questionnaire, scantily completed, David, a Jewish boy, not yet 17, responded to 'What do you expect to do when you leave (school)?' with 'Go to the shop + buy a coke! Ho Ho media studies at a University' [spelling corrected]. The elaboration of his self-account extended to five A4 pages (lined, with a margin) of small hand-written reflection. It was presented with the title *Fish*, his name, and signed and dated.

There are numerous spelling mistakes, words are crossed out and the handwriting is sometimes awkward, occasionally difficult to read. The *formality* of presentation expected of schoolwork was not, it seemed, a significant priority. The narrative exceeds and defies the constraint contained within the invitation (six tracks), naming whole albums and entire genres and only reluctantly settling for less. He talked confidently to the whole group about his selection and played the cassette that accompanied the writing. Clearly, the organization of his self-account can be read as an accomplished act of synthesis between the forms of school writing and those of more informal practices. The ordered, linear narrative, appropriately paragraphed, demonstrates the competence of a student whose continuing formation is achieved, sustained and confirmed in the production of essays. But the title defies school conventions, transitions are more representative of informal speech genres ('Lets jump a bit now . . .'; 'Another Leap forward now . . .') and, quite often, he produces lists of artists, as if detailing the extent of his collection and finding satisfaction in presenting more publicly a mostly private writing practice. Indeed, his private investment, a sustained gathering of music into himself, animated his display of informal knowledge, overwhelming the sanctioned generic artifice of selecting six tracks. It seemed as if the urgency of self-presentation as an expert exceeded any more disciplined self-positioning as strictly competent within the given terms of the task.

His writing combines introspection with an assertive attention to detail. He draws upon a discourse in which early childhood experience is equated with the fundamentally formative moments of individual subjectivity. He begins 'From very young . . .', and positions music as 'integrale' (sic), 'key', able to 'stick in my mind'. He claims 'My mother tells me I was able to clap to the rythm of records from about 6 months and I suppose that from then the influence realy was important' and, reiterating, continues 'From very young I remember certain tracks specificly . . .'. His account, thus framed, becomes a display of interiority and of competence in its recovery and analysis:

> By the next couple of years my tastes had turned to PUNK ROCK, *The Stranglers*. My parents had one of their albums and I was in love with the song, 'Golden Brown'. Again just realy because of repetitive play and familiarity with the track. At the time when I heared the record it conjured up an Image of a long, tiled passage, curving. This must have been a passage at a tube station in my mind's eye probably because at the end of the track there was a kind of echoy effect which must have played on my mind.
>
> Perhaps this is cheating but for my third choice I am choosing all three *Hit Factory albums* the best from PWL, Stock Aitken + Waterman. I cringe at the thought now but at the time I was so proud to be like part of this whole thing. I by purchasing this record, was part of the Hit Factory!

Such confessional and personal statement has a tactical value here: it is a condition of his claim to expert knowledge that such self-positioning be given depth and honesty and a history. The capacity to remember in detail, and to articulate such memory, also provides further confirmation of his scholastic credibility for, however trivial and ephemeral the recollected tastes might be, it is in his display of reflective self-distancing from them that his authority is constructed. Indeed, it is also likely that, in this highly competitive educational setting, he was willing to reveal so much because, in doing so, he positioned himself as that much more knowing than his fellow students.

A further tactic involved in sustaining his 'position of knowledge' involved what may be a distinctly masculine relation to music. For example, he writes

> As a Jew I had had my Bar Mitzvah and therefore gained a pretty lucrative sum of money. I spent nearly all over the next 2 years on cassette singles . . . I massed 119 cassette singles which I do pride myself on their diversity and variation . . .

As I noted in Chapter 5, there is some evidence (though insufficient within the scope of my own research) that it is boys who collect music and appear to enjoy opportunities to make public the quantity, and sometimes the range, of what they have accumulated. To have a collection may be a way of marking out a public, and individually differentiated, self in the context of family and friendship networks. It is also, plausibly, a support for a particular practice of remembering, strongly accented as *individual* by contrast with, for example, the practice of keeping a family photograph album (see Harvey, 1989; Radley, in Middleton and Edwards, 1990). Thus, though there are many ways in which a collection connects the collector to more broadly shared social identities, for boys this practice may signify a tactical separation from familial others, and thus have some importance in claiming a particular kind of masculine identity (see Chodorow, 1978).

David also asserted that:

> I realy don't have any records that have Emotional connotations for me and the reason I buy a record is because of the sound and the quality not just because everyone else likes it or its a particular genre.

Again, this reaffirms his self-construction as an 'expert' and it is possible to suggest that in relation to music, which is culturally constructed as emotional, it was important for him, in this educational context, to define knowledge in terms which emphasize the achievement of rational discrimination, choice and control. In some circumstances, it may be more imperative for boys to position themselves within the terms of such a knowledge because they thus locate themselves as less vulnerable to the implication that they may be positioned by others. In a school where the achievement of knowledge has been highly regarded, and striven for, not to espouse mastery in elite forms of knowledge could be problematic for both boys and girls. Within media studies, where an overtly theoretical discourse can reassure those devoting their time to the study of popular forms, pop music is an awkward object, untheorized and immediately a part of current everyday life. Distancing, by invoking memory for example, might thus become of some importance. For David, where distance is not claimed, the music is of a kind usually construed as hypermasculine and, in his account, is given a selective political credibility:

> Now I have one choice left. The only area I haven't touched is rap. I now consume more rap than anything else perhaps because of its alternativeness, its legendry qualities or perhaps the rebelios attitude that prevails.

> My diversity in this area is apparent too with like for Old-Skool (sic) so called Gangsta rap, Jazz rap, G-Funk, and newly created Horror rap. My final choice though is from none of these. It is British, anti-racism anti-homophobia anti-sexism yet still with a sharp rhyme and a unique quality leading to contraversy in the music press. The record's 'Call it What You Want' by Credit to the Nation.

Once again, this achieves several purposes. It sustains his self-representation as mobile across taste boundaries, itself a feature of the indeterminacy of adolescence, and confirms that he knows such hard, male music. However, it also displays an explicit act of choice which, in the same moment, reasserts a politics appropriate to his positioning as a serious student in a liberal educational domain. In his concluding comment, he explains that for several years:

> I had no TV therefore was an avid listener to radio and listened to music no one else had heard of. When It comes to music I like to think I know what I'm talking about and this has been the case since my early teens. It is and I hope it continues to be an integrale part of my life.

In effect, he represents his own relation to music as both personal and expert. The account, from early childhood through to his self-positioning within a continuing adolescence, translates the layering together of several distinctive phases of his experience into an implicit guarantee of the cultural authority to which he lays claim (see Ross, 1989: 81–2).

Caleb

Caleb's 'Media Studies. Most memorable music tracks', by its title, locates what follows as belonging both in the domain of popular discourse and in the subject media studies. Memory and acts of remembering are of considerable importance here. In this case, the narrative is not that of the self as expert, but as emergent adolescent. Like David, he presented much of his written account of himself to the whole group and was perhaps even more confident in doing so. There is also a similar tactical self-construction as the more mature, reflective self able to recall and retell emotionally accented events from an earlier period, almost as if the adolescent figure thus reconstructed was really a fiction. In fact, it would be plausible to suppose that these 'memories' are not Caleb's at all but are rather contrived in accord with the columns of teenage magazines. His act of public self-positioning combined humour and self-mockery with an implicit emotional authenticity. The text became both a script for a performance and, carefully word-processed, copy ready for publication:

When I was in junior school, I had mixed feelings about the school Christmas parties or discos. I would look forward to it because, there would always
be that chance of dancing (or not!) with that girl I was madly and passion-
ately in love with. However, there was the fact that my clothes were not
the height of fashion, but worse then that was that I never knew the words
of the songs . . . The song I remember the most from these discos was Michael
Jackson's 'Beat it'. All the boys knew the words, the girls only seemed to
like those boys that knew the words, and hey, I didn't. All except for 'So
beat it, beat it, beat it, beat it.' I remember lots of times when my worst
nightmare would seem to come true. After plucking up the courage to ask
my favourite girl to dance, the song would come on, and not wishing to be
humiliated I would pretend I needed the loo, and run and disappear there.
However, trying to keep my street cred, I would come back out again at
the chorus singing 'Beat it, Beat it', as if I knew the song like the back
of my hand. Realising, I couldn't go to the toilets again, I would last the
remainder of the dance by either turning around a lot, or covering my mouth
whilst in a coughing fit (naturally singing the words as well!).

The rest of his account is constituted through a similar remembering of particular songs in typical situations with parents, friends and girls. Writing as a school
student, sexuality is simultaneously claimed and disowned: an attribute of a self distanced by memory. In common with the talk of some radio DJs, music is represented
as giving access to that self and the emotions otherwise forgotten:

Overall the majority of the songs, seem to indicate the desire for a romance
with a girl when I was younger. Most of the songs have some reflection on
the feelings I used to have towards different girls. Music on the whole does
invite feelings of love and similar emotions to surface. However the songs
that really mean the most to me are songs that remind me of a friend or a
friendship, or some important time in my childhood.

Despite the tactical temporal distancing apparent here, it is worth recalling by contrast,
how impatient with being positioned as young adolescents the boys and some of the
girls in Hackney appeared to be. Caleb's appropriation of a discourse of 'adolescent
emotionality', though carefully contained by the framing of a male self, suggests a
continuing self-location somewhat within adolescence. By comparison, the boys in
Hackney, bored by their classroom bound predicament, and facing more immediate
adult futures, would have little coherent basis for representing themselves in this way;
to do so would probably be construed as both childish and effeminate.

When I began this phase of my research, I expected to be able to make some
clear connections between the choices of music students offered, features of their
social position and other aspects of their publicly displayed identities. In fact, it was
difficult to conceive of mapping relationships between forms of music and social

identities in any very reliable way.[9] Through comparisons with the Hackney group, it is possible to note some patterns of preference, constituted by class, gender and ethnic position. Such patterns are important. But, as the discussion of taste with the Hackney boys suggested, preferences could be very unstable and publicly declared preferences changed, tactically, with the circumstances. For some – such as Stephen in Hackney or David in Edmonton – distinct claims to musical knowledge were of some importance but, for many others, preferences were represented as more contingent and to attach much significance to particular choices would be unproductive. Again, then, the question of taste is better defined in terms of how these students represent their *relation* to music: *contingency* might thus be understood as one particular kind of *taste-relation*, a matter of particular cultural practices of self-presentation – if, also, sometimes an instance of individual disavowal.

Unlike either Stephen or David, Caleb did not make his choice of music a tactical claim to authority in the domain of popular music. His list was brief, eclectic but broadly popular: 'Beat It', 'Living Doll' and 'The Young Ones' (Cliff Richard), 'Tears of Heaven' (Eric Clapton), 'Die Zauberflote' (Mozart), 'End of the Road' (Boyz II Men), 'I've Had the Time of my Life' (from *Dirty Dancing*), 'Lady in Red' (Chris be Burgh) and 'Love Shack'. Of course, it would be possible to note what is not included here and to remark on its proximity to such bland categories as easy listening or middle-of-the-road but, in the end, explanation would have to return to the details of the circumstances which have been recalled in Caleb's selection and representation of these tracks.

It is important to note at this point, that for both David and Caleb and many of those students discussed subsequently, biographical organization of their writing does not produce a sharply delimited progression from one music to another. There is often, if not always, an unwillingness to allow one music to entirely displace another. As I have suggested, to make equations between their choices and their identities, on the basis of such evidence, would be very difficult. Identities tend to be represented by many of the students as insistently undecided. However, it is also the case that the nature of the connections between musical choices and identities are not available within the conscious repertoires of discourse they deploy.[10]

A further perspective on this is suggested by Roger Hewitt, who has argued that to visualize 'identity' in a 'polyculture' it may be helpful to compare urban graffiti with palaeolithic 'cave paintings' (Hewitt, 1992). In each case, images are superimposed within the same physical space and thus coexist in relations of cumulative 'destabilization'. I want to suggest that, to some extent, though chronologically ordered, the effect of these adolescent students' statements of musical interest is to accumulate layers of cultural identification without there being a core identity beneath any one of them. It seems unhelpful, therefore, to select one layer and declare it to be unequivocally more fundamental than the others. To some extent this argument converges to confirm, though not from a psychoanalytic perspective, the case made by Cohen (Cohen, 1986) against the notion of simple 'transitions': the idea of singular, and clearly separated, *stages* is inadequate to the description of identities.[11]

Nicholas

So far, I have discussed the writing produced by two boys and, of course, it is tempting to make generalizations about the gendering of the positions they adopt. To complicate this somewhat, I want to continue with further examples from the boys' writing before turning my attention to a selection of the girls' responses. '6 Tracks', by Nicholas, presents an account of his musical preferences which oscillates between choices seemingly located in an autonomous self, choices located in his family history and choices which are defined more by an occasion shared with friends. He produced a detailed and carefully hand-written account, adhering, even more closely than Caleb, to the prescribed instruction. The complexity of his response to the task is thus, remarkably, contained and ordered within three sides of A4. All six of his choices are represented in terms which draw upon a repertoire of distinctive emotions and, often, typically liminal experiences. Sometimes, it seems as if the encounter with a new and intensely emotive music is itself a liminal moment:

> (i) 'Back to One' recorded by Obituary taken from the album 'The End Complete' recorded in 1992 for Roadrunner . . . It really opened up my mind to a new form of music. At first I was shocked because I had never heard any music like this ('Death' metal) and it was such a departure from the music I'd heard before, it was much more brutal and extreme. Because of this album I went on to buy and become interested in more extreme forms of music and this has basically shaped my musical tastes of today and the other bands I used to listen to no longer interest me except maybe holding memories of when I was younger.

His interest in 'death metal', and related forms, is further illustrated with "Anaesthesia" Bass solo from the Album 'Kill Em All' recorded by Metallicas Bassist Cliff Burton . . .'; and '"World of Shit" Nailbomb from the album "Point Blank" released on Roadrunner records 1994', on which he comments:

> This song as well as appealing to me musically being a hybrid cross between punk and death metal also appeals to me lyrically. Nailbombs lyrics are very social and political . . . Also is a very violent + aggressive song + is a good song to listen to when youre angry, it has an almost cathartic effect on me a good way of neutralising my anger.

This particular characterization of music as intensely affective will emerge as common to many of these students in discussion of subsequent examples. But here it is notable that the violence and apparent nihilism of the music is, on the whole, subordinated to a rationalist political discourse; thus 'World of Shit' is:

> . . . about the violence racism hate etc which is 'bred' in the world by many of the worlds politicians + statesmen and how the earth as well as us

is suffering consequences and how the solution lies with us as does the future. I prefer lyrics to be meaningful and to have a point + that is why this song appeals to me

Like David, Nicholas achieves a mix of interests here. The aggressive masculinity of metal is celebrated but also, in school, assimilated to a discourse in which such music is both 'cathartic' and politically 'educational'. This might suggest a quasi-heroic self-construction, locating himself in an implicit narrative of discovery, trauma and subsequent development. Through the extremity of the metal domain, he has become a more mature and politically sophisticated person. At the same time, such a narrative doubles as an account of learning and, consistent with the explanatory mode of address, reconfirms both his present, and his future, as a student for whom adolescent experience has been explored and explained.

A further aspect of the construction of adolescent experience, in this case as an almost uniquely memorable biographical moment, is evident in many students' accounts of their summers out of school.[12] Memory, as one practice through which to sustain identity, clearly draws upon a broadly shared discursive repertoire, though there is also a distinctive individual inflection, an accenting of both remembered contents and of their retelling. In this case, Nicholas again, the evaluative emphasis on one track sustains the 'rational' subject position, reviewing experience and selecting from it to allow an aspect to stand as a public statement of taste:

'Fool to Cry' by the Rolling Stones originally recorded 1973 but rereleased on Jump Back . . . This song is another song I particularly like partially because of the memory and also because I think its a great song. The memory is of the first day of the Summer holidays after me and my friends finished our GCSEs. Met some of my old friends from primary school and some of my friends from this school all got together round one of my friends houses and decided to recreate Woodstock the festival in his bedroom seeing as we obviously didn't make it to the first one and it was summer of 35th [sic] anniversary. We just sat around listening to bands we would have liked to see play. (Rolling Stones, Doors, Pink Floyd, Jimi Hendrix etc.) It was a really nice sunny day and was a very 'mellow' experience. This song now always reminds me of that day and indeed the whole summer which was probably the best summer of my life. The song is possibly the best song I have ever heard memory aside.

A similar tactic is apparent in Nicholas' two remaining choices. Thus his account of 'Morricones "Good Bad + Ugly" [Ecstácy of Gold] taken from the soundtrack to the film' becomes a careful consideration of what part memory has played in forming a taste for such an apparently anomalous choice. The track is defined as enabling the recovery of an intense, 'atmospheric and epic', experience which has, like his own Woodstock, a distinct location in a liminal time: 'me and some friends went to see Metallica play at the Milton Keynes bowl. Before Metallica come on they always play this music . . . one of the highlights of 1993'.

Similarly 'Feed the World' / 'Do They Know It's Christmas?' (Band Aid), which has no musical connection with his other choices, is explained in terms of a distinctive biographical moment:

> At this time my mother was in hospital about to have my youngest sister Jessica. On the night Jessica was born me and my other two sisters spent the night at friends houses while my Dad went to see my sister. The next morning as we drove to the hospital to see our new sister we were listening to the radio . . . it reminds me of that day even now and I always associate it with my youngest sister.

Taste in this account is produced as the outcome of a particular practice of remembering, widely shared and culturally popular as I have suggested, but also inflected towards the inscription of a distinct, reflective, individual self, assessing what combinations of coincident circumstances have motivated the given selection. The rhetorical tactics of the account as a whole are to construct, not a kind of person, but himself as an individual.

To conclude this selective discussion of writing produced by boys, I want to turn now to a minority in whose accounts music was subordinated to sport. Given the biographical invitation, they responded with accounts in which they brought another variant of popular practices of remembering into what were carefully negotiated appropriations of the task. For these boys, a primary self-positioning through music was unwelcome, but they nevertheless produced self-accounts which were almost more committed to a repertoire of personal, liminal and emotive moments than several of those who positioned themselves as knowing about music. It may be that, in the context of this largely middle-class group of students, and in a school where musical knowledge and skill, though not of the popular kind, have been given a high prestige, the inscription of the self in accounts centred in sport was an assertion of a continuing class position. The competitive and bodily forms of male sport were drawn into an implicit refusal of the musical repertoire more widely shared in the group as a whole. Indeed, some evidence of self-conscious class positioning emerged in these cases.

Paul

Paul's selection of tracks, untitled, undated, was handwritten. Paul writes of songs which recall 'things that have happened to people or things that I can relate to'. In fact, he names only five tracks: 'Eye of the Tiger', from Rocky III, 'because when watching the film the adrenalin starts flowing and now that song has the same effect'; 'Simply the Best', 'kind of related to boxing because Chris Eubank has used [it] as his anthem'; 'Money for Nothing' by Dire Straits; 'Go West' by the Pet Shop Boys, 'it is not the song I like but the adaption of the song by the Arsenal supporters . . . it reminds me of when Arsenal won the European Cup Winners Cup last season and the happiness that went with it'; 'Abide with me', 'purely because of the fact that when they used to sing it in the FA cup final, the atmosphere must of been unbeli[e]vable with 120,000 people singing the song . . . I wish I could of been there.'

If 'Money for Nothing' seems incongruous among such explicitly sport related celebrations of competition and victory, his explanation draws it firmly into a class inflected discourse of individual aspiration: 'When I listen to it it gives me some inspiration because I know that some working-class people have made something of their life, they are stars and have made plenty of money, in some ways it gives me a bit of hope for the future.' Whatever other meanings, and other contexts, these songs may have becomes irrelevant to Paul's appropriation of them as emblematic of, and sustaining for, a class identity which is shared by only a very small minority of the group (see Walkerdine in Burgin, Donald and Kaplan, 1986).

Spencer

One of two other boys to make significant reference to sport is worth quoting in full here. His self-positioning is particularly exact, counterposing the repetitive inscription of the indexical pronoun 'I' to all who are not 'I', 'some people' (see Harré and Gillett, 1994: 107–8):

> I would not say that I was a music lover and for this reason I have found it extremely difficult to find any songs that either describe or say something about me. Some people listen to music all the time but I am not one of those people. Some people only listen to one style of music that they love, I am not one of those people. I listen to the radio to keep up with the latest tunes and I occasionally buy singles, but I hardly ever buy albums because I normally only like the song and not the artist.

These unspecified others are plausibly a majority of those in the larger group to which, in the production of this self-account, he belonged. There is, in this context, also some effort to refuse the implication that his identity might be fixed in a relation to a specific artist; in this respect, his insistence on a more partial and more ephemeral interest is comparable to that voiced by working-class boys in discussion together in Hackney. He, like them, refuses the risk of being taste-classified by others. Nevertheless, he does record, in a sparsely word-processed script from which he had omitted his name, some distinct preferences:

> One record that I have always like[d] is 'Chariots of Fire' From an early age I have been sports mad and extremely competitive and this tune always makes me want to go out and compete. It makes me think of the slow motion

scene from the film, which sends a tingle down my spine every time. I did not particularly enjoy the film but the tune is brilliant and would probably be one of my 'Desert island discs'.

Another song that inspires me is 'World in Motion' by New Order which was made with the assistance of the 1990 England world cup squad. This makes me think about the great world cup that England had and how we came so close to winning it. The song itself is not that great but the memories are. David Platt's last minute goal against Belgium in the quarter final was magical and Gary Lineker's in the semi final was superb. I have probably never felt better than the moment that goal went in.

The progression in each of the descriptions presented here is through the song to its effect: it 'makes me want to go out', 'makes me think about' – to compete and to win or to remember (almost) doing so. For Spencer, as for Paul, the emotional dynamic of self-positioning in such a discourse of competitive aspiration appears to arise out of the coincidence of coming from a working-class family and into an intensely competitive school – with upward mobility clearly on their horizons. Music, here, may serve to connect remembered contexts with the repertoire of emotions produced by such a competitive discourse, but it is not ever in itself the object of the emotions represented in this account. Music, for them, is not a primary symbolic resource in defining and representing their identities in this context and, to the contrary, some significant effort is apparent in their embedding of their chosen songs in other, nonmusical, scenes.

For example, in both of the following accounts, the songs are acknowledged as means to invoke or elicit particular fantasies or memories and to achieve a vicarious self-identification with male action scenarios. Despite listening to music, there is no self-positioning as a participant in music orientated youth cultures:

A more modern song that makes me think is Bon Jovi's 'Blaze of Glory' and it talks about the exploits of Billy the Kid who is someone that I would have liked to have known, I admire his style and the song says how he would not just die peacefully but he would like to go out in a blaze of glory and that is what I would like to do.

As football is my main hobby in life a song that I love to listen to is 'Alive and Kicking' by Simple Minds. This has only become a song that I would think of since SKY television used it in their campaign to promote the new FA Premier League and in the adverts they had the song playing and the pictures were of great goals, saves and tackles from the Premier League. So now whenever I hear the song, great memories of football come flooding back.

Spencer's last choices are entirely consistent with his earlier construction of a bounded self, set apart from the liberal middle-class milieu inhabited by the majority of the school's students:

My final two songs are the national anthems of both Great Britain and the United States of America. First that of the USA, the 'Star Spangled Banner' I like it because I admire the way that although it is a national anthem they allow popular singers to adapt it their own way as if it were an ordinary song. The anthem sung by Whitney Houston at a Superbowl a few years back was great and made me think that I would like to be American. The words of the song are also significant to me, at the end when it talks about 'the land of the free and the home of the brave' really inspires me. 'God save the Queen' is a song that will always make me feel proud to be British. Ever since I can remember I knew the words and I always stand when I hear it played. Perhaps the best rendition of the national anthem is heard at FA Cup Finals because football fans are mostly male and they all love there country so they sing loud. I am pleased to say I have been part of two FA Cup Finals and the singing of the anthem just before kick off was exhilarating and it gave me a real buzz. This also makes me think of representing my country in the Olympics and I imagine how great it must feel to be standing on the top of the rostrum with a gold medal around your neck, knowing that you have won for queen and country.

To choose the British and American national anthems, in this context, appears to be a double gesture, certainly of further separation from the culture of the students, but also of defiant subversion of teachers' assumptions about young people. Here, the songs are drawn into a discourse in which he further positions himself as a subject of, and actor for, nationhood and monarchy. Furthermore, sport is represented as a medium for the expression of loyalty to nationhood, just as, earlier, he submerged himself in the unified 'we' of England – '. . . the great world cup . . . and how we came so close to winning it'.

It is important, at this point, to recall that this piece of writing was a response to a specific and teacher imposed task. As I have argued, the particular response has some relation to the student's social position and to his location within the context of the school and the group. But it is also an attempt to do what was asked. In producing his response, he confirms himself as a student and thus his acceptance of the position assigned to him in a continuing, unequal, dialogue with the teacher. He was asked to represent himself in terms which were defined with reference to *Desert Island Discs*. The radio programme is open only to celebrities, to people who have achieved fame through sport, politics, music, theatre, literature and so forth. Here, the invitation to be positioned as a celebrity is engaged through a fantasy of ultimate victory in the Olympic Games, a fantasy identified realistically enough with the moment at which the British National Anthem is played. Read backwards from this achievement of celebrity, the rest of the account becomes a plausible fiction. This story of a sporting hero thus sustains his position as a student, responsive to the discursive regime imposed upon him, but also allows him to refuse some aspects of a liberal, middle-class culture.

So far, I have not examined the gendered features of these boys' self-accounts in any detail. However, before discussing examples of the girls' writing, some more expanded comments on the gender aspect need to be offered. For example, one feminist perspective on music, that of Susan McClary (1991; 1994, in Ross and Rose, 1994), includes the argument that an important tendency in centuries of discourse around music is to characterize it as a threat to social order and particularly to the maintenance of such order through regimes of masculinity. Among Plato's anxieties about music was:

> . . . the sensuous body as it can be aroused by the musics of women or ethnic groups noted for their 'laxness', such as the Lydians. What remain suitable for the Republic, then, are genres of music dedicated either to the martial discipline of the Spartans or to the moderate exchange of ideas through rhetoric (McClary, in Ross and Rose, 1994: 30).

Quoting St. Augustine, John of Salisbury and John Calvin, McClary argues that:

> One of the themes running through these citations is the fear of emasculation. In a culture rigidly structured in terms of a mind-body split, music's appeal to the body predisposes it to be assigned to the 'feminine' side of the axis . . . nothing less is at stake than masculinity itself and, by extension, the authority of church, state and patriarchy (McClary, in Ross and Rose, 1994: 31).

It could be argued that the boys who distance themselves from any explicit self-positioning within music are refusing an identification which, in this patriarchal tradition, would be read as feminine. However, the construction of music as 'bodily' and 'emotional', though familiar, can also be contrasted with its construction as abstract, mathematical and disembodied; either way, to pursue only one tendency in the cultural construction of music risks an essentialism. Thus when McClary proposes 'that music is foremost among cultural "technologies of the body", that it is a site where we learn how to experience socially mediated patterns of kinetic energy, being in time, emotions, desire, pleasure . . .' there is the possibility that she replicates the characterization of music central to 'masculinity itself' (McClary, in Ross and Rose, 1994: 33). It is possible that for these boys, rather than for others in the group, music may have a feminine connotation which they therefore overwhelm by subordinating music to male sport. But, as I have argued, that tactic does seem more motivated by class interests. The forms of masculinity to which they lay claim may be as important for their 'working-classness', in this context, as for their denial of femininity.

In fact, there were many more boys in the group who did engage positively with music of various kinds. Rather than essentialize music as feminine or physical, there is a need to consider music as a diverse phenomenon which, as a unified category, or as a collection of disparate genres, is remade with divergent meanings in its inscription within particular discourses. So, to conclude this discussion of the boys' writing, I want to reaffirm that an understanding of their choices cannot be accomplished simply at the level of generalized cultural polarities but requires some specification of the social relations of the particular context and of how they act to sustain and reinflect those relations.

I want to devote the remainder of this chapter to a consideration of the writing produced by several of the girls in the group. Like the boys, they were involved in a process of selective remembering which, in its presentation, involved them in constructing a public taste persona. As in the examples already cited, there is some degree of self-conscious construction of themselves as adolescent and as recalling liminal moments through the recovery of particular songs. However, it is apparent that these girls, to a greater extent than the majority of the boys, drew upon a discursive repertoire within which music seemed to be constructed as expressive of the self as interiority. Certainly, like the girls in Hackney, more evidence of self-positioning within discourses of sexuality was also present in their writing though, as already committed A Level students, the projection of themselves into educated futures was hardly a matter of equivocation. Here, the writing could tactically unite the demands of various discourses, notably those of femininity and of a popular psychology, to offer 'subjective depth', as itself the emblem of the personhood on which their futures turn. These middle-class girls are accustomed to expect to have a great deal to say about themselves and, in response to my request, it was quite 'natural' for them to do so.

Angela

Angela's account, a corrected hand-written text, began with this:

> 'Summertime' – Fresh Prince and DJ Jazzy Jeff.
> I can't remember when I first heard this song, but it was definitely on a sunny day. I managed to record it on to a compilation tape of summer songs, which I played all day, every day, throughout the summer, every summer. So its a very nostalgic song which I feel represents my 'laid-back' self. Its also my form of escapism during the colder seasons. Just listening to it creates the feeling of warmth . . . 'an air of love and of happiness . . .' that I associate with summer. I like the beat, the lyrics and the continuity of the lyrics.

As I have suggested, the summer motif recurs across a high proportion of the accounts produced by this group. It is evidence of the popularly circulated equation between the remembering of distinct seasons and the particular music at one time coincident with them. For the music radio audience positioned as adolescent, summers are constructed as a series of distinctive thresholds to be actively remembered, and to be self-consciously constructed as memorable as-they-are-lived. Such a motif is not at all peculiar to the girls, but, in Angela's account, it is used to represent a 'section' of her 'self'. Indeed, the assembly of her choices suggests the containment of difference and even contradiction within the depth of her subjectivity. This is an engagement with the discourse of adolescence which takes the implicit attributions of inconsistency and irresponsibility, of emotionality and fantasy, and incorporates them into the self-construction of a reflective, developing, interesting person. Like Margaret, in the Hackney group, Angela achieves a tactical compliance with her educational location as a successful female student. The next two choices exemplify this:

'Soul to Squeeze' – Red Hot Chilli Peppers
I first heard this while I was crammed in the back of a car with 2 other guys. We were on our way to an all-day rock festival with the last band being my favourite band at the time, 'Soundgarden'. Only last summer (1994) this happened during my holiday in Canada. The guy on my right was a close friend of mine and had paid for my ticket and organised the drive up there. It was his tape we were listening to, which he had made especially for the journey. The song came on, and immediately all the men in the car stopped conversation and mimed along to the words (playing the instruments too). It was the most perfect song in the world to be heard. The sun was shining, I was travelling at 90 miles an hour on a freeway, I was on my way to see the best concert of all time (fully paid for), no parents, no restrictions and lots of men!

'Daughter' – Pearl Jam
Not particularly one of my favourite tracks of all time (*that* changes according to mood and season), but it is a representation of a section of my personality concerned with the relationship between me and my parents. Coming from a close-knit, and often very protective, family I sometimes feel like wanting to break away and become independent so that I can do what I want all the time and not have to feel guilty or indebted towards my parents. Other times I am so desperate to please them and make them proud so that they can see the result of all their efforts. I also want them to see me as a 'person' not just their daughter, their possession, something they can control.

Angela's remaining tracks – 'Anna Begins' by Counting Crows, 'The Reality Bites Soundtrack' and 'Slide Away' by Oasis – are accompanied by a similar mix of locating commentary with reflection on the various sections of her personality. The text, as a whole, juxtaposes differently inflected self-representations:

- summer, nostalgia, my 'laid-back' self;
- a teen-movie scenario – 'no parents, no restrictions and lots of men!';
- intra-familial adolescent angst;
- 'Anna Begins' – 'I first heard it in my room when listening to the album' . . . 'a beautiful song . . . I listen to it when I'm feeling in a sensitive mood';
- 'the "Reality Bites" film . . . contains a character that I would like to be – a graduate with a job in the media, living with her 3 best friends and making a documentary about them';
- 'Slide Away' . . . 'the melody is surprisingly catchy and stays in my head throughout the school day – enabling me to get through it'.

Thus, as I have suggested, each song appears to anchor a distinctive way of representing herself, in part because of the particular lyrics and musical genre of each track, but also because of the way in which various desirable identities can be constructed around them – sometimes by recovering the memory of specific occasions, sometimes by suggesting the circumstances in which the song might be literally heard or remembered. As I will argue in the following discussion of Christina's writing, there is some basis for suggesting that this self-account is also an assertion that middle-class girls do have fun, that their identities are not contained by their academic futures.

Christina

Though particular bands, even particular tracks, do recur in the girls' accounts – Nirvana and Oasis for example – and can therefore be read as evidence of a particular socially differentiated and generational experience, rather more extensive similarities can be identified at the level of the shared categories through which their writing is organized: summer holidays, best friendships, relationships with boyfriends, relationships with parents, coping with intense emotions.

Christina's account, abbreviated here, usefully illustrates the typical repertoire of emotional thresholds and relational contexts drawn upon in the girls' production of their self accounts. Once again, summer emerges as a prominent motif, remembered in terms which seem derived from the common, informal and conversational exchange of such memories rather than from any particular experience. Indeed, the elements of memory become combined with imagined settings, 'a sandy beach late at night'. To some extent, such generic consistency suggests self-positioning within quite general, and popularly disseminated, accounts of what the lived experience of youth should be:

> 'Wild World' by Maxi Priest . . . a big hit in Cyprus while I was on holiday there a few years ago. Everywhere I went it was playing – in the bars and clubs and blaring from loud stereos on the beach. It reminds me of the people I met there and the great times we had together. Everytime I hear the song now it makes me feel as though I am back there – I can close my eyes and dream myself in Cyprus. It is also a song which epitomises the season of Summer. It is of the reggae genre, fresh and mellow, something you can really imagine dancing to on a sandy beach late at night.

This, in common with several others,[13] while undoubtedly representing some actual experience, is also an appropriation of a public discourse, to be found in teenage magazines. By reconstructing memory through such discourse, the writer positions herself, in this context, as belonging to one popular but also particular construction of youth. Her choice of 'Lithium' (by Nirvana) is similarly located, both geographically and discursively, and introduces the trope of friendship:

> This song reminds me of my holiday in Newquay last year. It was after my GCSE's and I was there with my friend Nici. The clubs in Newquay were quite grungey in their style of music and this song, a grunge anthem, was the favourite being played everywhere and reminds me of the fun Nici and I had.

Other choices more emphatically represent the intersection of friendships with liminal experience and, again, the effect is to position the writer as a girl with friends, who has 'a good time'. To some extent, therefore, her account seems to sustain the kind of social identity which, through from earlier childhood, is of such intense and public importance in the lives of girls (see Hey, 1997; James, 1993) but does so, again, by appropriating the popular discourse of teenage magazines. Christina thus positions herself as more like other 'ordinary' girls and less the 'brainy' special case at this highly selective school. It may be that to write in the forms of popular teenage magazines is to seek 'normalization'. Valerie Hey has commented on this:

> For the middle class girls the working class girls 'abnormality' centred upon their 'excessive' heterosexuality – 'jailbait' as one of them told me. Hence working class girls according to this discourse were *over-feminized*. Conversely, working class girls viewed middle class girls as '*under-feminized*' because their 'brains' disqualified them from the feminine category altogether, and thus from claims upon the 'really important' and central markers of (hetero)sexual self-identity (Hey, 1995).

Less elaborately than in the more substantial assignments produced by the girls in Hackney, here several of the girls adopt a more muted claim to a sexuality which, in the terms observed by Hey, they are not supposed to possess. So, in explaining her choice of 'Gett Off' (by Prince) she writes:

> This song takes me back to the third year in senior school. My best friend at the time Cassie and I were very much into dancing and Prince. When Gett Off was released it was our dream come true – a dance track by Prince. We choreographed our own dance for it. Later on that year we went to see Prince perform at Earl's Court and this song was the highlight of the evening.

By choosing a notoriously sexually explicit song and, more generally, by adopting a discourse more broadly shared by other 'normal', sexual girls, a self-positioning resistant to the academic and non-sexual connotations of the school context is suggested. Similarly, in attaching a particular anecdote to 'Always' (by Bon Jovi), she introduces a statement of her position as someone's girlfriend:

> This is one of those songs which makes my spine tingle every time I hear it. It makes me think of my boyfriend Paul and has quite a romantic story behind it . . . A few days later he gave me the single of Always accompanied by a single red rose and it has been one of our songs ever since.

However, as I noted above, to both retain friendships with girls and to move on into distinctively new phases, and acquire new friends, is also an important feature of her self-representation. For example, her account of 'Alive' (by Pearl Jam) is strongly marked as relocating her beyond those earlier phases of adolescence similarly disowned by the girls in Hackney (see, particularly, Chapter 5). She writes:

> This song signalled a new era in my life. It reminds me of new friends and a new style. This was the beginning of my love for indie music . . . My taste changed from mainstream pop to indie, grunge, acid jazz. It also marked the beginning of a special friendship with a girl named Steph and it is a song we both adore.

Finally, her account of 'Live Forever' (by Oasis) is further evidence of the importance in this context of being someone who goes out and participates in the public life of youth:

> This is one of my favourite songs off one of the best albums I have ever heard. It reminds me of the Oasis concert which I went to just before Christmas. This was the song everyone was waiting for and when Oasis performed it the entire audience erupted into verse in unison. It was an amazing atmosphere and experience marking a brilliant concert.

Thus, in this account of an adolescence by no means confined to the bedroom, she further confirms her public identity as more than a clever and conscientious student.

Emily

As I have suggested, other girls offered accounts in which much the same repertoire of elements is combined in explaining the selection of tracks. For both boys and girls, the request had involved asking them to represent themselves by selecting material from a cultural domain which is already heavily constructed as sexual, as bodily and as affective. Many of the boys did choose to write about songs which they could assimilate to various discourses in which bodily and, sometimes, intensely emotive states were integral features (listening to death metal in one case, to the National Anthem in another). If a consistent difference between the girls' and the boys' self-positioning in relation to such a domain can be identified, it is evident in the tendency of the majority of the boys to rationalize the states they describe and thus to recover some distance from, and implicit control over, the experience they recall. The girls, though certainly also achieving distance through the act of writing itself, produced accounts in which self-positioning as emotional, sometimes as implicitly sexual, was not qualified by the more overt social and political recovery of emotion evident in, for example, the writing of David and Nicholas. Consistent with the argument that, here, middle-class girls lay claim to sexuality, it is also the case that they position themselves as 'emotional' and 'physically moved' in ways which, again, contradict the negative equation, in popular discourses, of academic success with emotional depletion.[14] For example, this account translates the common attribution of adolescent emotional volatility into its affirmation:

> Manic St. Preachers – 'Suicide is Painless' and Dame Kiri Te Kanawa – 'O My beloved father' – Both are 'mood' songs. MSP is more of when in a depressed mood to put the song on full volume and lie on your floor listening to the words is probably the most moving thing. Putting on Dame Kiri manages to make me so relaxed when in any mood. Especially in an incredibly angry and physically tensed time putting on this song, deep meaningful breathing and then moving your arms and then whole body to this song makes me feel so completely overcome with a 'happiness of rage' – hard to put into words . . . But one song that I do want to mention apart from the above [Nirvana – 'All Apologies'] has to be Janis Joplin 'Piece of my Heart' because she sings it with so much feeling that you are just speechless after it. It is such a drive around on a hot day with windows open and music on full blast type of song.

Among her other selections, which she explained more publicly in her self-presentation to the group (her writing appeared to be primarily rough notes for such a presentation), Emily, like Christina, cited music which could represent the formation of a 'best friendship' ['Bangles – Olivia + Me']. She thus claimed a social position for herself which, in its public visibility, has more importance for girls than for a majority of the boys. But, to reiterate, she did so by also demonstrating how at ease and how fluently self-confident she could be in front of almost 30 people in an educational setting. So, whatever the interests fulfilled by the choices she declared and the experiences to which she connected them, her position as an accomplished student was never compromised.

Conclusions

Bourdieu's incisive comment that the young 'allow themselves to be kept in the state of "youth", that is, irresponsibility, enjoying the freedom of irresponsible behaviour in return for renouncing responsibility' should not, as I argued above, be given a transhistorical status (Bourdieu, 1986: 478). Even the belief that youth is a phase of life which should be both pleasurable and memorable has a particular historical inflection, though some elements of such a discourse on youth are undoubtedly enduring. Here, it is important to recognize how such a discourse is taken up by particular young people and what purposes they achieve in articulating it in preference to other possible, and available, discourses. I have suggested that, in every case, multiple interests are served by their self-accounts. Within this group, different discourses are invoked – some allowing a rhetorical self-positioning as political, others claiming an expertise in the domain of music, and others giving priority to pleasure and emotionality. Some of the students combined elements of all of these tendencies. There is the potential in this to raise, with the students, questions around the meaning of adolescence and youth for them and to pursue, more explicitly, the political and historical context of their expectations. Such a priority in teaching might also inform further research.

A further important emphasis of this chapter has been upon the embedding of music in the domain of popular discourse and the need, therefore, to consider tastes in music as features of discourse rather than in terms of a more abstracted relationship between the formal characteristics of music and particular subjectivities. In this context, taste has been reviewed in terms of its tactical definition between situated social actors and thus as a complex rhetorical feature of self-positioning. I have argued, therefore, that the overdetermined enactment of social relations within specific educational contexts significantly complicates the more generalized classification of taste categories in relation to class affiliations for adolescents with access to a wide array of cultural forms.

To conclude, this chapter has shown, in reporting the findings of a more narrowly focused period of research at a selective school, that there are significant gender differences in the relation to popular music claimed by these students but that such gender differences are also strongly inflected by processes of class positioning within a context defined by high levels of educational achievement. In relation to the more extensive Hackney study, I have emphasized a contrast between students positioned as working-class and negotiating their imminent departure from school, and the students, in this chapter, whose futures have been provisionally resolved by embarking on the A Level route through post-compulsory education (see Frith, 1983, discussed in Chapter 1). The A Level students, advancing towards an educationally framed horizon, and alert to every opportunity to make cultural capital of their experience, took up my requests willingly. In this sense, they put so much of themselves into the *Desert Island Discs* project because they were accustomed to seeing that what they give would be, if not immediately and literally, returned with cultural and educational value inscribed upon it. It was in this phase of my research that the difficulty of drawing working-class students into school work on transient knowledge became, by contrast, more evidently a feature of their non-investment in the educated career trajectories pursued by the Edmonton students. To some extent, the difficulties reported in Chapters 4–6 were a feature of the research process (awkward, tentative, exploratory) and should not be used to justify *rigid* generalizations about what 'working-class kids' are like. Nevertheless, as I have argued, many of their responses were also symptomatic of the students' relative disengagement, *at the age of 15 and 16*, from 'plans of life' grounded in continuing full-time education.[15]

In the next chapter, I want to consider further how teaching about popular music might seek both to go beyond what students already know and to provide them with the means to reflect on the place of music in their social experience.

Notes

1 This is taken from the Hole/Courtney Love album, *Live Through This* (Geffen Records Inc., 1994: EFA 04935–2).

2 Year 12 in 1994–95 (a cohort born 1977–78); the Hackney students in Year 11 (1992–93) belong to the birth cohort of 1976–77 and are thus, on average, one year older than the students discussed in this chapter.

3 This long-running programme invites a celebrity to talk about her or his life and to anchor the account through a choice of six records. The style of interviewing has become, in recent years, quasi-therapeutic.

4 An important aspect of this was the need to define myself by *not owning* the records my older brother liked – thus no Rolling Stones, for example.

5 Speaking of his sister, Aretha Franklin, the Reverend Cecil Franklin describes the inter-subjective character of her performance:

> It's a combination of electricity and empathy. She generates the electricity, and the empathy comes with her being able not only to feel what all those people are experiencing but able to really experience the same things they are experiencing. You listen to her and it's just like being in church. She does with her voice exactly what a preacher does with his when he *moans* to a congregation. That moan strikes a responsive chord in the congregation and somebody answers you back with their own moan, which means I know what you're moaning about because I feel the same way. So you have something sort of like a thread spinning out and touching and tieing everybody together in a shared experience just like getting happy and shouting together in church (Sanders, 1971: 126).

6 See Connell, 'The black box of habit on the wings of history', in Connell (1983); Frow (1987); Mander (1987): 427–53; and Shiach (1993). For more recent developments in Bourdieu's theoretical work, see Bourdieu 1992, especially Chapters 2 and 11.

7 Both of the media teachers involved with the class (Pete Fraser and Nikki Blackborow) acted as key 'informants', providing me with specific contextual knowledge to which I would not otherwise have had access.

8 Harvey (1989): 292.

9 Some of the problems of trying to make formal connections between subjectivity and music are discussed in Shepherd and Giles-Davis, 'Music, text and subjectivity' in Middleton (1990); Shepherd (1991); Willis (1978).

10 Middleton suggests:

> We do not . . . choose our musical tastes freely; nor do they reflect our 'experi-
> ence' in any simple way. The involvement of subjects in particular musical
> pleasures has to be constructed; indeed, such construction is part and parcel of
> the production of subjectivity. In this process, subjects themselves – however
> 'decentred' – have a role to play (of recognition, assent, refusal, comparison,
> modification); but it is an *articulatory*, not a simplistically creative or responsive
> role. Subjects participate in an 'interpellative dialectic', and this takes specific
> forms in specific areas of cultural practice (1990: 249).

11   . . . in sociologies of youth . . . transition is seen as a one way process – the
> transition from school to work, or childhood to adulthood. Freud's concepts
> of regression, compulsion to repeat, and transference, show that model up for
> what it is, an example of retrospective wish fulfilment, a convenient adult
> myth. Psycho-analytical research properly requires us to abandon the notion
> of transition, in favour of the notion of transposition (Cohen, 1986: 33–4).

12 My nephew, also in Year 12 studying A levels, responded to my written request to him
with the following:

> Oasis – Supersonic . . . It means a lot to me because it reminds me of last
> summer which was the best time I've ever had – I'd just finished my
> exams . . . and I spent 4 months just dossing about with me mates, every day
> we would hang about in town, then play footy and then get pissed – I can't
> think of anything else I'd rather do . . . This song reminds me of that summer
> because on the last day before I started at college, a busload of me and about
> 15 mates all went to watch Oasis at the Hacienda in Manchester there was
> something very special about the whole thing – the band, the venue, the City,
> the time. I will remember it forever.

13 Carrie, for example:

> 'No Woman, No Cry' – Bob Marley. This was my holiday song for this year.
> I went on tour to Israel for three weeks. A lot of the time was spent travelling
> around by coach. We played this song a lot as its very soothing and mellow.
> Most of the time we were extremely tired and we were travelling long dis-
> tances at night. We played this song whilst looking at the stars etc and falling
> asleep travelling through the middle of the desert.

14 In *Just Seventeen*, for example, one problem page letter complained of a girl's problem
with her 'brainy' reputation. The advice (with some irony?) was to read school books
concealed inside a copy of the magazine.

15 See Lindley, R. (1989): 92.

Chapter 8

Endtroducing[1]

I began this book with Simon Frith's study of young people's musical tastes re-searched in Keighley in 1972. He argued then that the differences between the various youth groups lay mainly in their varied 'leisure needs and interests', adding that 'Keighley's youth culture patterns were an aspect of the town's social struc-ture, its relations of production' (Frith, 1983: 212). I have not attempted to replic-ate Frith's survey or to follow his wider, sociological, framing of the relationship between taste/musical knowledge and social structure (for recent work, see Frith, 1996). However, there are clearly ways in which his distinction between middle-class Sixth Formers, working-class school leavers and a somewhat defiant, 'hip elite' can be seen to correspond to the divisions I have mapped across just two schools in North London. There are strong similarities between the students in Edmonton and the Keighley Sixth Formers, between *some* of the students at the Hackney compre-hensive and the working-class group described by Frith. Equally, some of the students in Hackney (Margaret and Abby, for example) and some of those in Edmonton (David, perhaps), can be compared to the hip figures in Frith's account. To some extent, it is undeniable that aspects of the social configurations outlined by Frith have persisted through to the present, some 25 years later. However, my interest has involved a more detailed attention to how individual students have variously posi-tioned themselves in the contexts made available by the teaching of pop music in media studies. This has involved more emphasis on mobility between positions within both popular and educational discourses and, though I do not deny the importance of Frith's sketch of the political economy of leisure, I have thus qualified his emphasis on the determination of identity by social position. Furthermore, despite taking up Frith's initiative, my intention has been to open up possibilities for future practice in media teaching, rather than to do 'the sociology of youth'. In effect, I have attempted to shift the focus of interest from sociology to educational practice, attending more to forms of self-representation within classrooms, than to the youth cultures outside them. I have wanted to re-emphasize that schools are those places in which much that constitutes the informal culture of children and young people is formed and sustained, just because that is where they spend so much time together.

A central theme in my reading of the students' work on popular music has been that of young people positioned as adolescent within the social relations of schools, tactically claiming various kinds of power. Clearly, popular discourses of sexuality figured in the discursive tactics adopted by many of these students. Against the view that these are the natural expressions of adolescent development, I have argued that they are rather highly overdetermined modes of self-identification in a cultural and institutional context where age-relations are organized through a division between childhood, adolescence and adulthood and the power relations they entail. Schools are thus somewhat implicated in the formation of the identities they seek to proscribe. For both teachers and students, considerable effort might be constructively applied to identifying and questioning many of the routine assumptions about social and sexual identity made in that institutional context. To amplify the point, the attraction of work and sexuality, as discursive resources, is that they provide a repertoire for the assertion of non-child identities and thus, in effect, ways of claiming a degree of social power denied by their location as 'adolescents in school'. I do not want to endorse such claims to social power as simply expressive of youthful agency. They are more problematic. How might teaching pop music help teachers to engage with these complicated and emotional matters?

It is now quite commonplace to argue that making popular culture an object of study does not simply, or automatically, produce a radical transformation of the social relations of teaching and learning (Buckingham, 1990; Richards, 1992). To teach about popular music may be no exception. But the distinctive importance and difficulty of putting music in the media studies curriculum is that it thus intersects more sharply with the 'privatized and private domain' (see Hey 1997: 143–5). Teaching about pop, which sounds so banal, actually takes teaching into questions of intimacy and affectivity, questions to which the practice of media education needs a more considered response. In earlier chapters, I have referred to 'social self-understanding' as one of the purposes of media education (see Buckingham and Sefton-Green, 1994: 109). I think media education should provide a means for students to reflect on their location in both the microcultural relations of adolescence and the integrally connected discourses of popular (music) culture. In this respect, teaching about pop music should aim to enable students to become more reflexively aware of how their routes from adolescence into adulthood are negotiated, in part, through the repertoires of difference available in such music. These are big aspirations. It is worthwhile to pause at this point to consider one possible way in which they could be realized.

I want to suggest that networks between media teachers in a variety of schools should be used to enable the exchange and circulation of their students' various media productions. It would have been valuable, for example, for the Hackney and the Edmonton groups to read, and situate, each other's comments – and for other groups, similarly differentiated, to do so. The writing discussed in Chapters 6 and 7 or other comparable pieces in which students represented their current, and past, experiences of popular music, could well be used to open up a sense of contrast and dialogue between differently located students. Broad questions around the social differentiation of tastes and of music audiences might thus emerge in terms of the particular evidence provided by the students themselves. Moreover, in transforming such research data into teaching materials, it would be productive to also make available the comparison which has framed this book – those passages, and some of the students' own words, from Frith's Keighley survey (Frith, 1983). In this respect, studying the social differentiation of audiences would be given a more concrete and exploratory turn. But such a practice of exchange might also further the effort to enable students to understand how their own self-accounts are constructed, in part, through the discourses of the self which teenage magazines and popular music make available.

In common with Valerie Hey (1997), I want to draw attention to the language in which subjects position themselves, but I also want such attention to be encouraged among students:

> This study suggests the crucial importance of language and discourse as constructing 'permissible' places from which to speak. We urgently need to interrogate which forms of discourse create what sort of places and how these positions encode cultural and social powers for their speakers and forms of powerlessness for those silenced.
>
> Bakhtin's theorization of the dialogic nature of ideology can provide us with a way into understanding how 'direct, face-to-face, vocalized verbal communication between persons' "interanimates" the utterance of another'. Self-evidently the social relations of cultural hegemony and their contestation are implicated in the speech genres and discourses mobilized by girls (Hey, 1997: 137).

The students' own learning about the social forms in which subjectivity is articulated is one possible outcome of a reciprocal working practice in which teachers could exchange students' productions rather than only ever return them to the producers themselves, within the constraints of a single classroom. Of course, such proposals may seem more plausible to teachers in highly academic schools like that in Edmonton and, in practice, there would be serious questions to pose about how reciprocal such exchanges might be and where the evidence of significant learning would be judged to have occurred. But, just because my own research has involved a strong contrast between only two, very differently located, schools I would not want to turn away from implementing this development in practice. Furthermore, though I was not able to repeat the more productive tactic – the *Desert Island Discs* project – in the Hackney school, I hope other teachers take it up and explore its possibilities in a wider variety of settings than those I have been able to investigate.

Practical Work

I want to move on now to consider other possible developments in practice and to do so by introducing some further interview extracts, from Richard and from Alison, both English teachers in the Hackney school. It needs to be emphasized again that, unlike the students whose words form the main object of study in this book as a whole, the teachers represented here drew upon a repertoire of social and discursive resources which substantially overlapped with my own. Even so, their words are quoted in the elaboration of an argument which fulfils purposes with which they may not entirely identify. As I suggested in Chapter 3, I am here reinscribing their words and reinflecting their meanings and not in any simple sense giving them a voice in this text.

I want to begin with two comments from Alison (quoted earlier in Chapter 6) because they introduce the importance, and her own experience of constraints on, the more practical features of media teaching:

> Well if it was easier to do more practical work then I think practical work would be a good way in, y'know if it was easier to use videos and to use tape-recorders and so on, I mean our groups are very large and there's no technical help with equipment and so it's really, you've got to really psyche yourself up and be feeling very energetic and on top of things and you've got no space either side of the lessons to get anything ready so you don't do as much practical work as you could, given the sort of conditions you're working in . . . it's easier to do the cutting and pasting . . .
>
> Well, I don't know, I mean for one thing technology is more difficult now because the technology has improved so much and people are really used to listening to a high standard of stereo in their own homes now . . . having a tape-recorder like that [pointing to my very basic cassette recorder] in your classroom and trying to play a tape of music on it is just crap – nobody wants to hear music like that including myself. So I mean in the old days there would be a Dansette record player in the school and you'd bring your LPs in, you'd bring it on the record player and everybody would gather 'round and listen and it wasn't that, that much worse than what you had at home but now everybody's used to . . . Even in your car you've got a decent, a decent . . . y'know everybody's perception of what sounds reasonable is much, much more advanced so as there is such crap listening facilities in school, that's probably why I don't play much music . . . if I had better facilities to play it then . . . a stereo system somewhere, even in a bookable room, I would use it far more but you can't hear the words with these things . . . so there are reasons why I don't use it.

These are mundane, but important, complaints. I introduce them here because, in many respects, they recall the dissatisfaction recorded by several of the students (see Chapters 5 and 6). It is also important to remember Lucy Green's argument for an understanding of music as a fully social medium which should not, therefore, be regarded as always requiring translation into, or explanation by, the supposedly more social medium of verbal language. There is a need to explore modes of teaching, and of learning, which make the re-presentation of musical sound more central to their practice. As I have suggested, such a practice might well draw on the popular forms of musical selection, appropriation and juxtaposition evident in hip hop culture or the, sometimes closely related, forms of radio DJ manipulation and talk-over. But this is not a practice that can thrive without quite fundamental improvements in the provision of technologies and, perhaps, in the minimum definition of what constitutes an adequate classroom.

Here, to some extent, teachers and students *share* their frustrations and can have similar perceptions of what kinds of change, what new arrangements and what new practices might make a difference. Stephen was perhaps the most explicit when he drew attention to the limits of the classroom as a context for studying popular music and suggested, if tentatively, that a studio might be a more useful place in which to learn. I want to derive from Stephen's comment, and from Alison's negative view of the meagre resources and time constraints of the classroom lesson, a wider argument for the provision of settings in which students can be more than 'pupils' – with less of the subordination the latter term implies.

Workplaces, of which I take a television or sound recording studio to be one example, appear attractive because they offer 'work-identities' and thus a greater degree of power than that allowed to young people in school. The educational experiences which are possible within school classrooms tend to confine children to being pupils and adults to being teachers. But it is necessary to explore arrangements in which, still as students, learning can be achieved through forms of production (see Buckingham, Grahame, Sefton-Green, 1995). This might also imply a re-positioning of students as more than the risky and irresponsible adolescents which, at 14, 15 and 16, schools expect them to be. But it can also make teachers more than just experts in educationally framed knowledge, skilled only in the internal discourses of the school and its subjects. I think Richard, for example, recognized this, if also therefore wondering if the media studies GCSE could be brought more within the frame of his academic knowledge:

> . . . I had more anxiety actually about . . . the practical side of things . . . setting the practical tasks up and getting them done, the pacing of them and the . . . I mean I'm not terribly clever with my hands myself and I'm not that brilliant with cameras and things so I was more anxious about that . . . but that's perhaps a reflection of the nature of the course that there isn't that much up front teaching of say views of news you know, what news is and things of the media that sort of kind of more theoretical input which perhaps there ought to be . . .

Other teachers, with more extended experience in media education, and in less under-resourced schools, spoke of practical developments with more confidence. For example, doing 'studio work' need not entail a literal removal from the classroom setting for, clearly, the actual space of a classroom can be, if only partially and temporarily, both physically and discursively reconstructed. In Edmonton, the head of media studies, Pete Fraser, had contrived an arrangement which made it possible to redefine a classroom space in terms of a working television studio. The physical and technical organization of the space made possible the effort to enact, and improvise around, positions in working relationships which, concomitantly, demanded of everyone some degree of relocation within a discourse otherwise un-spoken in the classroom context. Forms of production involving the selection and representation (sampling and mixing) of recorded music would provide a similar basis for a discursive reconstruction of the classroom context. Processes of learning, often regarded as peculiarly dependent on the contexts provided by formal education, still need to be more fully recognized as also occurring in, and through, other contexts and the working relationships they allow (see Buckingham, Grahame and Sefton-Green, 1995; Fornas *et al.*, 1995).

Historical and Institutional Knowledge

In this section, I want to draw attention to Richard and Alison's perhaps most insist-ent suggestions for further development in teaching about music. The case they made, on separate occasions, was that the students lack an adequate knowledge of the history of popular music and that their knowledge is selectively skewed by omissions in the popular representation of that history. Richard commented:

> . . . the contribution that black musicians have made y'know which is often not, they don't know about . . . I think some of that might be interesting, a kind of straightforward historical kind of input . . . not least because I know bugger all about popular modern music . . . I felt very alien somehow

and,

> . . . I think I'd want to address the idea of . . . a selective history of what gets left out of account . . . I mean it's interesting that a current advert's . . . a lot of people, my little son who's 9, for Christmas wanted tapes of, wanted a Beethoven tape, blues and jazz tapes and this seems to have been because, is it Budweiser? have been using, is it John Lee Hooker? and the Heineken one . . . his little friend has picked this up because his dad is into it, so it's actually become a recognized category for him and the two of them had exactly the same independently made up, the two had the same Christmas shopping lists and y'know we then bought him a, a ghetto blaster which he wasn't expecting at all and he actually does sit there listening to jazz or y'know Muddy Waters and he really seems to enjoy it . . . which abso-lutely left me gobsmacked y'know but he really seems to like it . . .

The concern here is partly that the reappropriation of black music by the media, and particularly by advertising, is compromised, creating some awareness and enthusi-asm for the music, but without acknowledging the larger context of its production or the longevity of the musical traditions from which such tiny fragments are taken. There is also, perhaps, an implicit anxiety that if these fragments are the sources of new identifications for young people then such identities might be as circumscribed and as disembodied as the material on which they draw (see Lipsitz, 1990). This is an important argument, pointing to the development and learning of larger contexts, both historical and institutional, for the fragmented and somewhat disparate knowledge of the students.

The difficulty here is that doing the 'straightforward history' of popular music will tend to reaffirm that school knowledge, and the knowledge teachers feel comfortable with, is at some distance from the currency of music in the 'private and privatized domain' of adolescent life. Steve Archer, writing recently in *The English and Media Magazine*, reported this in his account of teaching pop in GCSE media studies:

> Pupils seemed to have little knowledge of pop history, and indeed regarded all the extracts of music I played to them as just that . . . examples of history. The use of the term 'history' in this case implies their disapproval that a supposedly pleasurable subject was centred on texts that had no relevance or interest for them.
>
> As far as the Year 11 class were concerned, they were fans of a particularly new music, and much of their identity was defined in comparison with other, *debased* forms. This debasement focused on the music that adults such as myself were characterised as appreciating. I felt that music was a vital thing for them, the very substance of their identity was built on it, especially the jungle fans, one of whom would only listen to a particular 'pure' form . . . The fact is that music from the past – even the recent past – cannot reproduce the quality of sound and sheer volume and speed of composition that both jungle and hardcore can summon up. Perhaps it comes back to the nature of sound textures; youth *specifically* can still be addressed by the substance of noise, a substance that proclaims itself to be new, exciting and for them (Archer, 1996: 42, italics in original).

Alison identified very similar problems, despite her advocacy of both strongly historical and institutional versions of 'knowledge about music'. Like Richard, she seemed to want to circumvent the artifice of selves seemingly made through engagement with the media, but she was also, elsewhere, keen to emphasize the strength of affective commitment:

> . . . the other thing is that kids feel uncomfortable about being construed as audiences so when you're sort of teaching genre and marketing and 'how is this music reaching its audience' and you know 'you have been told . . . sucker, come and spend your money on this because you're black or because you're female or whatever', they feel very uncomfortable about that and they sort of say 'no that's not true I buy it because I like it, it's nothing to do with that' and yet how come you've got your black kids who're only into some kind of sub-sub-culture of American black music that is not distributed by any mainstream, which you would not be able to

hear about or even know about unless you knew a black person who could actually tell you about it and where to get it and stuff because it's so sort of minority that it's under under-ground and yet they're saying 'well y'know 'cause I like it, I'm not targeted', you know, it's . . . how do you teach that sort of thing?

As I've argued, it is through popular music that adolescents claim some degree of distinctive social and affective space, and a degree of power in and through that space. As Alison suggests, and as my discussions in Chapters 4 and 5 confirmed, they do not want to be positioned by others, explained as members of marketing categories. Unfortunately, a critical discourse representing every choice in popular music as manipulated and determined, or as coming out of a history about which the teacher knows (or claims to) and the class does not, looks likely to take us back to those problems and to the arguments with which I began in Chapter 1. But I do not think that media teachers should forget history, or drop efforts to teach about the 'industry'.

In teaching about pop music, there is necessarily a struggle to achieve several purposes simultaneously. Such teaching has to work with the kind of assertive self-positionings reported by Archer, identified in my own research, and acknowledged by Richard and Alison. The emphasis on practical activities and forms of production, is significant just because it recognizes the need to enable young people to use their own cultural experience in engaging with processes structured and supported by teachers (see Buckingham, Grahame and Sefton-Green, 1995). Without succumbing to excessively gloomy warnings of manipulation by the media industries or exclusively historical retrospectives, it is essential to recognize that the forms of knowledge which both Richard and Alison invoke are fundamental to media education. Historical and institutional perspectives on pop music should be integral to the development of a *social* self-understanding. But to keep alive the sense of immediate and emotive microcultural meanings in the opening of dialogues around music may well depend on teachers being painfully explicit about their own musical knowledge, history and taste. Archer ends his article with this:

Perhaps my students resisted knowledge about music itself for the same reasons they might resist French New Wave Cinema. This ignorance may be compounded by the approach of the Music teaching in the school which generally ignores pop music in favour of folk forms from around the world and classical music.[2] Perhaps a closer relationship between Music and Media Studies could produce a better model for encouraging creativity, fandom and knowledge. As it is, I ended up teaching much more about what *surrounds* pop music – the discourses on image, style and promotion – rather than the substance itself.[3] My own contempt for artists such as Bon Jovi makes it hard for me as an educator to positively teach about him, just as in English, I could never teach books I personally dislike.

This leads me to the final challenge: owning up to my own fandom. If I can have the courage to admit to my interests in music at the beginning of the unit of work, then perhaps a more open and flexible attitude to learning about music will develop. By exposing my own fandom, by making what I like and value explicit, I can provide an immediate model for a discourse about music. All these challenges face me the next time I teach pop music. I look forward once again to the chance to encourage a meaningful fusion of fan creativity and critical value . . . the evolution of a stringent pop music criticism in the classroom (Archer, 1996: 44).

Who we are, as teachers, and where we are located culturally, becomes more uncertain, and more open to our students' questions, in moving out of the apparent security, and bounded discipline, of English and into media studies. In fact, in the recent controversies around the National Curriculum, and in rapidly changing cultural circumstances, that supposedly stable identity – an English teacher – is itself suffering, but also sometimes thriving upon, a protracted crisis in which it is difficult to reclaim singular or pre-defined identities. The advantage of this, for teaching about pop music, is that the need to more directly represent our cultural positions to our students is less the isolated anomaly that it once was. Perhaps, then, we are now a part of a more widely recognized sense of crisis around cultural legitimacy in the school curriculum.

Conclusions 1

In *Changing the Future* (1991), it is argued that a future curriculum:

> . . . would aim to move between – on the one hand – issues arising from the lives of learners and – on the other – the general relationships which structured those issues and those lives. Likewise, it would move between everyday common sense and formally-organized conceptual systems. It would not centre itself on a universalism that concealed the presence of specific social interests; nor would it limit itself to a 'curriculum of everyday life', confined to the local and particular (Chitty, 1991: 85).

I want to review and reassess the classroom research represented in earlier chapters in the light of this formulation. In my initial enquiries, there was a marked tendency to make a priority of eliciting the 'local and particular'. However, even in the discussions reviewed in both Chapters 4 and 5, there were within the mix of anecdote, evasion and tactical self-positioning, connections with larger debates. As a teacher, I would want to make explicit and extend those debates. Out of the discussions in Chapter 4, there was plenty of scope to explore family histories, migrations, and the partially overlapping experience of transnational cultural networks (see Lipsitz, 1994). Within that framework, and not excluding our own explicit involvement here as teachers, there would be some value in considering how such particular histories locate and differentiate us in relation to the marketing of music. Here too, the polarity of the authentic versus inauthentic (see McRobbie, 1994: 174), or of the immediate and the debased (Archer, 1996), could be anchored concretely in terms of lived social relations, both familial and more widely inter-generational. References to parents' collections of music, and to their tastes, which I did not follow up in any detail, would allow a productive movement back and forth from the immediacy of student interests to more broadly historical matters. The dynamics of Alan's aesthetic 'conservatism' (see Chapter 4) was just one intriguing starting point. The domestic context itself, its physical organization and the technologies it contains could become a focus for further investigation. Recalling Margaret's account, it is not difficult to see that students might well find representing the internal divisions of household space, its social uses, and the intricacy of intra-familial negotiations of both tastes in and access to music, a matter of compelling interest. Starting from diagrams, drawings, maps of the domestic, it would be possible to move into questions of gender and age relations, of tactics of unification and separation (see Bourdieu, 1997; Moores, 1993; Silverstone, 1994; Silverstone and Hirsch, 1992). These could be complemented by getting students to chart both sibling relations and friendship networks, building a knowledge of the flows of musical interest and taste on that basis. Thinking more of tactics of individuation, there is scope here as well to encourage some documenting and reflection on habits of collection and use in relation to tapes and CDs and records (see Harvey, 1989; Middleton and Edwards, 1990). How and why do collections (or 'pile-ups' as a recent student of mine called them) get made?

In autobiographical mode, I might well want to talk about *buying*, at 15, Memphis Slim and John Lee Hooker LPs, while listening to (but not buying) Motown and soul on pirate radio. What did this mean in the youth cultural divisions of 1967? What consequences did it have? Why did I subsequently sell both LPs, only to replace them years later? Why did I let my brother take my copy of *Blues Breakers* (John Mayall) when he left home? Why did I not go to see Jimi Hendrix in Hull when I had the chance? I am not going into the answers to these questions here but, just to make it clear that the issues are not just idiosyncratic and personal (which of course they are), I can explain that, in 1967, Memphis Slim, rather than Motown, meant choosing folk authenticity against commercial debasement. Beginning to collect old blues records, starting an archive, must have seemed a better investment than a party stained Motown (dance) compilation. Of course, buying Memphis Slim was also a (gendered) act, privileging the masculinity of blues against the effeminacy of Motown and its (mod) followers. It didn't work. The superiority of my record collection seemed meaningless to the girl I was trying to impress. And of course, there are writers whose fictional handling of these issues could usefully complement accounts worked up by teachers and by students. Nick Hornby's (1995) novel, *High Fidelity* would be a good place to look.[4] Questions of gender and sexuality variously explored by the students in Chapters 5, 6 and 7 are well interwoven with matters of musical taste throughout Hornby's extremely funny story of anguished masculinity in North London.

Whatever my misgivings about always anchoring classroom practice in writing, I think a wide ranging search for varieties of writing about socially embedded musical experience ought to be a priority for media teachers. Steve Archer, critically review-ing his own efforts, suggests that he devoted too little time to:

> . . . helping them to develop an adequate language to express their indi-vidual concerns. My biggest mistake was in largely ignoring the wealth of pop writing styles that already exist in magazines such as *Smash Hits* and *Melody Maker* . . . (Archer, 1996: 44).

In Chapter 5, and elsewhere, I have placed some emphasis on the limitations of current talk about music, and the need for other ways of representing musical experi-ence. Of course, there is a case for a more formally organized conceptual system in the discussion and teaching of music (Green 1988, 1997; McClary, 1991). But for students, or for ourselves as media teachers, struggling to engage in talk about music, with those for whom it is an immediate, transient and everyday medium, these formal vocabularies are very unlikely to offer attractive places to begin. However desirable a language of formal description may be, there is a sense in which music is always already replete with social meanings and these cannot easily be bracketed out. A language of description has to be attentive to the social produc-tion of particular music forms (see Goodwin, 1993) and the diverse meanings produced in their contexts of reception and use. Writing which is ethnographic (see Geertz, 1973, on 'thick description'), or which may be journalistic or fictional, and represents music's social currency is likely to be an essential resource. To some extent, *Desert Island Discs* and other radio talk shows also provide, as was evident in Chapter 7, productive models for exploring more individuated features of musical experience. But, in all of this, I am sure that writing which also invites laughter, like *High Fidelity*, is essential to encourage talk about pop music. In classrooms, such talk can be stifled by just a bit too much gravity, by both the 'seriousness' and the 'classical' tastes commonly attributed to teachers by their students.

Conclusions 2

The approach to teaching about pop music suggested here is one which takes up a discourse of education as change and innovation. But I want to emphasize that teachers really do need to put themselves within that discourse, placing themselves along with their students, rather than always and only seeing themselves (ourselves) as the agency of change in others. Looking back over the research for this book, some of it carried out almost five years ago, I want to emphasize how differently I would do it now. Most obviously, listening to music and taking more risks with forms of representing musical experience would be a priority. As a teacher, if not as a researcher, I would also, in common with Archer, be much more upfront about my own sense of musical location and the complexities of both long past and continuing experience. Moreover, as I suggested earlier in this chapter, media education and especially teaching about pop music, can move teachers into a more radically un-settled curricular space than that previously provided by most English teaching. The struggle to conceive of a more flexible practice, attentive to the forms and the detail of the emergent and disparate cultures in which school students locate themselves can thus demand innovation.

The effort of teaching and of sustaining the discursive coherence and credibility of media education involves teachers in some work on themselves, drawing on experi-ences of change and possibility in the past, but also necessarily rethinking the more settled features of their own formation as, often initially, teachers of English. To some extent, new forms of teacher identity are achieved in this process.[5] Ken Jones, in a discussion of the 1993 boycott of testing (Jones, 1994: 84–110), has argued that those events, in which the teachers interviewed here also participated, can be interpreted in terms of a social movement in which new kinds of teacher identity were created. My own view is that, within the larger political context of English teaching, media education has continued to suggest other kinds of practice, both potential and actual. Media education has been a discursive resource for teachers, enabling them to redefine what they might be and might achieve. Of course, this has not just been a peculiarity of the recent past but, as Jones argues:

> . . . the categories employed by a collective agent are not all provided for it by the central struggle in which it is involved: agents are formed by their participation – usually, over a number of years – in a multi-discursive, multi-conflictual context. It is this many-sided engagement which supplies agents with the material from which to construct complex and effective discourses (Jones, 1994: 101).

Both Richard and Alison have histories which confirm this observation.[6] Like myself, they were in their early 40s at the time of the research, and thus shared, biographic-ally, adolescence in the 1960s and entry into teaching in the 1970s. But the present circumstances were not simply read from within fixed 'symbolic moulds' (Willis *et al.*, 1990) formed in earlier decades of educational politics. Of course, traces of such politics have informed the broader concerns of these teachers. But the effort has been to sustain the social purposes of education within contexts shaped by both the unfamiliar cultural worlds of the students and, less welcome, by the disorgan-ization of Conservative educational policy in the early 1990s. It is important to stress that, even in the midst of the more urgent conduct of the boycott, the *effort* of making media education more attentive to the forms of popular culture it has tended to neglect – pop music in this case – was also a kind of struggle against the strictures of Conservative educational policy.

To reiterate, my argument is for a more determined engagement with the detail of microcultural meanings through the practice of teaching about pop music. But it is also, necessarily, for movement beyond the more bounded forms of iden-tity within the professional domain of English teaching, in which media studies has been anchored. The question of what kind of teacher to be – and of what kinds of knowledge to recognize and develop in dialogues with students – remains a live issue.

Notes

1   I have taken this title from DJ Shadow (J. Davis) *Endtroducing* – Mo Wax Recordings, A&M Records Ltd. London, MW059CD, released 1996.

2   See my review of music education Chapter 1.

3   See Green, 1988 and my review of her work in Chapter 1.

4   As I was finishing this chapter (April 1997), I heard him remark (BBC Radio 4) that the trouble with psychoanalysts is that they don't seem to know about popular culture so you spend 23 minutes out of 45 explaining who Aretha Franklin is!

5   However, see Bernstein, 'On the classification and framing of educational knowledge', for a seminal essay which mixes advocacy and warning: '. . . deep-felt resistances are called out by the issue of change in educational codes' (1973: 249).

6   Nikki Blackborow and Pete Fraser, in Edmonton, belong to a somewhat younger generation: Nikki was born in the mid-1960s, Pete a few years earlier.

Teachers, Research and Popular Culture

It was by working with teachers that I did the research for this book. In this post-script, I want to address the issue of how the practices of teaching and research might be more effectively connected. The polarity of academic discourse and popular culture is one strand in this: as I suggested in Chapter 1 (see, especially, 'Putting Cultural Studies in Its Place?') I can share a little of the suspicion with which teachers might meet the theoretical contemplation of the everyday. Their misgivings are grounded in the conditions of their working lives and the sense of routine familiarity surrounding what, in my research, was selected out as of special interest. To engage the perspectives of teachers, placed somewhat between academic researchers and the students themselves, highlights the issue of what research is for and what outcomes it might be intended to have, and for whom. A variety of perhaps divergent interpretations of what is happening may become established in the process of a school-based research project. One problem, then, is that of how some reciprocally agreed purposes might be recognized and achieved.

My own position, in teacher education, has sustained a sense of disjunction between educational domains. Specifically, I have been made continuously aware of the contrast between the research anxious demands of higher education and school teachers' need to make lessons work – to give priority to teaching that feels credible and looks successful. There has been some tension between my priorities and those of teachers: *research* has become a necessary element in the construction of an academic future, accompanied by a sense of urgency and demand, and sometimes impatience at the other priorities of those whose working lives are not governed by a sense of individual distinction as a voice with a name. I want to acknowledge, therefore, the different expectations which intersect in research. For teachers it is a matter of what the research is for and how it might make a difference to what they do; for academics it also has a place in a projected career. To get beyond this recognition, I want to consider the terms on which more common purposes might be negotiated. I want to ask how a common understanding of research, and particularly research into popular culture, might be negotiated between teachers and researchers.

There is only space to consider one interview here. I have conducted several others and have drawn on one other, with Richard, in Chapters 4 and 8. I have chosen not to introduce an interview with one of the Edmonton media teachers,

Nikki Blackborow, in this context, because it represents a somewhat exceptional instance. That interview, along with several others, will be discussed in a further publication.[1] Here, the interview, with Alison, represents issues which are not entirely peculiar to just one individual but arose as critical moments in the context of educational politics in 1993–94. I have selected it to illustrate the institutional and occupational disjunctions which arise in seeking to connect research with teaching and to suggest some of the problems which many teachers face in their everyday practice.

To establish a way of reading the interview it is useful to recall C. Wright Mills' stress on the importance of biography, history and structure (Mills, 1959). His discussion of what might constitute an adequate understanding of 'the life of an individual' suggests the historically variable terms in which people might explain their own lives (Mills, 1959: 162). In discussing the interview here I am necessarily working with a kind of evidence which is both complex and partial: it is one kind of account and needs to be considered in terms of its 'vocabularies of motive' and its location within a biography lived out in particular institutional and historical circumstances.

The interview took place in school, early in February 1994. In representing the interview I have selected those moments which illustrate broader institutional relations and constraints rather than the biographical axis. Nevertheless, a part of my purpose was to recover something of the teacher's relation to her own schooling and, tentatively, to connect this with her location and practice as a teacher in the present. Like myself, and several of the other teachers I talked to, she could recall some degree of ambivalence about her own schooling and some uncertainty about why she had become a teacher. It is suggestive of a distinctive history – that of the relation between the traditional culture of schools and the emergence of post-war popular culture, and, within that, of some degree of diversification in the routes into becoming a teacher:

> *CR*: When did you actually first start to think about becoming a teacher? . . . when you were knee high, don't tell me!
>
> *Alison*: No, no . . . it was the last thing I ever thought about doing 'cause I was really very naughty at school . . . I was a really disruptive pupil.
>
> *CR*: Really, which school were you at?
>
> *Alison*: Henrietta Barnett
>
> *CR*: Oh I didn't think they had naughty girls there
>
> *Alison*: I was very naughty. I was always in trouble, constantly outside the headmistress's office . . . I was a real . . . when I went back to a sort of reunion they said, they were very surprised, they said I was the last person in the world who would become a teacher . . . I think it was by default. I just left university and I didn't know what else to do.
>
> *CR*: So how did you think about your future when you were at school – what did you reckon you'd do? . . . perhaps you didn't think about . . .

Alison: I had no ambition . . . you know I was a typical sort of casualty of being a girl in the 60s, in that sort of everybody always said that you know there were so many opportunities . . . and I had a total lack of ambition which I still suffer from a bit, I never wanted to do anything.
[brief section omitted]

Alison: I didn't want to do anything, I wanted to be a writer . . . from when I was about eight but I don't know what really put me off or why I didn't really try to be a writer.

This could be read as personal memory; in one sense, all of this is true. But it is also a particular kind of explanation which is familiar and which I and other teachers, with similar conviction, would offer in response to the question. There are here particular discursive motifs: the 1960s, the disruptive pupil, lack of ambition, wanting to be a writer. This is one 'vocabulary of motive' which has wide popular currency. It is a vocabulary which forms the retrospective understanding of a period and of how lives were shaped through that coincidence of being at secondary school in the 60s. Many other kinds of explanation might be brought into play, varying with context, addressee and purpose, and without denying the credibility of that offered here. In some settings, I might explain my own entry into teaching, and that of some others, as the outcome of a combination of class and familial circumstances with the provision of extended state education, in a period of high employment and material confidence, circumstances which made possible an indifference to, and distance from, work as a main reality of adult life. Becoming a teacher, though never consciously intended and perhaps unwillingly chosen, is, in this view, one way to exchange cultural capital, accumulated through a relatively lengthy education, for the means to an adult life sufficiently independent of family and reasonably immune to any serious economic hardship. But there is a sense in which both explanations serve a similar purpose in positioning the self as teacher for they minimize responsibility, intention and aspiration. Therefore being a teacher, acquiring that work identity, is represented more as a *position* within an institutional domain than as the attainment of an earlier identification projected into an adult future. I know that either explanation outlined here, however convinced I am of their truth, does not exhaust the many other additional, not alternative, explanations I could offer. What matters here is what explanation was offered at that time and in that context, and how such an explanation positions her in relation to her teaching.

There is evidence that some of those who take up positions in media teaching have histories of ambivalence towards their own schooling.[2] Many who now work as teachers have, as adolescents, lived through the conflict between their involvement in popular cultural forms and the demands of a traditional school curriculum. Not imagining their futures in conformity with the social and cultural aspirations such a curriculum assumed, they have tended, as adults, to take up positions where the obligation to transmit traditional culture has not been enforced: in schools with a substantial working-class composition and in areas of the curriculum where cultural orthodoxy could be refused (see Kuhn, 1995: 98–103). In doing the research for this book, I found that teachers positioned in this way have been most likely to engage with, and to make sense of, my intentions.

Alison presents quite sharply contrasting accounts of her own teaching at various points in the past 20 years. There are two key instances in which, in very different ways, she explored innovations in her teaching. The first is from very early in her career:

> *Alison*: ... now when I first taught English in '74, it was very creative writing orientated and I was a sort of ... a bit of a hippy, although we never called ourselves hippies at the time ... we were just dope freaks I suppose, who liked all the music that was around, you know Hendrix and everything else, what our generation grew up listening to. And all I could do with some of the classes I had was sort of play them my records and sort of study song lyrics ... I used to sort of play them a lot of Bob Dylan songs and make them listen to the words and ... I can remember teaching a kid to read off the cover of *Quadrophenia*, Bell Boy, 'carry the bleedin packages up' – do you know that album? And in fact I even wrote to Pete Townshend and told him that, and I even got a reply from him which I think I've still got, about how I taught this kid to read from the cover of his album. You know, we just used to listen to the records, the words, and actually I mean there are kids that teach themselves to read like that using *Smash Hits* or something ... they've just discovered that that's a good way to learn, you know, spelling and things ... they listen to the songs on the radio and they wait for the words to come out in *Smash Hits* and then they see, they learn how to spell them all, you know, it's a very, it's a good way [of] helping kids who aren't motivated to read, so I discovered that very early on ... that was nothing to do with teaching media studies ...

The terms in which these lessons are recalled, then connected with the present, are those of an English teaching struggling to define itself in the public domain and defensive of its practices. Creative writing is not claimed and argued for but is rather distanced as belonging to an entirely different time when, for no explicit reason, that was what English teachers did. The use of pop music is represented as a device to facilitate basic literacy, to motivate the illiterate then (at Moulsecoomb, in Brighton, on a council estate with a factory) and in the present, in Hackney. It is striking that no defence is made of her introduction of music in the 1970s in terms of ideological content and that no argument is made for making the classroom a context in which the students' popular culture can be valued; both arguments could draw upon long familiar discourses within English teaching but here that does not happen, despite the particular description of practices which such discourses form and legitimate. I am not suggesting that this is an inadequacy in Alison's understanding of her own work but that it is consistent with the difficulty which English teachers have in representing what they do to others, in the public domain (Jones, K., 1992). The interview took place at a time when the political meanings of English teaching had rarely been more visibly contested and when, despite some considerable successes for English teachers, there were continuing uncertainties.

The second instance is one which is introduced quite specifically as authorized by experts from beyond the school:

Alison: I don't really know how I got interested, but I went on the one year course [media studies] that Jenny Grahame used to do with Chris Mottershead, it was after school every evening, I . . . did it to develop my career I suppose . . . [section omitted] . . . I actually got an au pair girl so, just to facilitate me doing that course but, but I really liked the course . . . [section omitted] . . . it certainly changed the way that, it really sharpened up my own viewing of the media, definitely, it gave me a very different perspective, it's made it sort of really made me realize how much a part of my life it was and sort of . . . it made it much more enjoyable.

Later in the interview, she offered this outline of what she does in teaching music within media studies:

CR: . . . it may be good fun but why bother allocating . . . time to it?
Alison: . . . what I do think is useful is to make them aware of it in terms of an industry . . . I think that's useful . . . to make them aware of it in terms of an industry, that everything's thought about, that everything's calculated, that everything's planned, it didn't just happen like that, that all the designs . . . So I think it's, it's interesting to make them think of the end product as part of a package that has been designed and constructed to promote this kind of music with this kind of audience in mind. I think it's helpful for them to have that kind of awareness and sharpen up their perceptions a bit, of what's happening on popular television when they see music on TV . . . it's a kind of sadder but wiser sort of thing because it's very nice to be naive and to sort of not know all that stuff but that's the real world. Then I also think it's good for them to think a bit about the decisions that people make when they design covers or posters and I think it's good for them to think of it as an industry and know all the different kinds of jobs that there are in it so if they're interested they can actually think about it in terms of their possible career because it's not an industry that's suffered a lot from the recession that I can see and there are obviously a lot of openings in all that . . . so partly you can encourage people to go on and study media in further education as well . . .

The contrast here is clear: from the outline of a minimal literacy in her account of popular music within English, she moves to the presentation of a media studies discourse which proposes the 'demystified, critical, subject' as a projected outcome. Here, a perspective in which 'naive' consumers are positioned by an overwhelmingly manipulative industry enables a construction of teaching as revelation – the real processes which lie behind the products offered for consumption are known through forms of knowledge which teachers can provide for their students (see Buckingham, 1986; Eagleton, 1983; Leavis and Thompson, 1933; Masterman, 1985; Mulhern, 1979). This is an important and powerful discourse and it is one which, with a variety of political inflections, has been crucial to the credibility of media studies. It connects with arguments for the role of education in the formation of citizens in a democracy and both assumes and extends a belief in the priority and value of rational analysis of what is represented as the fundamental layer of reality – industry, and thus the economic. But the account here is also wary of counter-argument: if the notion of the critical citizen is challenged by a vocationalist demand for some plausible role in training for jobs, then, by still turning the argument around the pivotal term *industry*, such a challenge can be met by showing that this approach is also a way of connecting schooling with work and with particular occupational destinations.

Given my not entirely hypothetical anxiety – to justify the time devoted to media studies on grounds other than mere fun – this is exactly the kind of public statement which any teacher concerned with media studies has to be prepared to offer. It is not, however, an account which engages in the degree of doubt, speculation and tentative explanation which those concerned to further research, from outside teaching, find productive of the appropriate academic discourse. From my position, therefore, the response, though I asked for it, is disappointing – it does not translate easily into my concern with informal knowledge and the agency of consumers in forming their own cultural domains, always somewhat at odds with the undoubted power of media industries to profit from popular culture (see de Certeau, 1984; Fiske, 1989b; Jenkins, 1992: 26; and Willis *et al.*, 1990).[3] Nor, indeed, is the sense in which knowledge might be so relativized as to be destructive of teachers' authority recognized and engaged here; the possibility of such a displacement of teacher expertise is not easily made a part of most teachers' everyday working concerns. To establish a shared basis for research when teachers are institutionally positioned as 'bearers of knowledge' and researchers as entitled to produce questions, is, as I have argued, necessarily a struggle.

To some extent, research can be conducted on the basis of collaboration with a teacher, or teachers, whose projected career path is orientated towards the concerns of higher education and who may already be a participant in a particular research culture; this is a model promoted with much success by David Buckingham and is exemplified in his work with Julian Sefton-Green (1994). Indeed, in schools to be seen to have an interest in research is to imply a wish to leave, to project a future of work other than in classrooms; the consequence is that such an interest repositions the teacher in relation to the school and the people with whom she or he works. In my discussion with Alison, I found the word 'research' difficult to speak without hesitation; I felt that it was not likely to be construed as having much to do with the work of classroom teaching and would be unequivocally an assertion of my interest, and perhaps somewhat to the disadvantage of the teacher. It is in this that questions of time, of power, and of outcomes are critical, and might therefore be given more consideration in the pursuit of *collaborative* action research projects. As I suggested in Chapter 3, I locate my own enquiries within *action research* but collaboration does involve tensions between differently situated participants. Moreover, in media education, where there is no tradition of classroom research comparable to that in English, the precedents are not obvious and, as yet, still relatively unfamiliar to the wider body of English (and media) teachers.

Continuing with the interview, and still pursuing my wish to make a curiosity about the everyday musical culture of school students central, I asked:

> *CR*: ... what kinds of things do you feel as if you need to know more about in relation to their music or the teaching of music?
>
> *Alison*: Well it's not so much that I need to know more about ... I think the big thing that I lack is planning time, it's time to actually think things through, preferably with another person, to actually plan things properly ... I mean, I read everything that's written in the papers about the media, I read enough to sort of keep me informed reasonably well ...

and, again:

> *CR*: Right, so how would you make use of another person, if you had somebody else working with you, preparing stuff on music?
>
> *Alison*: Well, to sort of plan, sit down and plan, units and make proper worksheets, use sort of more, you know, make worksheets with illustrations on them, or some sort of factual research on anything ... just thinking on my feet all the time ...

Alison's comments evoke an urgency and restlessness which certainly connected with my own experience of teaching, but were also more particular allusions to the working conditions imposed in the early 1990s. However, such conditions are also represented through a discourse of teaching which is pragmatic but also, typically, apologetic: a way of understating what is achieved, and of minimizing the knowledge and experience on which those achievements depend, appears to have an enduring place in teachers' repertoires of self-representation. Of course, Alison does identify real needs but, at the same time, anything more than a teacher identity, defined within the pragmatic limits of the presently constituted job, is somehow disallowed. The material and institutional differences between schools and universities do much to restrict an expanded conception of the teacher's identity and practice but I also want to suggest that there is no secure discourse in which to speak of a composite *teacher-as-researcher* or *researcher-as-teacher* identity. To speak of research, as a teacher in a school is, as I have suggested, to indicate a future elsewhere; to be a teacher, unless framed and circumscribed by a research project, is, for an academic, to lose status – the right to professional visibility. Of course, a discourse does not bring about, of itself, the material infrastructure and the institutional relations through which to constitute newly productive identities. It is only in combination with the development of sustained intellectual contact – through meetings, reciprocal visits, shared reading and discussion – that it is possible to work with a common discourse and to argue for an identity otherwise denied by the intensification of the discursive separation between academics and teachers.

Time, and its differential allocation within hierarchically separated working practices, is among the most substantial of material constraints on the development of joint research. Indeed, time became an ever more elaborated motif in the latter part of the interview.

> *CR*: . . . do you feel as if it's got a lot worse, that the style of teaching you'd like to do is actually being squeezed more and more?
>
> *Alison*: Oh I think it has, oh definitely yes, I mean there used to be provision for having collaborative learning, they used to put two teachers in together and they used to plan it a bit better in my old school . . . [section omitted] . . . this head has come in and he's looked at all the time-tables and 'oh you're not teaching enough, you're not teaching up to your full quota . . . We must have collaborative learning, we must have differentiated work, we must (you know) have equal access to the whole curriculum for everybody, you're not teaching enough!' you know, and so they're just sort of filling up all your free periods even more, I mean I can't find any time to have meetings, I've lost all my frees this week one way or another, I now don't have any free periods doesn't matter about this one, I don't have any anyway.

A little earlier she remarked that 'collaborative learning is not just making kids learn in groups, it's actually teachers collaborating and it actually has resourcing implications like planning time . . . it's a whole ethos, it's a whole way of working.' In this inflection of a theme seemingly imposed from above, there is precisely a kind of discursive innovation in play. Indeed, the multiaccentuality (Volosinov, 1973) of collaboration is turned somewhat against managerial efforts to secure a singular meaning. The shift to teacher collaboration, and the demand for time, opens up a sense of what an enlarged conception of teaching might be.

Among a variety of suggestions, the need to explore the relationship to media studies of those whose linguistic and cultural experience is not primarily in English emerged as an immediate focus for research and teaching which might combine and change the skills and knowledge of teachers, and researchers, working together.[4] Such a project might also produce a constructive space between the intellectual practices of teaching and research and the identities they sustain. School teaching is an intellectual practice in need of more space for theoretical work; meanwhile, academic intellectual life constantly risks a clever, self-regarding, sequestration. The effort to join them in some common, socially and politically productive project is essential to both.

A Conclusion

There is an urgent need to continue a dialogue between research and teaching. In such a dialogue, the academic disciplines of media and cultural studies need to be open to revision and reconstruction. A more sustained dialectic between these disciplines and the work of teachers in schools might be achieved through the effort and difficulty of a shared research practice. In such a shared context, the questions posed from within research might thus be more readily negotiated in the particular circumstances of teachers' work and in the light of their very specific knowledge of their own institution and the young people they teach. Indeed, as I noted in Chapter 7, the *context-specific* knowledge made available by my 'teachers-as-informants' in Edmonton contributed significantly to my analysis of the writing produced by their students. Similarly, in those chapters devoted to the Hackney research, it was often the case that I drew upon discussions with teachers in reformulating my readings of the classroom context. However, it is worth noting that the Edmonton teachers[5] were more specialized in media education than those in Hackney, for whom English was still their primary discipline. Thus, an easier reciprocity, somewhat grounded in a more common discourse, was perhaps more apparent in the Edmonton phase of my research.

The autobiographical elements in this book, though relatively slight, are more than an explanation of my motivation. My argument is also that any research has a somewhat submerged history in the lives of those individuals involved – the researcher just as much as the respondents. It is important to present and reflect on individuals' histories in the process of identifying both what moves one individual to do research and in defining what it may be that the researcher already shares with those who, inevitably, have the status of 'others'. The *otherness* of those who are researched can, through such biographical means, be diminished. In this case, of course, the very sharp distinction between the institutional locations of those involved persists. But it is because of this that I have made a case for documenting the perspectives of teachers rather than expecting them to be no more than willing facilitators, intermediaries between myself and the young people with whom I have discussed popular music and its cultural significance in their lives. Teachers, and the work that they do, need to be rendered as more than institutional background. Their own histories of schooling and of involvement with popular culture, though only glanced over here, do have a more than nostalgic relevance to the terms in which they inhabit their working lives.

Notes

1　Provisionally entitled, *'The cool thing to do?' The Making of Media Teachers.*
2　Richard Bingham (1993) confirms this impression through interviews with three media teachers. Also of relevance is Fornas *et al.* (1995) see p. 247.
3　The lesson I learned in my first year of teaching was that readings of texts, in this case images in *Ways of Seeing* (Berger, 1972), could well be at odds with my own educationally 'authorized' interpretations; but such other readings, however socially marginal, were not wrong.
4　For example, the cultural identity of Asiye, discussed in Chapters 4, 5 and 6, but only marginally placed in terms of the main concerns of this book, would demand far more detailed attention in further research.
5　My main informant, Pete Fraser, is also a member of the Media Teachers' Research group at the Institute of Education, and a contributor to *Watching Media Learning* (Buckingham, 1990).

References

This list is a more comprehensive guide to relevant reading than one confined only to those texts explicitly cited in this book. Though not exhaustive, it represents a wide variety of sources in media education and beyond.

ABERCROMBIE, N., HILL, S. and TURNER, B.S. (1980) *The Dominant Ideology Thesis*, London: Allen and Unwin.

ABRAMS, M. (1959) *The Teenage Consumer* LPE Papers – Number 5 – July, London Press Exchange.

AGGLETON, P. (1987) *Rebels Without a Cause? Middle-Class Youth and the Transition from School to Work*, Basingstoke: The Falmer Press.

ALTHUSSER, L. (1971) *Lenin and Philosophy and other Essays*, London: NLB.

ALVARADO, M. and BOYD-BARRETT, O. (1992) *Media Education: An Introduction*, London: BFI/Open University.

ALVARADO, M., GUTCH, R. and WOLLEN, T. (1987) *Learning the Media*, London: Macmillan.

AMIT-TALAI, V. and WULFF, H. (Eds) (1995) *Youth Cultures: A Cross-cultural Perspective*, London: Routledge.

ARCHER, S. (1996) Pop, pleasure and pedagogy, *The English and Media Magazine*, **34**, pp. 39–44.

ATTALI, J. (1985) *Noise: The Political Economy of Music*, Manchester: Manchester University Press.

BAKHTIN, M. (1988) *The Dialogic Imagination*, Austin, TX: University of Texas Press.

BAKHTIN, M. (1994) *Speech Genres and Other Late Essays*, Austin, TX: University of Texas Press.

BARTHES, R. (1972) *Mythologies*, New York: Hill and Wang.

BARTHES, R. (1977) *Image–Music–Text*, London: Fontana.

BATES, I., CLARKE, J., COHEN, P., FINN, D., MOORE, R. and WILLIS, P. (1984) *Schooling for the Dole?* London: Macmillan.

BAZALGETTE, C. (1991) *Media Education*, London: Hodder and Stoughton.

BAZALGETTE, C., BEVORT, E. and SAVINO, J. (Eds) (1992) *New Directions: Media Education Worldwide*, London and Paris: BFI, CLEMI, UNESCO.

BAZALGETTE, C. and BUCKINGHAM, D. (Eds) (1995) *In Front of the Children*, London: BFI.

BENNETT, R.C. (1993) Why is the romance of dance so absent from academic discourse? in BRACKENRIDGE, C. (Ed.) *Body Matters: Leisure Images and Lifestyles*, Eastbourne: University of Brighton – Leisure Studies Association.

BENNETT, T., FRITH, S., GROSSBERG, L., SHEPHERD, J. and TURNER, G. (Eds) (1993) *Rock and Popular Music: Politics, Policies, Institutions*, London: Routledge.

BERGER, J. (1972) *Ways of Seeing*, London: BBC/Penguin.

BERNSTEIN, B. (1973) *Class, Codes and Control*, London: Paladin.

BERTAUX, D. (Ed.) (1981) *Biography and Society: The Life History Approach in the Social Sciences*, London: Sage.

BINGHAM, R. (1993) Our lives: Cultural biographies of media studies teachers, unpublished PGCE Dissertation, University of London – Institute of Education.

BLACKMAN, S.J. (1995) *Youth: Positions and Oppositions*, Aldershot: Avebury Press.

BLAKE, A. (1992) *The Music Business*, London: Batsford.

BLANCHARD, T., GREENLEAF, S. and SEFTON-GREEN, J. (1989) *The Music Business*, London: Hodder and Stoughton.

BOURDIEU, P. (1986) *Distinction: A Social Critique of the Judgement of Taste*, London: RKP.

BOURDIEU, P. (1992) *Language and Symbolic Power*, Cambridge: Polity Press.

BOURDIEU, P. and PASSERON, J.C. (1977) *Reproduction in Education, Society and Culture*, London: Sage.

BOWKER, J. (Ed.) (1991) *Secondary Media Education: A Curriculum Statement*, London: BFI.

BRACKENRIDGE, C. (Ed.) (1993) *Body Matters: Leisure Images and Lifestyles*, Eastbourne: University of Brighton – Leisure Studies Association.

BRADLEY, D. (undated) The cultural study of music, CCCS Stencilled Paper No. **61**, University of Birmingham.

BRAKE, M. (1980) *The Sociology of Youth Culture and Youth Sub-cultures: Sex and Drugs and Rock 'n' roll?* London: RKP.

BRENNAN, D. (1993) Adolescent girls and disco dancing, in BRACKENRIDGE, C. (Ed.) (1993) *Body Matters: Leisure Images and Lifestyles*, Eastbourne: University of Brighton – Leisure Studies Association.

BRYANT, I. (1996) Action research and reflective practice, in SCOTT, D. and USHER, R. *Understanding Educational Research*, London: Routledge.

BUCKINGHAM, D. (1986) Against demystification, *Screen*, **27**(5), September–October.

BUCKINGHAM, D. (1987) *Public Secrets: EastEnders and its Audience*, London: BFI.

BUCKINGHAM, D. (Ed.) (1990) *Watching Media Learning: Making Sense of Media Education*, London: Falmer Press.

BUCKINGHAM, D. (1993a) *Children Talking Television*, London: Falmer Press.

BUCKINGHAM, D. (Ed.) (1993b) *Reading Audiences: Young People and the Media*, Manchester: Manchester University Press.

BUCKINGHAM, D. (1993c) *Changing Literacies: Media Education and Modern Culture*, London: Institute of Education/Tufnell Press.

BUCKINGHAM, D. (Ed.) (1997) *Teaching Popular Culture: Beyond Radical Pedagogy*, London: UCL Press.

BUCKINGHAM, D. and SEFTON-GREEN, J. (1994) *Cultural Studies Goes to School*, London: Taylor and Francis.

BUCKINGHAM, D., GRAHAME, J. and SEFTON-GREEN, J. (1995) *Making Media: Practical Production in Media Education*, London: English and Media Centre.

BURGIN, V., DONALD, J. and KAPLAN, C. (Eds) (1986) *Formations of Fantasy*, London: Methuen.

BUTLER, J. (1990) *Gender Trouble: Feminism and the Subversion of Identity*, London: Routledge.

CARROLL, J. (1995) *The Basketball Diaries*, New York: Penguin.

CCCS EDUCATION GROUP (1981) *Unpopular Education*, London: Hutchinson.

CCCS EDUCATION GROUP II (1991) *Education Limited: Schooling and Training and the New Right Since 1979*, London: Unwin Hyman.

DE CERTEAU, M. (1984) *The Practice of Everyday Life*, Berkeley, CA: University of California Press.

CHAMBERS, I. (1980) Rethinking 'popular culture', *Screen Education*, **36**, Autumn.

CHAMBERS, I. (1981) Pop music: A teaching perspective, *Screen Education*, **39**, Summer.

CHAMBERS, I. (1985) *Urban Rhythms: Pop Music and Popular Culture*, London: Macmillan.

CHAMBERS, I. (1986) *Popular Culture: The Metropolitan Experience*, London: Methuen.

CHITTY, C. (Ed.) (1991) *Changing the Future – Redprint for Education*, London: Tufnell Press.

CHODOROW, N. (1978) *The Reproduction of Mothering: Psychoanalysis and the Sociology of Gender*, Berkeley, CA: University of California Press.

CLIFFORD, J. and MARCUS, G.E. (1986) *Writing Culture: The Poetics and Politics of Ethnography*, Berkeley, CA: University of California Press.

COHEN, P. (1986) *Rethinking the Youth Question*, London: Institute of Education Post 16 Education Centre/Youth and Policy.

COHEN, P. (1990) *Really Useful Knowledge: Photography and Cultural Studies in the Transition from School*, Stoke-on-Trent: Trentham Books.

COHEN, S. (1972) *Folk Devils and Moral Panics: The Creation of the Mods and Rockers*, London: MacGibbon and Kee 1972.

CONNELL, R.W. (1983) *Which Way Is Up? Essays on Class, Sex and Culture*, Sydney: Allen and Unwin.

CONNELL, R.W. (1995) *Masculinities*, Cambridge: Polity Press.

CONNELL, R.W., ASHENDEN, D.J., KESSLER, S. and DOWSETT, G.W. (1982) *Making the Difference: Schools, Families and Social Division*, Sydney: Allen and Unwin.

CORRIGAN, P. (1979) *Schooling the Smash Street Kids*, London: Macmillan.

CROSS, B. (1993) *It's not about a salary – Rap, Race and Resistance in Los Angeles*, London: Verso.

CUBITT, S. (1984) Top of the pops: The politics of the living room, in MASTERMAN, L. (1984) *Television Mythologies*, London: Comedia/Routledge.

DENZIN, N.K. (Ed.) (1996) *Cultural Studies: A Research Volume*, Greenwich, CT: JAI Press.

DEWDNEY, A. and LISTER, M. (1988) *Youth, Culture and Photography*, London: Macmillan.

DONALD, J. (1992) *Sentimental Education: Schooling, Popular Culture and the Regulation of Liberty*, London: Verso.

DRUMMOND, P. and PATERSON, R. (Eds) (1988) *Television and its Audience*, London: British Film Institute.

DU GAY, P., HALL, S., JANES, L., MACKAY, H., NEGUS, K. (1997) *Doing Cultural Studies: The Story of the Sony Walkman*, London: Sage/Open University.

DUTTON, B. (1989) *Media Studies – An Introduction*, London: Longman.

EAGLETON, T. (1983) *Literary Theory*, Oxford: Blackwell.

EDWARDS, D. and MERCER, N. (1987) *Common Knowledge – The Development of Understanding in the Classroom*, London: Methuen.

ELLSWORTH, E. (1989) Why doesn't this feel empowering? Working through the repressive myths of critical pedagogy, *Harvard Educational Review*, **59**(3), August.

FAIRCLOUGH, N. (1989) *Language and Power*, London: Longman.

FARBER, P., PROVENZO, E.F. and HOLM, G. (Eds) (1994) *Schooling in the Light of Popular Culture*, Albany, NY: SUNY Press.

FELD, S. (1982) *Sound and Sentiment: Birds, Weeping, Poetics and Song in Kaluli Expression*, Philadelphia, PA: University of Pennsylvania Press.

FERRARI, L. and JAMES, C. (1989) *Wham! Wrapping*, London: BFI.

FISKE, J. (1989a) *Television Culture*, London: Routledge.

FISKE, J. (1989b) *Understanding Popular Culture*, London: Unwin Hyman.

FLEMING, D. (1993) *Media Teaching*, Oxford: Blackwell.

FORNAS, J. and BOLIN, G. (1995) *Youth Culture in Late Modernity*, London: Sage.

FORNAS, J., LINDBERG, U. and SERNHEDE, O. (1995) *In Garageland: Rock, Youth and Modernity*, London: Routledge.

FOUCAULT, M. (1976) *The History of Sexuality – Volume 1*, Harmondsworth: Penguin.

FOUCAULT, M. (1982) *Discipline and Punish*, Harmondsworth: Penguin.

FRITH, S. (1978) *The Sociology of Rock*, London: Constable.

FRITH, S. (1980) Music for pleasure, *Screen Education*, **34**, Spring.

FRITH, S. (1983) *Sound Effects: Youth, Leisure, and the Politics of Rock 'n' roll*, London: Constable.

FRITH, S. (1992) The cultural study of popular music, in GROSSBERG, L., NELSON, C. and TREICHLER, P. (Eds) *Cultural Studies*, London: Routledge.

FRITH, S. (1996) *Performing Rites: On the value of popular music*, Oxford: Oxford University Press.

FRITH, S. and GOODWIN, A. (Eds) (1990) *On Record: Rock, Pop and the Written Word*, London: Routledge.

FRITH, S. and HORNE, H. (1987) *Art into Pop*, London: Routledge.

FRITH, S. and MCROBBIE, A. (1978/9) Rock and sexuality, *Screen Education*, **29**, Winter.

FRITH, S., GOODWIN, A. and GROSSBERG, L. (1993) *Sound and Vision: The Music Video Reader*, London: Routledge.

FROW, J. (1987) Accounting for tastes: Some problems in Bourdieu's sociology of culture, *Cultural Studies*, **1**(1), January.

GAUTHIER, G. (undated) Introduction to the semiology of the image, London: BFI paper.

GEERTZ, C. (1973) *The Interpretation of Cultures*, New York: Basic Books.

GEORGE, N. (1989) *The Death of Rhythm and Blues*, Omnibus Press.

GIDDENS, A. (1979) *Central Problems in Social Theory*, London: Macmillan.

GIDDENS, A. (1991) *Modernity and Self-Identity: Self and Society in the Late Modern Age*, Cambridge: Polity Press.

GILLIS, J.R. (1981) *Youth and History – Tradition and Change in European Age Relations, 1770–Present*, Academic Press.

GILROY, P. (1987) *There Ain't No Black in the Union Jack*, London: Hutchinson.

GILROY, P. (1993) *The Black Atlantic: Modernity and Double Consciousness*, London: Verso.

GIROUX, H. and SIMON, R. (1989) *Popular Culture, Schooling and Everyday Life*, Bergin and Garvey.

GOODSON, I. (1992) *Studying Teachers' Lives*, New York: Teachers' College Press.

GOODSON, I. and WALKER, R. (Eds) (1993) *Biography, Identity and Schooling: Episodes in Educational Research*, London: Falmer Press.

GOODWIN, A. (1993) *Dancing in the Distraction Factory: Music Television and Popular Culture*, London: Routledge.

GREEN, L. (1988) *Music on Deaf Ears: Musical Meaning, Ideology and Education*, Manchester: University of Manchester Press.

GREEN, L. (1997) *Music, Gender, Education*, Cambridge: Cambridge University Press.

GREIG, C. (1989) *Will You Still Love Me Tomorrow? – Girl Groups from the 50s on . . .* London: Virago.

GRIFFIN, C. (1993) *Representations of Youth: The Study of Youth and Adolescence in Britain and America*, Cambridge: Polity Press.

GROSSBERG, L. (1992) *We gotta get out of this Place*, London: Routledge.

GROSSBERG, L., NELSON, C. and TREICHLER, P. (Eds) (1992) *Cultural Studies*, London: Routledge.

HALL, S. and JEFFERSON, T. (Eds) (1975) *Resistance Through Rituals – Working Papers in Cultural Studies*, **7/8**, CCCS, University of Birmingham.

HALL, S. and WHANNEL, P. (1964) *The Popular Arts*, London: Hutchinson.

HALL, S., CRITCHER, C., JEFFERSON, T., CLARKE, J. and ROBERTS, B. (1978) *Policing the Crisis*, London: Macmillan.

HALL, S., HOBSON, D., LOWE, A. and WILLIS, P. (1980) *Culture, Media, Language*, London: Hutchinson.

HALL, S., HELD, D. and McGREW, T. (1992) *Modernity and Its Futures*, Cambridge: Polity Press/Open University.

HAMMERSLEY, M. and ATKINSON, P. (1983) *Ethnography: Principles in Practice*, London: Tavistock.

HANNERZ, U. (1969) *Soulside – Inquiries into Ghetto Culture and Community*, New York: Columbia University Press.

HARDING, S. (1991) *Whose Science? Whose Knowledge? Thinking from Women's Lives*, Buckingham: Open University Press.

HARRÉ, R. (Ed.) (1986) *The Social Construction of Emotions*, Oxford: Blackwell.

HARRÉ, R. and GILLETT, G. (1994) *The Discursive Mind*, London: Sage.

HARRIS, D. (1992) *From Class Struggle to the Politics of Pleasure: The Effects of Gramscianism on Cultural Studies*, London: Routledge.

HART, A. (1991) *Understanding the Media – A Practical Guide*, London: Routledge.

HARVEY, D. (1989) *The Condition of Post-Modernity*, Oxford: Blackwell.

HATCHER, R. and JONES, K. (1996) *Education after the Conservatives: The Response to the New agenda of Reform*, Stoke-on-Trent: Trentham Books.

References

HEATH, S.B. (1983) *Ways With Words: Language, Life and Work in Communities and Classrooms*, Cambridge: University of Cambridge Press.

HEATH, S.B. and MCLAUGHLIN, M.W. (1993) *Identity and Inner-City Youth – Beyond Ethnicity and Gender*, New York: Teachers' College Press.

HEBDIGE, D. (1979) *Subculture – The Meaning of Style*, London: Methuen.

HEBDIGE, D. (1986) *Hiding in the Light*, London: Comedia.

HEBDIGE, D. (1987) *Cut 'n' Mix – Culture, Identity and Caribbean Music*, London: Comedia.

HENRIQUES, J., HOLLWAY, W., URWIN, C., VENN, C. and WALKERDINE, V. (1984) *Changing the Subject: Psychology, Social Regulation and Subjectivity*, London: Methuen.

HEWITT, R. (1986) *White Talk Black Talk: Inter-racial Friendship and Communication Amongst Adolescents*, Cambridge: Cambridge University Press.

HEWITT, R. (1992) Language, youth and the destabilisation of ethnicity, in PALMGREN, C., LOVGREN, K. and BOLIN, G. (Eds) *Ethnicity in Youth Culture*, Stockholm: Youth Culture at Stockholm University.

HEY, V. (1995) 'Bitching' and 'little bits of garbage': Resituating ethnographic evidence of girls' friendships, CREG Seminar Paper, University of London Institute of Education.

HEY, V. (1997) *The Company She Keeps: An Ethnography of Girls' Friendship*, Buckingham: Open University Press.

HOARE, Q. and NOWELL-SMITH, G. (Eds) (1971) *Selections from the Prison Notebooks of Antonio Gramsci*, New York: International Publishers.

HOBSON, D. (1982) *Crossroads: The Drama of a Soap Opera*, London: Methuen.

HODGE, B. and KRESS, G. (1988) *Social Semiotics*, Cambridge: Polity Press.

HOLLANDS, R.G. (1990) *The Long Transition: Class, Culture and Youth Training*, London: Macmillan.

HOLLWAY, W. (1994) *Subjectivity and Method in Social Psychology*, London: Sage.

HOLLY, L. (1989) *Girls and Sexuality: Teaching and Learning*, Buckingham: Open University.

HORNBY, N. (1995) *High Fidelity*, London: Gollancz.

HUMPHRIES, S. (1981) *Hooligans or Rebels? An Oral History of Working-Class Childhood and Youth 1889–1939*, Oxford: Blackwell.

HUNT, J.C. (1989) *Psychoanalytic Aspects of Fieldwork*, Beverly Hills, CA: Sage.

JAMES, A. (1993) *Childhood Identities: Self and Social Relationships in the Experience of the Child*, Edinburgh: University of Edinburgh.

JAMES, A. and PROUT, A. (1990) *Constructing and Reconstructing Childhood: Contemporary Issues in the Sociological Study of Childhood*, London: Falmer Press.

JENKINS, H. (1992) *Textual Poachers: Television Fans and Participatory Culture*, London: Routledge.

JENKS, C. (Ed.) (1982) *The Sociology of Childhood: Essential Readings*, London: Batsford.

JONES, K. (1983) *Beyond Progressive Education*, London: Macmillan.

JONES, K. (1989) *Right Turn: The Conservative Revolution in Education*, London: Hutchinson Radius.

JONES, K. (Ed.) (1992) *English and the National Curriculum: Cox's Revolution?*, London: Kogan Page.

JONES, K. (1994) A new kind of cultural politics? The 1993 boycott of testing, *Changing English*, **2**(1), Institute of Education.

JONES, K. (1995) Across the great divide? Culture, economic life and the rethinking of education policy, *Curriculum Studies*, **3**(3).

JONES, S. (1988) *Black Culture, White Youth: The Reggae Tradition from JA to UK*, London: Macmillan.

JORDIN, M. and BRUNT, R. (1988) Constituting the television audience: A problem of method, in DRUMMOND, P. and PATERSON, R. (Eds) *Television and its Audience*, London: British Film Institute.

KEIL, C. (1966) *Urban Blues*, Chicago, IL: University of Chicago.

KRESS, G. (1985) *Linguistic Processes in Sociocultural Practice*, Oxford: Oxford University Press.

KRESS, G. (1993a) Against arbitrariness: The social production of the sign as a foundational issue in critical discourse analysis, *Discourse and Society*, **4**(2), pp. 169–191, London: Sage.

KRESS, G. (1993b) No time for nostalgia, *Times Educational Supplement*, February 12, 18.

KRESS, G. (1994) *Learning to Write*, London: Routledge.

KRESS, G. (1995) *Writing the Future: English and the Making of a Culture of Innovation*, Sheffield: NATE.

KUHN, A. (1995) *Family Secrets: Acts of Memory and Imagination*, London: Verso.

LACAN, J. (1993) *Ecrits*, London: Routledge.

LEAVIS, F.R. and THOMPSON, D. (1933) *Culture and Environment*, London: Chatto and Windus.

LEES, S. (1986) *Losing Out: Sexuality and Adolescent Girls*, London: Hutchinson.

LEPPERT, R. and McCLARY, S. (Eds) (1987) *Music and Society*, Cambridge: Cambridge University Press.

LEWIS, L.A. (1992) *The Adoring Audience: Fan Culture and Popular Media*, London: Routledge.

LINDLEY, R. (1989) Teenagers and other children, in SCARRE, G. (Ed.) *Children, Parents and Politics*, Cambridge: Cambridge University Press.

LIPSITZ, G. (1990) *Time Passages – Collective Memory and American Popular Culture*, Minneapolis, MN: University of Minnesota.

LIPSITZ, G. (1994) *Dangerous Crossroads*, London: Verso.

LULL, J. (Ed.) (1987) *Popular Music and Communication*, Beverly Hills, CA: Sage.

LUSTED, D. and DRUMMOND, P. (Eds) (1985) *TV and Schooling*, London: BFI/Institute of Education.

LUSTED, D. (Ed.) (1991) *The Media Studies Book*, London: Routledge.

LUTZ, C.A. and ABU-LUGHOD, L. (1990) *Language and the Politics of Emotion*, Cambridge: Cambridge University Press.

MAC AN GHAILL, M. (1994) *The Making of Men: Masculinities, Sexualities and Schooling*, Buckingham: Open University Press.

McCLARY, S. (1991) *Feminine Endings – Music, Gender and Sexuality*, Minneapolis, MN: University of Minnesota Press.

McCLARY, S. (1994) Same as it ever was – youth culture and music, in ROSS, A. and ROSE, T. (Eds) *Microphone Fiends: Youth Music and Youth Culture*, London: Routledge.

McROBBIE, A. (1980) Settling accounts with subcultures, *Screen Education*, **34**, Spring.

McROBBIE, A. (Ed.) (1989) *Zoot Suits and Second-Hand Dresses*, London: Macmillan.

References

McRobbie, A. (1991) *Feminism and Youth Culture*, London: Macmillan.

McRobbie, A. (1994) *Postmodernism and Popular Culture*, London: Routledge.

Mander, M.S. (1987) Bourdieu, the sociology of culture and cultural studies: A critique, *European Journal of Communication*, **2**, London: Sage.

Marcus, G. (1990) *Mystery Train*, London: Omnibus Press.

Marcus, G.E. and Fischer, M.M.J. (1986) *Anthropology as Cultural Critique*, Chicago, IL: University of Chicago.

Massey, D. (1991) A global sense of place, *Marxism Today*, June.

Masterman, L. (1980) *Teaching about Television*, London: Macmillan.

Masterman, L. (Ed.) (1984) *Television Mythologies: Stars, Shows and Signs*, London: Comedia.

Masterman, L. (1985) *Teaching the Media*, London: Comedia/Routledge.

Middleton, D. and Edwards, D. (Eds) (1990) *Collective Remembering*, London: Sage.

Middleton, R. and Horn, D. (Eds) (1981) *The Popular Music Yearbooks* (Five Volumes) Cambridge: Cambridge University Press.

Middleton, R. (1990) *Studying Popular Music*, Buckingham: Open University Press.

Mills, C.W. (1959) *The Sociological Imagination*, Oxford: Oxford University Press.

Moores, S. (1993) *Interpreting Audiences: The Ethnography of Media Consumption*, London: Sage.

Morley, D. (1992) *Television, Audiences and Cultural Studies*, London: Routledge.

Morse, D. (1971) *Motown and the Arrival of Black Music*, London: Studio Vista.

Moss, G. (1989) *Un/Popular Fictions*, London: Virago.

Mulhern, F. (1979) *The Moment of 'Scrutiny'*, London: NLB/Verso.

Mungham, G. and Pearson, G. (Eds) (1976) *Working-Class Youth Culture*, London: Routledge and Kegan Paul.

Murdock, G. and Phelps, G. (1973) *Mass Media and the Secondary School*, London: Macmillan/Schools Council.

Nava, M. (1992) *Changing Cultures: Youth, Culture and Consumerism*, London: Sage.

Nava, M. and McRobbie, A. (Eds) (1984) *Gender and Generation*, London: Macmillan.

O'Brien, K. (1995) *Hymn to Her: Women Musicians Talk*, London: Virago.

Palmer, M. (1981) *New Wave Explosion*, London: Proteus.

Palmgren, C., Lovgren, K. and Bolin, G. (Eds) (1992) *Ethnicity in Youth Culture*, Stockholm: Youth Culture at Stockholm University.

Points, C. (Ed.) (1985) *Working Papers for 16+ Media Studies*, Clywd: Media Studies Unit/ CCCS.

Polsky, N. (1971) *Hustlers, Beats and Others*, Harmondsworth: Penguin.

Potter, J. and Wetherell, M. (1987) *Discourse and Social Psychology: Beyond Attitudes and Behaviour*, London: Sage.

Radway, J. (1988) Reception study: Ethnography and the problems of dispersed audiences and nomadic subjects, *Cultural Studies*, **2**(3).

Raphael, A. (1995) *Never Mind the Bollocks: Women Rewrite Rock*, London: Virago.

Redhead, S. (1990) *The End-of-the-century Party: Youth and Pop towards 2000*, Manchester: Manchester University Press.

Redhead, S. (Ed.) (1993) *Rave Off: Politics and Deviance in Contemporary Youth Culture*, Aldershot: Avebury Press.

RICHARDS, C. (1981/82) Classroom readings, *Screen Education*, **40**, Autumn–Winter.

RICHARDS, C. (1982) Topicality, *Teaching London Kids*, **19**, pp. 20–2, London.

RICHARDS, C. (1983) Media-race-riots, *Teaching London Kids*, **20**, pp. 2–7, London.

RICHARDS, C. (1986) Anti-racist initiatives, *Screen*, **27**(5).

RICHARDS, C. (1990) Intervening in popular pleasures, in BUCKINGHAM, D. (Ed.) *Watching Media Learning: Making Sense of Media Education*, London: Falmer Press.

RICHARDS, C. (1991) Review of The media pack, The media manual, Mediafile, *Screen*, **32**(4), Winter.

RICHARDS, C. (1992) Teaching popular culture, in JONES, K. (Ed.) *English and the National Curriculum: Cox's Revolution?* London: Kogan Page.

RICHARDS, C. (1993) Taking sides? What young girls do with television, in BUCKINGHAM, D. (Ed.) *Reading Audiences*, Manchester: Manchester University Press.

RICHARDS, C. (1994) The English curriculum: What's music got to do with it?, *Changing English*, **1**(2), Institute of Education.

RICHARDS, C. (1995) Room to dance, in BAZALGETTE, C. and BUCKINGHAM, D. (Eds) *In Front of the Children*, London: BFI.

RICHARDS, C. (1996a) Review of FORNAS, J., LINDBERG, U. and SERNHEDE, O. (1995) *In Garageland: Rock, Youth and Modernity*, London: Routledge and SHUKER, R. (1994) *Understanding Popular Music*, London: Routledge, in *The English and Media Magazine*, **34**, p. 51.

RICHARDS, C. (1996b) Labouring to learn: Notes on work, identity and adolescence in media teaching, in HATCHER, R. and JONES, K., *Education After the Conservatives: The Response to the New Agenda of Reform*, Stoke-on-Trent: Trentham Books.

RICHARDS, C. (1997) Beyond classroom culture, in BUCKINGHAM, D. (Ed.) *Teaching Popular Culture: Beyond Radical Pedagogy*, London: UCL Press.

RICHARDS, C. (1998) *Questions of youth, identity and social difference in the classroom study of popular music: a case study in the development of media education*, unpublished PhD thesis, University of London Institute of Education.

ROBINS, D. and COHEN, P. (1978) *Knuckle Sandwich: Growing up in the Working Class City*, Harmondsworth: Penguin.

ROE, K. (1983) *Mass Media and Adolescent Schooling – Conflict or Coexistence?* Stockholm: Almqvist and Wiksell.

ROMAN, L.G. and CHRISTIAN-SMITH, L.K. with ELLSWORTH, E. (Eds) (1988) *Becoming Feminine: The Politics of Popular Culture*, Basingstoke: Falmer Press.

ROSALDO, R. (1993) *Culture and Truth: The Remaking of Social Analysis*, London: Routledge.

ROSE, J. (1984) *The Case of Peter Pan, or The Impossibility of Children's Fiction*, London: Macmillan.

ROSE, T. (1994) *Black Noise: Rap Music and Black Culture in Contemporary America*, Hanover, NH: Wesleyan University Press.

ROSS, A. (1989) *No Respect: Intellectuals and Popular Culture*, London: Routledge.

ROSS, A. and ROSE, T. (Eds) (1994) *Microphone Fiends: Youth Music and Youth Culture*, London: Routledge.

SANDERS, C.L. (1971) Aretha – A close-up look at sister superstar, *Ebony*, December.

SARLAND, C. (1991) *Young People Reading: Culture and Response*, Buckingham: Open University.

SCARRE, G. (Ed.) (1989) *Children, Parents and Politics*, Cambridge: Cambridge University Press.

SCHOSTAK, J. (1992) *Dirty Marks – The Education of Self, Media and Popular Culture*, London: Pluto Press.

SCOTT, D. and USHER, R. (1996) *Understanding Educational Research*, London: Routledge.

SENNETT, R. and COBB, J. (1972) *The Hidden Injuries of Class*, Cambridge: Cambridge University Press.

SHEPHERD, J. with GILES-DAVIS, J. (1991) *Music as Social Text*, Cambridge: Polity Press.

SHIACH, M. (1993) 'Cultural studies' and the work of Pierre Bourdieu, *French Cultural Studies*, **4**, Part 3, (12) October.

SHOTTER, J. and GERGEN, K.J. (Eds) (1989) *Texts of Identity*, London: Sage.

SHUKER, R. (1994) *Understanding Popular Music*, London: Routledge.

SILVERSTONE, R. (1994) *Television and Everyday Life*, London: Routledge.

SILVERSTONE, R. and HIRSCH, E. (Eds) (1992) *Consuming Technologies – Media and Information in Domestic Spaces*, London: Routledge.

SOUTHERN EXAMINING GROUP (1994) *General Certificate of Secondary Education: Media Studies (2164)*, Guildford: SEG Publications.

SPENCE, J. and HOLLAND, P. (Eds) (1991) *Family Snaps: The Meaning of Domestic Photography*, London: Virago.

STANLEY, L.A. (Ed.) (1992) *Rap – The Lyrics*, Harmondsworth: Penguin.

STANLEY, L. (Ed.) (1990) *Feminist Praxis: Research, Theory and Epistemology in Feminist Sociology*, London: Routledge.

STRINATI, D. and WAGG, S. (1992) *Come On Down? Popular Media Culture in Post-war Britain*, London: Routledge.

TAYLOR, J. and LAING, D. (1979) Disco-pleasure-discourse: On 'Rock and Sexuality', *Screen Education*, **31**, Summer.

THOMAS, H. (Ed.) (1993) *Dance, Gender and Culture*, London: Macmillan.

THOMPSON, J.B. (1990) *Ideology and Modern Culture*, Cambridge: Polity Press.

THORNTON, S. (1995) *Club Cultures – Music, Media and Subcultural Capital*, Cambridge: Polity Press.

TOOP, D. (1984) *The Rap Attack: from African Jive to New York Hip Hop*, London: Pluto Press.

TURNER, G. (1990) *British Cultural Studies: An Introduction*, London: Unwin Hyman.

VOLOSINOV, V.N. (1973) *Marxism and the Philosophy of Language*, New York: Seminar Press.

VOLOSINOV, V.N. (1987) *Freudianism*, Bloomington, IN: Indiana University Press.

VULLIAMY, G. and LEE, E. (Eds) (1976) *Pop Music in School*, Cambridge: Cambridge University Press.

VULLIAMY, G. and LEE, E. (1982a) *Popular Music: A Teacher's Guide*, London: Routledge and Kegan Paul.

VULLIAMY, G. and LEE, E. (1982b) *Pop, Rock and Ethnic Music in School*, Cambridge: Cambridge University Press.

VYGOTSKY, L.S. (1962) *Thought and Language*, Cambridge, MA: MIT.

VYGOTSKY, L.S. (1978) *Mind in Society*, Cambridge, MA: Harvard University Press.

WEEKS, J. (1981) *Sex, Politics and Society: The Regulation of Sexuality since 1800*, London: Longman.

WEXLER, P. (1992) *Becoming Somebody: Toward a Social Psychology of School*, London: Falmer Press.

WHITELEY, S. (1992) *The Space Between the Notes: Rock and the Counter-Culture*, London: Routledge.

WHITTY, G. and YOUNG, M. (Eds) (1976) *Explorations in the Politics of School Knowledge*, Driffield, Nafferton Books.

WIDDICOMBE, S. and WOOFFITT, R. (1995) *The Language of Youth Subcultures*, Sussex: Harvester Wheatsheaf.

WIDGERY, D. (1986) *Beating Time*, London: Chatto.

WILLIAMSON, J. (1981/2) How does girl number 20 understand ideology?, *Screen Education*, Autumn/Winter 1981/2, 40.

WILLIS, P. (1977) *Learning to Labour: How Working-class Kids Get Working-class Jobs*, Farnborough: Saxon House.

WILLIS, P. (1978) *Profane Culture*, London: Routledge and Kegan Paul.

WILLIS, P., with JONES, S., CANAAN, J. and HURD, G. (1990) *Common Culture: Symbolic Work at Play in the Everyday Cultures of the Young*, Buckingham: Open University Press.

WINTER, R. (1989) *Learning from Experience*, London: Falmer Press.

WOLFF, T. (1990) *This Boy's Life – A Memoir*, New York: Harper and Row.

WOLPE, A. (1988) *Within School Walls: The Role of Discipline, Sexuality and the Curriculum*, London: Routledge.

WOMEN'S STUDIES GROUP (CCCS) (1978) *Women Take Issue: Aspects of Women's Subordination*, London: Hutchinson.

YOUNG, M. (1971) *Knowledge and Control*, London: Collier-Macmillan.

Index

Note: 'n.' after a page reference indicates the number of a note on that page.